SIGNS OF NEW LIFE IN CENTRAL AMERICA AND THE CARIBBEAN

Christian Revitalization amid Social Change

Karla Ann Koll
Editor

First Fruits Press
Wilmore, Kentucky

TABLE OF CONTENTS

CONTRIBUTORS

Carlos Aguirre Salinas. Professor and researcher at Martin Luther University, Managua, Nicaragua; researcher at the Center for Social and Cultural Analysis (CASC), Central American University (UCA); member of the Latin American Network for Pentecostal Studies (RELEP).

Herbert Mauricio Alvarez Lopez. Roman Catholic layman who teaches theology at the Rafael Landivar University and at CEDEPCA (Evangelical Center for Pastoral Studies in Central America) in Guatemala, member of the AMERINDIA theology network in Guatemala. Master in Sciences of Charity (Social Theology) from the Albert Ludwigs University, Freiburg, Germany; Master in University Education and Licentiate in Theology from the Rafael Landivar University, Guatemala.

Priscila Barredo Pantí. Communications Director for the Latin American Biblical University (UBL) and communications coordinator for the Together with Children and Youth Movement. Master in Bible from the ESEPA Seminary and a master's student in Latin American Studies at the National University of Costa Rica.

Robert Brenneman. Associate Professor of Sociology, St. Michael's College, Colchester, Vermont, USA. Ph.D. from the University of Notre Dame.

H. Fernando Bullon. Professor emeritus, Nazarene Seminary of the Americas, and adjunct professor at the Evangelical University of the Americas, San Jose, Costa Rica. Specialist in religion and development. Ph.D. from the Faculty of Economic and Social Studies of the University of Manchester, England.

Ondina Cortés, rmi. Assistant Professor of Practical Theology, St. Thomas University, Miami, Florida, USA. Ph.D. from

St. Thomas University.

Jordan Dobrowski. Research assistant, Latin American Program for Socio-religious Studies (PROLADES), San Jose, Costa Rica. B.A. in anthropology from Augustana University, Sioux Falls, South Dakota, USA.

Laura María Fernández Gómez. Lay Leader, Diocese of Santa Clara, Cuba.

Bryan T. Froehle. Professor of Practical Theology, St. Thomas University, Miami, Florida, USA. Director of research and lead facilitator for the consultation in Costa Rica on which this book is based as well as many of the consultations funded by two grants from the Luce Foundation to Asbury Theological Seminary's Center for the Study of World Christian Revitalization Movements. Ph.D. in Sociology from University of Michigan, USA.

Wanjiru M. Gitau. Visiting scholar, Asbury Theological Seminary, Wilmore, Kentucky, USA. Graduate of the University of Nairobi. Doctorate in Cross-Cultural Missions from Africa International University, Center for World Christianity, Nairobi, Kenya.

Clifton L. Holland. Director, Latin American Program for Socio-religious Studies (PROLADES), San Jose, Costa Rica. M.A. from Fuller Theological Seminary, Pasadena, California, USA. Doctoral studies in cultural anthropology, missiology and church history.

Karla Ann Koll. Professor of History, Mission and Religions, Latin American Biblical University, San Jose, Costa Rica. Ph.D. in Mission, Ecumenics and History of Religions from Princeton Theological Seminary, New Jersey, USA.

Nestor Medina. Visiting scholar, Emmanuel College Center for Research in Religion, University of Toronto, Canada. Specialization in theology and culture. Ph.D. from Toronto School of Theology, University of Toronto, Canada.

America Gabriela Ochoa. Instructor in Spanish, St. Michael's College, Colchester, Vermont, USA. M.A. in

Latin American History and Literature, Rafael Landivar University, Guatemala City, Guatemala.

Stephen Offutt. Associate Professor of Development Studies, Asbury Theological Seminary, Wilmore, Kentucky, USA. Ph.D. in Sociology from Boston University, Boston, Massachusetts, USA.

Pablo Richard. Chilean theologian. Former director of the Ecumenical Department for Research (DEI), San Jose, Costa Rica. Doctorate in sociology of religión from the Sorbonne University, Paris, France.

Hilda Romero. Director, A-Brazo Association, San Salvador, El Salvador.

Adrián Tovar Simoncic. Mexican anthropologist and sociologist specializing in religious diversification in Latin America, Pentecostalism, and indigenous theologies. M.A. in Cultural Studies from the University of Bayreuth, Germany.

INTRODUCTION

The Global Conversation on Religion and Revitalization in the Latin American and Caribbean Context

Bryan T. Froehle

This volume enters the global conversation on religion and revitalization from the perspective of Latin America and the Caribbean. It builds on a conversation flowing from specific cases and contexts across different confessional and historical traditions. As such, it engages the ongoing work of renewal, both within Christianity and within social life, and the inextricable link between the two. This is ultimately a comparative conversation that embraces difference and the plurality of Christian expression globally, recognizing how differences in the larger religious and spiritual context in each place add to the depth of understanding and possibilities for social transformation.

This introductory chapter discusses approaches to religion and revitalization, proposing ways of moving toward a more integrated engagement. It introduces the chapters and conversation partners in the text that follows, contextualizing the conversation while situating it within the final of seven global conversations engaging Christian revitalization movement in the world today. The final section offers some thoughts on the role of scholars of religion as public intellectuals contributing in processes of social transformation.

Approaches

This book is the final product of a project designed to advance the conversation around religious renewal in a global Christian context. It represents the culmination of a series of seven consultations conducted around the world in as many years.[1] During that time, various theoretical models and methods were tested, some intentionally, others quite accidentally. The project began when the work of the Center for the Study of World Christian Revitalization Movements moved from a previous

---

1 The Center for the Study of World Christian Revitalization Movements of Asbury Theological Seminary, Wilmore, Kentucky, gratefully acknowledges the generous support of the Luce Foundation for these seven consultations conducted between 2009 and 2016. The Luce Foundation provided two grants, an initial one that provided for the first three consultations and a follow-up grant that supported the final four consultations. The consultations took place in Wilmore, Kentucky; Edinburgh, United Kingdom; Toronto, Canada; Nairobi, Kenya; Dehradun, India; Manila, Philippines; and San Jose, Costa Rica.

frame of a particular narrative informed by an historical focus to a more missiological one informed by relatively more theoretical understandings of revival and revitalization.[2] It concludes in this book, which represents the development of insight from specific and profound empirical theological study in the specificity of particular cases. This represents the best of an approach to missiology that reflects the ecumenical and even inter-religious engagement of the emerging discipline of World Christianity. It presents a contemporary practical theological approach that is intentionally intradisciplinary, borrowing from a critical realist approach to link various disciplines in an epistemologically respectful fashion, including sociology, history, and theology, for the collective engagement and development of all.[3]

Framing Spirituality, Theology, Religion, and Religiosity

The reduction of spirituality or religion to a single sphere of life is purely heuristic and artificial. Reified, closed, or overly specialized frames prevent rather than enhance understanding of human meaning-making at the heart of the human spirit and consciousness. Spirituality in this sense is shared by all humanity precisely because the human mind neurologically allows for the experience of consciousness and meaning-making. Theological frames flow from this reality, engaging lived expressions of faith and traditions that enhance this meaning-making. Just as the word "theology" can be translated from the Greek as "God-talk," the much newer term "religion" offers insight from its Latin etymology meaning "re-linking." Religion can be seen in more structural terms, including external manifestations or behaviors, action that can follow from moral codes or rituals or both, including organized power structures and other aspects tied to religions. Religiosity dwells on the social or psychological dimensions of personal levels of identity and commitment. Clearly all these concepts can be studied through various intellectual disciplines. This work and the research and consultations that have informed it, and

2 This is the history of the Center itself, which began as the Wesleyan Holiness Studies Center. In 2006, the Center took on a name emphasizing world Christian revitalization and changed the name of the newsletter it had produced since 1992 to Revitalization.

3 For more on intradisciplinarity, see Johannes van der Ven (1998). For more on critical realism, see Margaret Archer, et. al. (1998).

the vision of the Center that sponsored it, intentionally engage these frames in dialogue so as to advance mutual understanding within the intellectual disciplines but also across theological and religious and spiritual traditions.

Some aim to avoid contentious debates in these areas by nesting all of these conversations within culture. However, this merely exchanges one set of problems for another, typically sacrificing the clarity of understandings expressed in theological rigor or analyses of religious structuring as well as religiously inflected moral codes and rituals. In other cases, reframing spiritual, theological, or religious conversations as cultural ones takes them from an over-specialized, over-constructed frame into an amorphous, under-defined one. In some ways, the contemporary reality of what is called "spirituality," "theology," "religion," or "religiosity" may be differently and more adequately understood in newer, broader concepts such as these. The problem remains of by-passing limitations of disciplinary or "sphere" language in order to have a properly holistic conversation about something simultaneously at the heard of all human experience—meaning-making—and yet lending itself to distinctive, rigorous study proper to the contexts of human expression of spirituality. In this sense, spirituality cannot be only a privatized or individualistic expression but ultimately a generously inclusive way of denominating all that is contained within the concepts of theology and religion and more besides, open to the rigor of particular intellectual disciplines as well as transdisciplinary engagement.

Disciplining Frames

Frames can be narrowly or widely construed and need not be identified with a single intellectual discipline. Just as a frame is visual and a spatial field, disciplines offer themselves as habits – ways of habituating study. Such habits produce new insight even while they necessarily contain inadequacies and put forth new constraints.

World Christian revitalization can be studied within missiology, the theological discipline that focuses on the missio Dei both as the "sending forth" of the Christian gospel around the world and as the sending forth of God's very self throughout all of creation, including all humanity. This model is both useful and inadequate as a disciplinary focus. However, some aspects are better captured from an historical or sociological discipline. This book, and the larger conversation of which it is a part, suggests the value of multiple, mutually critical ways of disciplining the frames at the heart of the conversation.

Disciplines can also be limited by the sheer weight of the literature within them, suggesting a need, from time to time, for a kind of revolution within the paradigm that upends the discipline itself. This could be seen in how the discipline of missiology is, in part, giving way to an emerging discipline increasing termed "world Christianity." Certainly, limitations can be seen in the dualism implicit in much of the missiological literature that frequently emphasized those places where Christianity, or specific forms of Christianity, arrived on the scene relatively more recently. Some aspects of the literature are grounded more within a focus on evangelizing and others on God's gracious self-revelation across time and place, but often still with a focus on areas outside of a "Christian core" in relation to a "periphery." This can lead to a reductionist dualism that segregates consideration of Christianity in contexts that have long been its heartlands, implying that such contexts contain the criteria by which others are to be compared or judged in some way. Characteristically missiological tools derived from anthropology and language study, for example, are utilized less in those areas imagined as Christian heartlands, introducing an implicit "othering" within the Christian theological enterprise itself.

Sociology offers another way to discipline study of these frames. Here, too, as in all disciplinary approaches, limitations can be seen. These limitations also have origins, in part, within the accumulated literature of the field. This scholarly inheritance is instructive but can also distort when it is not brought into dialogue with other disciplines. Intellectual insight, in this sense, is always relative, and in this sense theology, religious studies, and all disciplines have a mutually critical role to play. Consider sociology, for example. Classic sociological theory reflected its nineteenth century European origins in its emphasis on secularization and the declining power of religious institutions just as rational choice theory reflects its origins in the late twentieth century United States in its emphasis on individual decision-makers and the specifically religious associational life. Both literatures offer insights, but the inadequacies of both become evident when Northern European secularization processes are generalized to the world or when homo economicus is treated as a built-in inevitability of the human condition. Secularization takes a certain European experience as normative and rational choice theory does the same with U.S. experience, though in both cases it is altogether unclear why this experience should be privileged globally or seen as normative across time and place. While it may have appeared that the sheer power and privilege of Europe or the United States should make one or the other, or both, of these theories or realities preeminent, the multiplicities of emerging paradigms today call that into question.

Method

Method is a way of proceeding that engages certain tools, and an understanding of those tools, within an overall research design. It need not offer a higher reflection on methodology – underlying epistemological and hermeneutical understandings may be taken for granted or simply ignored. Yet considerations of method are never superficial and raise questions of adequacy encountered throughout the research described here on religious revival and revitalization.

Levels of Analysis

Approaches informed by sociology often take sides in the secularization and rational choice theory debates to the point of confusing levels of analysis between the institutional level implicit in secularization approaches with the individual level implicit in rational choice approaches. Both can easily miss a cultural level. The habitus that flows from institutional and individual level phenomena interactively shapes emerging cultural patterns. Religious worship is culturally embedded and culturally formative at a communal level. As such, it transcends self-imposed limits customarily stemming from an exclusive focus on the institutional or individual levels. More than that, there are serious methodological limitations in constructing a purely institutional or individual level of analysis. The artificiality of these levels of analysis, useful at a heuristic or conceptual level more than a more fully descriptive or narrative one, can be resolved in part by a more robust account of the nature of culture and the human person as creative agent in the ongoing shaping and reshaping of patterns of acting and understanding.

Contingent Comparisons

Case-based approaches, whether current or historical, need not do anything other than tell their story. Literary and historical narration has its place in understanding, and comparison, direct or indirect, advances insight. Further, contingencies are defining to the story itself. It is only when multiple stories – historical or contemporary – are brought together comparatively that one can see patterns that move away from pure contingency without ever eliminating seeing the contingencies. Case study approaches thus demand comparative methods as well as methodologies adequate to them. The problem is that comparative methods are often applied after the fact – after data are gathered and conclusions made within a single, particular case. True mixed methods approaches offer another way, allowing for comparison every step of the way, including in the design of data collection as well as in the design of primary and secondary analysis. Combining survey or demographic data analysis, in-depth interviews, and documentary or participant observation in this way assures that each case is a dialogue in itself.

Revitalization and the World Christian Conversation

Different worldviews, most definitely including different religious and theological understandings, resource different intellectual approaches. A worldview nourished in the context of various Christian theological traditions would emphasize a view of human flourishing that foresees forward-looking, ongoing renewal, on the one hand, paired with a backward-looking normativity that sees a series of "oughts" or "taken-for-granted" principles as grounded in a certain revelation or historical time and place.

Renewal beyond Revitalization Theory

Revitalization need not be applied exclusively in a backward-looking revivalist context or as functionalist anthropological theorizing. Yet there is something deeply religious and spiritual about retrieval. As noted earlier, the word "religion" itself refers to a re-connecting. An attention to renewal or return seems built into religious experience, even consciousness itself. Spirituality thus builds on a sense of connection that transcends any one time or place even while it connects across time and place. Many different world religious traditions express this, from the Abrahamic to dharmic, including the most ancient and traditional of human religious expression, whether African, Aboriginal, or any of the deeply rooted indigenous traditions around the globe. This certainly can be seen in Christianity within contemporary Spanish-speaking Central America and the Caribbean, from which the cases of this book are drawn.

World Christianity beyond Confines

Certain concepts are related to language and cultural areas in which they first spring up. Negritude had an origin in French-speaking areas of the world, and the post-colonial conversation developed and deepened in English-speaking areas, particularly South Asia, at first. In the Anglophone world, including those parts of the world where English is a lingua franca such as Asia and much of Africa, World Christianity is a relatively more discussed phenomenon that generally studies and is understood as a largely evangelical-Protestant phenomenon. As such, it came to be extended to Francophone and Lusophone parts of Africa as well as Spanish and Portuguese-speaking Latin America, but still with a focus on various forms of independent or evangelical Christianity. This has been in spite of the fact that Catholicism, Orthodoxy, and Anglicanism express considerable diversity within themselves and often have many more adherents and faith communities, depending on how they are defined as well as the context. In any case, all these forms are certainly a part of World Christianity, as is Christianity in a North Atlantic context or that of Australia and New Zealand for that matter.

Clearly, the intentional engagement of diverse expressions of Christianity and Christian understanding wherever they are found and in whatever tradition offer a basic and critically important means to extend the world Christian conversation. This includes going beyond English-language scholarship and evangelical or Pentecostal cases.

Indeed, a focus on World Christianity in this context suggests a value in going further, beyond the formal bounds of Christianity itself. Islam grew up in interaction with Christianity. Contemporary Hinduism was shaped in some critically important ways by its encounter with Christianity under the British Raj. The comparative examination of Buddhism and other spiritual expressions, including ones that are entirely this-worldly, as in the case of Chinese Confucianism and Daoism, may further advance understanding of World Christianity. The same could be said for those religious forms that are simply disinterested in theism, as in the case of Jainism or Buddhism. Indeed, some forms of Christianity themselves are relatively more this-worldly or less interested in theism.

A focus on World Christianity, in other words, must open itself to a truly global comparative Christian approach, a truly ecumenical or inter-confessional approach, but also to an inter-religious one since World Christianity cannot but be understood in the context of other religious traditions that are often built into Christian and other religious understandings in various ways around the world. These forms and types might not be as clearly seen except when Christianity in one part of the world, for example, is compared to Christianity in another part of the world. Christianity itself, the most globally extensive form of religion, further lends itself to comparative study with other forms of spiritual meaning-making precisely because it offers a common point of comparison. This is all the more the case given that the single largest form of World Christianity, Catholicism, has a diocese-and-parish organizational arrangement that covers the world, thus further facilitating comparative work all the more within this form of World Christianity.

Advances Suggested by this Book

This book follows on a series of consultations conducted around the world on the theme of World Christian Revitalization. It is the last word of those consultations even as it aims to be the start of future conversations. It builds on seven consultations over seven years and two major grant-funded projects.

New Comparisons

This book focuses on Spanish-speaking Central America and the Caribbean with its core cases drawn from Guatemala, El Salvador, Nicaragua, Costa Rica, and Cuba. Additional cases are included in the initial, global view, drawing particularly on cases from previous consultations in East Africa, North India and Nepal, and the Philippines. Comparisons are drawn across megachurches and microchurches, Catholics and evangelicals, churches of the poor and churches of the professional classes, and diverse forms of government and political power.

New Conversations

These globally oriented consultations began in Wilmore, Kentucky in 2009, Edinburgh in 2010, and Toronto in 2011. The second series of consultations were conducted under a second grant-funded project, this time with a focus on world regions, first in Nairobi in 2013, Dehradun, India in 2014, the Philippines in 2015, and Costa Rica in 2016. Every consultation aimed to create new conversations across various confessional traditions, such as evangelicals and Catholics, as well as between academics and practitioners, seminaries and church leaders.

This final consultation in Costa Rica in 2016 built on that legacy in the theological dialogues between diverse perspectives and traditions. Each moment was itself a conversation, from the opening dialogue between an African scholar and a Central American scholar of mission and World Christianity, to the jointly authored papers and presentations in extended sessions. The conversations were strengthened by in-depth remembrances of the growth of evangelical churches in Costa Rica and the on-going liberationist vitality of churches of the poor throughout the region. The final panel offered new syntheses on the findings regarding revitalization, cultural change, and transformation. The final conversation was led by a Pentecostal scholar of Guatemalan origin who pointed forward to new challenges and possibilities suggested by this consultation and the six previous ones of which it was the culmination.

Bringing Theology Back In

This book shows how theology can be an equal and essential partner in advancing understanding of religious change in Latin America. Engaging theology and theologians does more than help advance needed understanding of the various religious traditions and the ways in which their members believe, live, and worship. Theology is a critical contributor to the method of understanding itself. Theological method and methodological understandings bring a robustness to existing approaches.

Practical and Empirical Theological Approaches

Practical and empirical theology are theological disciplines that emphasis a dialogue with the social sciences just as biblical theology emphasizes a dialogue with linguistic and cultural studies or dogmatics engages historical studies. Practical theologians often use something like the "circle method" described later in this book, which itself has space for engaging social scientific understanding as well as understandings found in religious teaching and scriptures. This typical critical realist methodology encourages conversation among sources of insight that are not so opposed but simply different. The circle method allows for both focus and sharing across various movements, described as paired terms, each of which is critical in its own way: identity and insertion; assessment and analysis; correlation and confrontation; and, finally, empowering and extending.

Inter and Intradisciplinarity

Such an approach means that all disciplines of thought are in partnership together. Theology is in interdisciplinary engagement with other disciplines such as history, sociology, and political science. At the same time, theology itself needs to be open to intradisciplinarity, meaning that sometimes theologians themselves need to be engaging questions of historical narrative, social analysis, and power relations within their theological work. This book illustrates exactly that in the power analysis of Offutt and Romero, the historical analysis of Cortes and Fernandez Gomez, and the sociological approach of Ochoa and Brenneman. All, including the case study, survey research approach of Holland and Dobrowski, are as theological as they are sociological. The historical work and in-depth interviews of Aguirre Salinas and Tovar Simoncic similarly advance theological understanding even as they contextualize the development and growth of an emerging church. Pablo Richard's use of power, history, and social theory undergird his theological argument. And Wanjiru M. Gitau's global perspective, together with Karla Ann Koll's regionally oriented contextual focus, is as much a contribution to missiology and the study of World Christianity as to comparative historical analysis.

Methodological Engagement

Ultimately, these methods fit together, and make important contributions to diverse areas of scholarship, precisely because they engage deep methodological questions. Rather than simply addressing merely technical questions of method, they shed light on philosophical understandings of method – that is, methodology. This book, its authors, and the conversations that fueled their contributions, underline the critical role of a deep understanding of method. Rather than a simple empiricism, these studies take the empirical seriously without denying underlying questions of knowing and understanding.

Phenomenologically integrated

Methodology offers a means of encompassing a range of methods and disciplines when it takes a phenomenological turn. That is, accepting the phenomenon as observed and understood by participants and others allows one to enter into the thought-world of others. In this way, one can bring everything together insofar as it is all part of collective life and experience.

Critically Realist

Methods that follow a taken-for-granted empiricism can miss the much deeper questions of knowing and perception. Such questions cannot deny a common sense reality but neither do they take it as the only reality. Critical realism does not deny the common experiences that one's senses describe nor the common understandings derived from observational experience. Further, critical realism does not deny that our senses and common understanding have limitations, and that empiricism is no less a construction, made all the more tenuous when it denies realities commonly known or experienced simply because they cannot be measured. Reality is simply more complicated, in spite of what simplistic empiricist ideologies might claim. A critically realist approach thus pursues truth more than it claims to possess knowledge of all truth.

Public Intellectual Engagement of Public Issues

The point of serious methodological and theological engagement is to advance understanding in a way that serves more than religious leaders and institutions or academic debates and disciplines. The point of this book, and the consultation and project from which it sprang, is to bring the voice of the scholar and practitioner together, as one, in service of public questions and social needs. The purpose is ongoing social transformation through deeper, more reflective conscious activity. The public intellectual recognizes other audiences, including academic and spiritually focused ones.

The public intellectual is open to surprises since contributions are made in the open dialogue of the public forum. Such surprises are exactly what emerged from the consultation in which these cases and contributions were considered. As practitioners and scholars engaged in several days of conversations built around a practical theological method, new insights were generated. Speaking as public intellectuals informed by a variety of intellectual disciplines ranging from theology to social science and social communications, they offered new, forward-looking syntheses. By the conclusion of the consultation, Alvarez Lopez, Koll, Bullon, and Barredo Pantí offered interventions that suggested a kind of unanticipated convergence of new understanding. This was further embodied by Nestor Medina in a rich integrative final statement that was drafted though ongoing observation of the unfolding of the method and engagement with the context of the consultation.

Academic Engagement

The voice of the public intellectual requires academic engagement. It goes without saying that scholarship itself is the sine qua non of the intellectual, whether a university-related or independent scholar, whether degreed in one's specialty or earned through self-taught research and writing. The main audience of the public intellectual may be the society in general or thought leaders and readers of one kind or another, but an intellectual inevitably also engages with the academy. There are many ways of doing so, and this book illustrates those multiple ways in which practitioners, action researchers, and more contemplative thinkers might come together to the mutual benefit of an emerging understanding. In that way they, as public intellectuals, further serve scholarship as well as the society in general.

Spiritual Engagement

The voice of the public intellectual also requires spiritual engagement at some level. Whether one is adheres to a specific religion or not, or is observant or not, the public intellectual's identity has a spiritual dimension insofar as it engages and serves a reality larger than the buffered, individual self. For members of distinct religious traditions, as in this book, the result of one's public intellectual voice involves distinctive religious contributions. This includes those contributions specifically within religious organization(s) or tradition(s) with which that person identifies. This can take the form of spiritual engagement and contributions to a spiritual life or understanding in a sense that could be recognized as shared by all human persons when understood in sufficiently open terms. Ultimately, the public intellectual and theologian, as much as the reader of this book, has a role to play in advancing human progress, resourced from within a spiritual foundation and developed through the salutary effects of a plurality of expression.

References:

Archer, Margaret, Roy Bhaskar, Andrew Collier, Tony Lawson, and Alan Norrie, eds.
1998. Critical Realism: Essential Readings. London: Routledge.

van der Ven, Johannes.
1988. Practical Theology: An Empirical Approach. Leuven: Peeters.

CHAPTER 1:
"ALL OVER THE WORLD, THIS GOSPEL IS GROWING."

Making Sense of Revitalized Christianity in Asia, Africa and Latin America

I. A Global View

Wanjiru M. Gitau

II. Approaching Christianity in Latin America and the Caribbean

Karla Ann Koll

I. A Global View

Wanjiru M. Gitau

The vibrant street markets of San Jose, Costa Rica, remind me of some years ago when I lived in a five-story building, from the top of which I could survey a bustling open-air market sprawled below. From up there, the market seemed cluttered and too crowded. But how different it was when I walked through the stalls to shop! In this Kenyan soko you can find almost anything: clothes, food, utensils, books, car spare parts, even an (imitation) Gucci bag, all at a price within reach. And if a vendor didn't have the needed item, there was no problem—he would disappear around the corner for a couple of minutes and get it.

The Christian scene in our world over the last one-hundred years is a bit like this crazy and colorful place. Many scholars have pointed to the worldwide transformation of Christianity, which today is the religion most widely dispersed across the globe as well as the most diverse. A century ago, sixty-eight percent of the world's Christians lived in Europe. Today, seventy-five percent of Christians are to be found outside of Europe (Jacobsen 2015, 106). What a dramatic turnaround.

This aerial view is not new, because there is now a rich body of literature pointing to factors behind the shift of Christianity from north to south, which include the work of missionaries (described by scholars such as Brian Stanley 1990 and David Bosch 1991); Bible translation (Lamin Sanneh 1989); the rise of indigenous churches (Ogbu Kalu 2008, Allan Anderson 2010); inculturation (Edward Cleary 2007, Steve Bevans 2011, Robert Schreiter 1985); and the fact that Christians joined in the struggle against injustice, thus generating contextual theologies everywhere.

All around the world, Christian activity is part and parcel of everyday life. Churches are found every few blocks or right opposite each other. They offer a range of activities pointing to the deep commitment of participants. The Church of the Black Nazarene in Quiapo, Manila, where mass is conducted every day on the hour from 8:00 AM to 8:00 PM, is packed for each service.

At New Theological College in India, students meet at 5:30 AM every morning to pray, as do students in many parts of Africa. At the Basilica of Our Lady of the Angeles in Cartago, Costa Rica, pilgrims visiting La Negrita crawl to the altar on their knees in penance and prayer.[4] Megachurches in Manila run services inside high-end shopping malls. In Africa, youth fellowships, students' movements, children's camps, businessmen's breakfasts, women's guilds, and pastors' conferences are everywhere. Hospitals, schools, publishing agencies, houses of hospitality, social and economic development schemes, non-profit advocacies, political parties, and large numbers of theological colleges are part of this brisk Christian presence. A bustling market indeed.

I loved to shop in the tightly packed stalls of Toi market in Nairobi. It was burned to the ground in January of 2008 following a political controversy. Several months later, the market was reconstructed. The city council arranged and allocated the stalls neatly, created wider passageways, added drainage and garbage control, all which made it easier to walk and shop. This was good. The market could be approached in a new way. The same is true for world Christian revitalization. Our pressing need now is to understand this market and to gain a perspective that shapes how we engage with it. I believe we need to imagine a kind of walk to Emmaus. After the events of crucifixion and resurrection, the disciples were trying to make sense of the things that had happened recently among them. Jesus joined the conversation quietly and gave them perspective from the scriptures. In my own small way, I offer a perspective to help shape how we think about Christian revitalization. I will consider two dynamics. The first is the social volatility within which the Christian gospel grows. The second examines how timing shapes the rise of leaders, the message and the movement.

Social Volatility

In the wisdom of African elders, "A man who cannot tell where the rain started beating him cannot know where he dried his body." This means that if we are to make sense of our tragedy

4 Our Lady of the Angeles, a small statue of the Virgin Mary holding Jesus, is the official patron of Costa Rica. Due to the nearly black color of the stone, she is often called La Negrita, the little black one.

and, at the same time, of our blessing, we must understand what has happened to us. Since Columbus "discovered" and laid claim to the New World, and since European powers carved up Africa in "the scramble for Africa", our communities have experienced a profoundly destabilizing period, particularly over the last one hundred years as we have increasingly been forced into the circle of global consciousness.

Our foreparents had no idea that we had been co-opted into a global order. When the first white men showed up in Kikuyu land, the local people saw the pale men as ghosts. Then they were amused by their foolish ways as the white men grabbed fertile land and settled down. Young Kikuyu men who confronted the rude strangers were felled by bullets. Those who remained were herded into crowded reserves. When Kikuyu refused to help farm the stolen land, settlers introduced a tax for every wife and her children. Where would the Kikuyu get money? They cleared forests for the white man to plant coffee and tea and build roads. Eventually, they congregated in cities, places of dislocation from kinship networks, social control and order. This negative narrative of the rise of cities has happened over and over again.

Kibera in Nairobi is known as the biggest slum in Africa. Nairobi, now a city of four million people (in a country of forty million), was founded in 1899 as a railway station town. The colonial administration intended to keep Nairobi a home for settlers only. African migrant workers could only live in "native reserves" at the edge of the city. One such group was soldiers of Sudanese origin who, having served the British government during World War I, were settled five kilometers from the city. As the city intended for half-a-million people grew to be home to more than four million, Kibera has grown to more than 160,000 people living in a space of 2.5 square miles.

The list of challenges brought by subsequent global events is long. According to historian Niall Ferguson, "The 100 years after 1900 were the bloodiest century in history.... The victims of organized violence (wars, colonial massacres, holocaust, starvation, ethnic conflicts, genocides) in those 100 years are estimated to be more than 150 million - 200 million all over the world." (2006, xxxiii-xxxiv) The tragedy is that when the European societies turned against each other in wars, economic meltdowns and cultural revolutions, the retribution and consequences of their sins were sent to the wrong address—to Africans, Asians and Latin Americans.

Where the rubber meets the road for us is that Christianity has come as part and parcel of this volatile encounter. The unique compression of space-time in what sociologists call globalization has sharpened the pressure on local communities, especially in cities. This consultation process on Christian revitalization movements has a preferential nod towards the cities. Not only is social change most concentrated in cities, but it is cities that shape what happens in far-flung rural communities. Everywhere, people have had to adapt at an unnatural pace, which has resulted in a worldview dissonance for the majority of people who are working hard to make sense of life in paradoxical situations. The problems of violence and injustice, poverty and social dislocation are actually symptoms of societies in psychological conflict. The case of Belice Bridge Labor and Educational Project run by the Society of Jesus illustrates this very well (chapter 3). Father Iznardo works with youngsters trapped in violence and poverty in a country that has a wide variety of natural resources. Unfortunately, that wealth is concentrated in the hands of a minority upper class who live in gated communities while the nature of social stratification makes it difficult for indigenous communities to create a better future. The youth resort to violence and other vices as the only option they feel is open to them. As this case study shows, the church is not removed from these inequalities; a megachurch campus valued at fifty million dollars stands side by side glaring poverty—the story of Nairobi, Delhi, Manila, and every city we know.

How can the gospel be implicated in these glaring disparities? It is because the gospel's encounter with cultures is a dynamic reality. As we can observe from Jesus' ministry in the gospels, God meets people where they are. Gentile or Jew, barbarian, Scythian, slave or free, Christ came and preached peace to all who were far away and to those who are near (Col. 3:11). Andrew Walls calls this indigenization, which means that the Christian faith always enters a society that is conditioned by its particular time and place (1996, 7). In our contexts, the gospel was planted for the very first time into what were already religiously fertile cultures. It then acquired its own dynamic as it came into creative and critical encounter with continuously lively cultures. The result has been great varieties of Christian responses. One of the most recent form of creativity is seen in the megachurches. Large churches are not new in the history of Christianity, but their numbers, and concentration, is a new fact of our time. Megachurches are described as churches of more than two thousand people; in the Philippines, Korea, and Nigeria, there are churches of twenty, thirty and even eighty thousand! What do you expect when you have a city of six, ten or twelve million people? There are not even enough churches to go around for all these millions. Not only do megachurches reflect demographics of the huge cities, they also reflect a moment in history when there is a newly ascendant, newly aspiring but not yet rich middle class. The megachurch message of prosperity, success, self-fulfillment, and artificially constructed communities is highly appealing to this emerging class.

Scholars identify the creative attempts to use the gospel to rebuild society as revitalization movements. Revitalization movements emerge out of traumatic situations, which give birth to high levels of chronic dysfunction (alcoholism, broken homes, crime, conflict between older and younger generations, moral crises, etc.). They are called "revitalization" because they connect the present to the past—trying to retrieve a golden past—and give a vision for the future. The radical nature of activities, led by discerning leaders, during a crisis moment is what distinguishes the nascent movement as a revitalization, which is in contrast to gradual, chain-reaction processes involving the slow wheel of time. In Christian revitalization, the Holy Spirit is central to spiritual awakening through prayer, preaching, repentance, restoration and formation of a revived community. Christian leaders or clergy then reform theology, structures of church leadership, and methods of engagement with the wider world.

In the twentieth century, fluctuations within capitalism, colonialism and world wars affected so many local contexts that instability and fear were in large supply. In the face of this, Christianity has provided large numbers of people with mechanisms for coping with fundamental social and psychic disturbances by offering not only a new set of values, but also new family-like relationships when people feel rejected by their families or their worlds. New institutions replace the old. An example is the Bharat Susamachar Samiti and New Theological College (BSS-NTC), a 25-year-old Christian revitalization movement that was examined in our consultation in the northern part of India.[5] This movement began as a simple effort by a team led by George Kuruvilla to evangelize scheduled castes. Soon the evangelists recognized that evangelism was not enough. To bring people out of the intractable hopelessness of poverty and structural social exclusion of the caste system would require introducing formal education, helping people put rice and lentils on the table, and building up the self-esteem of the excluded. The BSS-NTC movement now not only plants churches, but also has a network of schools, development projects and a theological college, out of which a whole new generation is growing up with confidence that they are included in God's good plan for a future full of hope.

The Time Factor

Twentieth-century revitalization movements have been vehicles for helping people cope. A consideration of the time factors helps us conceptualize the process of revitalization.

Kairos moment

Revitalization movements usually begin at "the right moment", which New Testament theologians refer to as a kairos moment, and social scientists call a "liminal" or compelling moment during a crisis. It is that decisive moment in time such as when Mordecai discovered the Jews were to be destroyed and told queen Esther, "who knows if you were raised for such a time as this" (Esther 4: 14 NIV).

The key to a kairos moment for a revitalization is the emergence of a leader as a crystallizing point for a movement. Such a leader, defined as a charismatic personality, has

5 This consultation was held in mid-2014 at New Theological College in Dehra Dun, India. The volume based on the consultation is forthcoming.

extraordinary gifts of the Spirit, and is driven by a sense of being called (Gerlach and Hine 1970, 106). Revitalization leaders are gifted intellectuals who analyze and often internalize the social crisis through a personal crisis, at the end of which they see reality in a new way and share that as a vision of renewal. New leaders also connect their intuitive reading of the times with the work of Jesus in the gospels (Shaw 2010, 61-62).

A good example of this is pastor Magdalena (chapter 2). The exclusion and misunderstanding she experienced from her church community after her personal crisis of divorce with two young children led her to identify with the crisis of garbage pickers in La Chureca in Managua, Nicaragua. In that moment, lonely, abandoned, and mistrusted, she developed a radical unconditional love that led her to found the Church of New Jerusalem at the garbage dump. The crisis of a woman and the crisis of dehumanized families living off the garbage dump sparked a movement. Pastor Magdalena did not need any power or finances; leaders do not found movements because they have resources. Those come later. All Magdalena did was stand at the landfill and share her testimony, convincing the people there of their own self-worth. As her faithfulness carried beyond the skepticism and doubt, she mobilized the goodwill and financial resources of those in power such as the vice president of Spain, Maria Teresa Fernandez de la Vega, to construct dignified residences and provide work for these families. It was the church, the New Jerusalem Church in Managua, led by a woman no less in a context where women were formerly excluded from leadership, that inspired the dreams of a new generation, the desire to learn, to serve and to find more dignified job opportunities.

The variety of movements reflects different perceptions of the crisis and the social locations of those in need. The rise of each movement reveals insights into the most basic need of the person on the street and the conviction that the answers lie with Jesus (even when the question and answer do not seem to fit!): Jesus as savior of a soul otherwise condemned in a world that has newly creative ways to sin (Billy Graham's era of cultural revolution), Jesus as answer to material needs (the prosperity gospel in a world of poverty), Jesus as a revolutionary who subverts the unjust governments of this world (liberation theology in Latin America), Jesus as suffering kinsman (Watchman Nee of the Chinese house church), Jesus as Son of a mother who cares deeply in a world where family values are at stake (Juan Diego and the Virgin of Guadalupe, la Negrita, Our Lady of the Assumption), Jesus as the one who loves unconditionally, and the list can go on and on. All these answers are to be found in Jesus' teachings and in the New Testament. The restoration of hope through a vision of a new future helps people feel responsible and capable of doing something about their broken world.

Muriithi Wanjau of Mavuno Church is an example of a leader who emerged at just the right moment. He was a brilliant young man at the university when he was invited to attend a little church. Subsequently, he was mentored by another young pastor in the 1990s when Kenya was in a profound national economic, political, health and social crisis. Oscar Muriu recognized that the solution to the problems of the nation lay in training Muriithi's generation of students to think like Africans (in contrast to urban youth who are enamored with newly imported liberal media), to be problem solvers (rather than expecting the older generation to come up with solutions), to create opportunities (rather than complaining there are no jobs), to train and to delegate leadership to others (rather than to hold onto power) and to raise funds for ministry (rather than expect financial aid from abroad). When Kenya had its own renewal moment, Muriithi and several other leaders trained by Oscar Muriu had a significant impact on the general Kenyan society (Gitau 2015).

Followers and the laity

A revitalizing idea crystallizes around a leader, yet the real agents of renewal, who will never hit the headlines of the evening news, are itinerants, parish priests, pastors of small communities and lay volunteers. In his research on how gang members are able to exit gangs in Central America, Robert Brenneman came across a considerable number of priests and pastors who are at work in their own communities to keep young people out of the gangs or to help them leave the gangs. Most of these pastors and priests do not belong to any formal association or movement

(2012). Few are able to mobilize the kind resources the Jesuits at the Belice Bridge project have been able to obtain, but all serving as bridges to abundant life merely by inspiring hope and opening doors for these otherwise marginalized youngsters. Isn't this the experience in history, too, that the earliest evangelists were unnamed disciples "who were scattered by the persecution" and preached everywhere they went? (Acts 11:19 NIV)

A popular movement may arise at a kairos moment, yet for long-term renewal of community and society to take place, there must be a process beyond the kairos moment. Some theologians will call this the chronos time, the Greek word for chronological or sequential time. Over the course of time, the leaders and the laity must develop structures to facilitate growth.

A popular movement has been going on for a long time at the Quiapo Church of the Black Nazarene, one of the most popular Roman Catholic churches in the Philippines. This parish church is home to the Black Nazarene, a much venerated four-hundred-year-old statue of Jesus Christ. The statue is clad in a maroon-colored robe with a crown of thorns from which extend three silver rays. His face is contorted in pain and he is carrying a large wooden cross in a semi-kneeling position. Each year, there is an annual fiesta on January 9th where up to twelve million devotees march on a "pilgrimage experience" in honor of and in prayer to the Nazarene. The devotion to this image is quite outside of the Catholic Church's theological framework of prayers and liturgy, but the resilience and the devotion of millions reflect something of the experience of millions of poor people. The official church held some degree of disdain towards this expression of popular piety and stayed aloof to it, often coming into conflict with the devotees. In 2008, a discerning priest in charge, Father Jose Clemente Ignacio, recognized this piety as a seed for renewing the whole church. He consulted widely with leaders of the devotees, then he empowered a movement of lay catechists who organized education classes, Bible studies, parish ministries, all to deepen the spirituality of the devotees. As a result, the Church of the Black Nazarene has experienced a remarkable revitalization. There is mass every hour of the day run by lay leaders and numerous spiritual formation activities which have greatly renewed the church.[6]

Structural renewal or self-reformation is especially necessary for revitalization of pre-existing church communities. We see something similar in the case from Cuba (chapter 4). The devotion to Our Lady of Charity became a rallying point for the Mambises, the rebels; she herself was seen as a rebel fighting for Cuban freedom. The independence movement led by Carols Manuel de Céspedes dedicated itself at the shrine of this image. This act of personal and collective religious devotion took root throughout Cuba during the independence struggle. Our Lady of Charity was named the patroness of Cuba in 1915. As Cuba faced many challenges in its recent history, with the church reduced to silence and an officially imposed atheism, renewal was occasioned by the pilgrimage of the cross. That event, followed by a pilgrimage with the image of Our Lady of Charity, the Mambisa, reinitiated spiritual conversations and church attendance, and revitalization had begun in earnest. The visit of Pope John Paul II to the Diocese of Santa Clara opened a wider door for re-evangelization, the diocesan training center, and charitable activities throughout the diocese. Here the structural work of renewal includes both welcoming popular piety and also strengthening the structural identity of the church.

Implication of the New Realities for Our Witness

I began by pointing to the global reality of Christianity today, an interdisciplinary conversation about demographics, numbers, racial and ethnic composition, geographical and denominational distribution of the new Christians. I noted the implications of this shift in politics, economics, and culture. At a fundamental level, this is perhaps best seen as a theological conversation critical to the life of Christianity today. Of course, scholars and all of us continue to debate so many issues. Is the prosperity theology a

6 Case study presented at the consultation held at the International Graduate School of Leadership in Manila, the Philippines in July of 2015. The volume from the consultation is forthcoming.

good thing or not? Should Neo-pentecostal megachurch leaders run for political office? Should church-related development projects continue to be funded from outside?

This consultation on revitalization organized by Center for the Study of World Christian Revitalization Movements is part of an ongoing conversation on what God doing in specific contexts to transform our world. We are witnesses that God is at work, whether it is revitalization as response to crises of violence and marginality in the larger society as reflected in the case study from Guatemala, or revitalization as restoration of basic human dignity as in the community at La Chureca in Nicaragua. Revitalization can also be resilience and self-reformation as in the case of the Roman Catholic Church in Cuba following structural ideological challenges such as communism. Or revitalization can be experienced in the reconstruction of worship styles and the organizing of new churches as in the case of the megachurch Vida Abundante (chapter 5). Revitalization might come by linking as the new transnational networks are now offering new ways of connecting local communities to needed resources (chapter 6). God is at work everywhere.

We can say together with Paul, who wrote during the very first century of Christianity, "All over the world, this gospel is bearing fruit and growing just as it has been doing among you since the day you heard it and truly understood God's grace." (Col. 1:6, NIV) As we recognize that God is at work through us, how should we frame our community conversations as a body of Christ? I suggest three ways. First, Jesus prayed for unity for the sake of witness. How can we enhance a local collaborative conversation so as to strengthen one another and our witness? Secondly, Paul taught that we are all part of one body, each bringing different gifts. What gifts in worship, service, resources, leadership, radical community and so on do we each have? How can we learn from each other and share these lessons with our communities? Thirdly, Christians face new and unique challenges today in a world of choices more diverse than ever. How can we contribute to world Christian revitalization in our own work and through the work of the world-wide body of Christ?

II. Approaching Christianity in Latin America and the Caribbean

Karla Ann Koll

It's true. During the last century, Christianity became a world religion. I say it this way to my students. "Isn't it marvelous to be a Christian today in the 21st century, when more people from more cultures are followers of Jesus Christ than ever before?" Each group understands the gospel within their own worldview and contributes their unique perspective to the universal church of Christ. There is so much to discover and learn now. Those of us who try to study religious phenomena have the enormous challenge of explaining this great diversity. We should enter into this terrain with a great deal of care to avoid jumping to easy conclusions or adopting triumphalist positions.

I wish to locate our reflection within the Latin America and Caribbean context. The new academic field known as "World Christianity", within which this project of Asbury Theological Seminary is located, has emerged in the last few decades from the recognition that the center of gravity of the world's Christian population migrated to the south during the twentieth century. However, the experience of Latin America does not fit neatly into this narrative, one that is based on the experiences of Africa and Asia as well as postcolonial studies.

Christianity didn't arrive in Latin America in the nineteenth century. It was brought more than five hundred years ago as the religious and ideological justification for the conquests carried out by the Iberian powers. This first globalization, which constructed the Atlantic world under the control of European powers, brought death and slavery to the invaded peoples not only in the Americas, but also to African peoples. In the so-called "New World", the Iberian powers were able to impose the Christendom that was fragmenting in Europe. By the end of the first century of colonization, almost the entire population identified as Christian. Latin America, in contrast to the growth of Christianity in Africa and Asia, has been the most Christian area of the world for centuries. If it is possible in many places in

Africa and Asia to celebrate the arrival of Christianity as a new experience and to find parallels between the experiences of the new Christian communities and the situations of the churches in the first century of the Christian era, in Latin America the people who want to be followers of Jesus have to carry the weight of the all that has been done in the name of Christ in the past.

The nations of Latin America achieved their political independence in the course of the nineteenth century, but the social power relationships and the structure of knowledge that were established through the colonizing process have not changed. This leaves Latin America in a state of continuing "coloniality" (Quijano 2000). We are not in a postcolonial situation. In much of the region, a functional Christendom continues to exist that in some case is maintained on a formal level such as here in Costa Rica with its Roman Catholic confessional state.

In addition to the historical processes in the region, we need to take into account the fact that religious practices in Latin America, even before the arrival of the Spanish and the Portuguese, were eclectic. The institutional hegemony of the Roman Catholic Church has hidden this reality from view, but the church never had sufficient men on the ground to control the religious practices of the conquered peoples, much less their beliefs. Indigenous religious leaders incorporated what they understood of Christianity into their worldviews. The Iberian invaders and migrants brought forms of popular religiosity that had been influenced by centuries of interaction with Judaism and Islam. In addition, the Africans who were brought in chains reconstructed their religious practices in their new Latin American and Caribbean contexts. In spite of all of this diversity in religious beliefs and practices, almost the entire population of Latin America identified as members of the Roman Catholic Church. The arrival of organized Protestant groups, who allied themselves with the liberal political parties to fight for freedom of worship, broke the institution control of the Roman Catholic Church and made the religious diversity visible. Religious options continue to diversify even more, a situation that has led various researchers utilize the metaphor of a marketplace to describe the plethora of offerings.

How does this eclectic nature of religious practices manifest itself in Latin America today? Years ago, I heard the African theologian John Mbiti at a conference at Princeton Theological Seminary speak of those he called "ecumenical Christians", people who in the course of their lives have passed through several faith communities of different Christian traditions. The life stories of my students from different Latin American countries indicate the importance of migration in these changes in religious affiliation, whether from the countryside to urban areas, from one barrio to another, or from one country to another. I notice as well that in many cases people no longer feel the need to maintain an exclusive religious affiliation. Instead, they participate in diverse religious spaces according to the needs they feel. I think of a woman I know in Quetzaltenango, Guatemala. On Sundays, she attends one of the worship services in a Neopentecostal megachurch. During the week, she participates in the women's fellowship at the Presbyterian church in her neighborhood. When someone in her family becomes ill, she looks for a traditional Mayan healer. In addition, she listens to an evangelical radio station or watches the sermons transmitted by television from one of the megachurches in the capital. I suspect there are many more people like her. The way we evaluate this situation depends on our own perspective. We might consider these people to be religiously confused or we can see them as religious subjects that are taking advantage of the religious offerings on hand to construct a spiritual life that responds to their own needs. At a minimum, this diversity of religious practices should encourage us to offer only tentative conclusions about religious affiliation and its significance today in Latin America.

In order to study religious phenomena, is it imperative that we focus on social location. In Latin American theologies, as in other contextualized theology, social location has been a fundamental concept. The social location is given in each situation. Indigenization, also called contextualization, is the process by which Christians, as individuals or in groups, in a more or less conscious way, appropriate the gospel into a given context and construct their identities as believers. Social location conditions, but does not determine, the form that contextualization takes.

Social location is comprised of various factors, some of which are evident in the cases studies. However, other factors require more attention.

The celebration of a consultation in this region of the world has already lifted up the geographic component of social location. We are interested in discerning what is happening in Central America and the Caribbean. ¿How do experiences here compare with those in other parts of the world and what does this teach us about Christianity in the world today?

Latin America and the Caribbean are pluricultural spaces. The good news of the gospel has been appropriated into a great variety of cultural situations. In August of 2015, the political constitution of Costa Rica was amended to declare that Costa Rica is a multi-ethnic and pluriculutral nation. However, the different ethnic groups have not had the same access to social power. The relationship between ethnicity and religious preference in the construction of identities in Latin America is a topic of academic debate. In the case of Guatemala, some studies have suggested that conversion to an evangelical church allows individuals to leave behind a Maya ethnic identity and assume new ladino identity in order to participate in the dominate culture (for example, see Cabarrus 1998). Other researchers see conversion to an evangelical church as a way of reconstructing a Maya ethnic identity in new circumstances, that is to say as a form of revitalization (Samson 2007). It seems evident to me that both processes are occurring, though in different contexts. What does it mean that ethnicity did not emerge as an explicit topic in the case studies included in this book?

Gender is another aspect of social location that has not received much treatment in the case studies. What gender roles, for men as well as for women, do these religious institutions promote, be they churches or non-governmental organizations? Are they supporting traditional gender roles or are they proposing changes? Do they offer alternative forms of masculinity for young men to challenge the dominant machismo? Do the situations of poverty and violence impact women in the same way they affect men? Who has access to the resources the different networks are able to mobilize? It is vitally important to keep in mind the question of gender when studying religious phenomena.

The same century that saw the center of gravity of the world's Christian population migrate to the south, also witnessed the greatest concentration of wealth ever seen in human history. I don't want to suggest a direct causal link between these two phenomena, but we need to keep this situation in mind. We are in a context marked by growing inequality in the distribution of income and wealth. At the socio-economic level, we must ask if the religious experiences we have studied for this consultation process are part of the cultural transformations that theories of revitalization have encouraged us to seek. Or are these experiences perhaps religious accommodations to the neoliberal economic system? We also need to ask if the work of the faith-based non-governmental organizations with marginalized and impoverished populations is playing the role the system assigns to religious groups, to care for people on the margins of society while wealth continues to concentrate in fewer and fewer hands.[7] Some analysts here in the Central American region have suggested that emigration and the work of non-governmental organizations serve as escape valves to inhibit the buildup of social pressures and thus prevent the population from demanded radical changes. I suspect that we will need not only the theoretical tools offered by Weber, Durkheim and Wallace to understand what is happening in the region, but also tools developed by Marx, Gramsci, Bourdieu and Maduro, among others.

Each researcher who attempts to analyze religious phenomena should acknowledge her or his own social location from which she or he is reading these situations. At the same time, it is important to un-locate or decenter yourself, to listen to the perspectives of other people, especially the persons whose religious practices we wish to examine. The people from the churches and organizations that were studied in this consultation process have offered us their faith testimonies. I invite you to

7 In their book Empire, Michael Hardt and Antonio Negri (2000) suggest that today's NGOs play the same role as the mendicant orders did during the mercantile phase of capitalism in Europe.

receive them with gratitude and reverence. Without a doubt, in each one of the case studies, lives were transformed. However, this does not free us from the responsibility of doing an in-depth analysis.

The question of location is fundamental for those of us who are believers. This goes far beyond the desire to define our own location. We must also ask, "Where is God?" In the incarnation, God not only assumed the history of a particular human being. At the same time, God revealed that history is the space in which God encounters us. By discerning where God is, we discover where we should be. Many years ago, I came to Costa Rica as a theology student to study at the Latin American Biblical Seminary. I took a course in Christology with Professor Saul Trinidad, a Methodist from Peru. Saul insisted that the text of Matthew 26:10, in which Jesus says to his disciples that "the poor you will always have with you", is a text about location. The function of the text is not to justify the continuing existence of poverty. Rather, the text indicates where the followers of Jesus must be, with people who have been impoverished as long as poverty exists.

In Latin America, the revitalization that Christianity needs is not an attempt to return to an idealized glorious past. As we have seen, the past of Christianity here in Latin America is stained with blood, especially that of the indigenous peoples. The decolonization of Christian faith starts with repentance for this past and with the effort to construct a different kind of future with more just and more inclusive societies. We need a renewal of Christian faith that will permit women and men to construct new identities and new relationships, both on a personal level and on a political social level. We are seeking a revitalization of Christianity that will be good news.

References:

Allan Anderson, Allan, et al., eds.
2010. Studying Global Pentecostalism: Theories and Methods. Berkeley: University of California Press.

Bevans, Stephen B.
2011. Constants in Context: A Theology of Mission for Today. Maryknoll, N.Y.: Orbis Books.

Bosch, David Jacobus.
1991. Transforming Mission: Paradigm Shifts in Theology of Mission, American Society of Missiology Series, no. 16. Maryknoll, N.Y.: Orbis Books.

Brenneman, Robert.
2012. Homies and Hermanos: God and Gangs in Central America. New York: Oxford University Press.

Cabarrus, Carlos Rafael.
1998. Lo maya, ¿una identidad con futuro? Guatemala: CEDIM-FAPO.

Cleary, Edward L. and Timothy J. Steigenga, eds.
2007. Conversion of a Continent: Contemporary Religious Change in Latin America. New Brunswick: Rutgers University Press.

Ferguson, Niall.
2006. The War of the World: Twentieth-Century Conflict and the Descent of the West. New York: Penguin Press.

Gerlach, Luther P. and Virginia H. Hine.
1970. People, Power, Change: Movements of Social Transformation. Indianapolis: Bobbs-Merrill.

Gitau, Wanjiru M.
2015. "Revitalization of Christianity in Nairobi: The Mavuno Church". In Africa Urban Christian Identity: Emerging Patterns, edited by Philomena Njeri Mwaura and J. Steven O'Malley, 56-81. Nairobi: Acton Publishers.

Hardt, Michael and Antonio Negri.
2000. Empire. Cambridge, Mass.: Harvard University Press.

Jacobsen, Douglas G.
2015. Global Gospel: An Introduction to Christianity on Five Continents. Grand Rapids: Baker Academic.

Kalu, Ogbu.
2008. African Pentecostalism: An Introduction. Oxford: Oxford University Press.

Quijano, Anibal.
2000. "Colonialidad del poder, eurocentrismo y América Latina". En Lander, Edgardo, comp., La colonialidad del saber: Eurocentrismo y ciencias sociales, 201-245. Buenos Aires: CLACSO-UNESCO, 2000.

Samson, C. Matthews.
2007. Re-enchanting the World: Maya Protestantism in the Guatemala Highlands. Tuscaloosa: Univ. of Alabama Press.

Sanneh, Lamin O.
1989. Translating the Message: The Missionary Impact on Culture. American Society of Missiology Series, no. 13. Maryknoll, N.Y: Orbis Books.

Schreiter, Robert J.
1985. Constructing Local Theologies. Maryknoll, N.Y.: Orbis Books.

Shaw, Mark.
2010. Global Awakening: How 20th-Century Revivals Triggered a Christian Revolution. Downers Grove, IL: IVP Academic.

Stanley, Brian.
1990. The Bible and the Flag: Protestant Missions and British Imperialism in the Nineteenth and Twentieth Centuries. Leicester, England: Apollos.

Walls, Andrew F.
1996. The Missionary Movement in Christian History: Studies in the Transmission of Faith. Maryknoll, N.Y.: Orbis Books.

CHAPTER 2: NEW JERUSALEM IN A GARBAGE DUMP

Religious Revitalization of Urban Space in Managua

Carlos Aguirre Salinas
and
Adrian Tovar Simoncic

So the law was put in charge to lead us to Christ that we might be justified by faith. Now that faith has come, we are no longer under the supervision of the law. You are all sons of God through faith in Christ Jesus, for all of you who were baptized into Christ have clothed yourselves with Christ. There is neither Jew nor Greek, slave nor free, male nor female, for you are all one in Christ Jesus. (Galatians 3: 24-28 NIV)

In the Nicaragua of the 1980s, three young girls—Carmen, Reina and Magdalena—walked near Matagalpa toward a crowd moved by the Spirit. It is an evangelization campaign led by the Assemblies of God in Rancho Grande. "Just go to sell candy," their Catholic mother had warned them. "Don't accept Jesus." Her words made no difference. "The power of the Spirit was so strong that soon I realized I was accepting Christ," recalled Pastor Magdalena. She was eleven years old. Although deeply upset by her daughters' disobedience, the mother urged her daughters to keep their new commitment as long as they did not neglect their work on the farm. Perhaps she held out hope that her daughters would abandon their new faith after a time, given the demands made by evangelical activism. But she was mistaken. Years later, Pastor Magdalena's spirit of inspired transgression and perseverance would mark her ministry and with it, the emergence of the Pentecostal Mission New Jerusalem on the site of the largest garbage dump in Central America, "La Chureca."

Magdalena's Call: Origins

In 1986, the terrors of the Contra War[8] led Magdalena's mother to send her daughters to a friend in the capital, for she feared for their safety. Magdalena worked as a maid and at night attended night school where her employer had enrolled her.

8 In 1986, the war intensified in Nicaragua after the re-election of Reagan in the United States. Reagan authorized the CIA to finance the Contra, an act that was condemned by the International Court of Justice at The Hague. Between 1980 and 989, more than 30,000 Nicaraguans died in the conflict between the Contra and the Sandinista government. The migration of Magdalena's family to Managua coincided with the most intense part of the war.

There she learned how to read the Bible. At the age of 14, she was baptized in a congregation of the United Brethen of Christ. During the difficult experience of migrating from the countryside to the city during her adolescent years, and having been separated from her mother, religious socialization as an evangelical Christian played an important role in her life. Between work, school, and church, the life in the congregation represented for Magdalena not just a discipline but a lifestyle that allowed her to focus and protect herself from the multiple vulnerabilities experienced by a young female migrant in the city.

It was through her congregation that Magdalena acquired her first experiences in leadership and service to the community, watching over the children of the congregation. At 17, she was called by her mother to return to help with the rearing of her younger siblings and the reorganization of the farm after the war. By then she was in the third year of her secondary education, which she had to interrupt.

The pastor of her congregation in Managua followed her home and after a week of instruction, charged her to open a preaching point in the countryside near her mother's home. She replied that she did not know anyone, and that it would be especially awkward if she had to lead services at a home where she was the only evangelical. "Here you will start a congregation because God is needed!" was the reply of the pastor upon leaving. Magdalena relates that indeed—albeit with great difficulties and without fully understanding what was happening—she began to preach and she continued preaching until, eventually, a congregation was formed.

At 21, she returned to Managua to marry a member of her congregation and to serve in the women's council. But by age 27 she was in the midst of a severe marital crisis that ended in separation, leaving her on her own with two small children. Her only source of income was working at a small food stand in a city market. Magdalena then made the most improbable of decisions.

"This is not Nicaragua, it might as well be Africa or something, but it can't be Nicaragua," thought Magdalena one November afternoon in 1998 when she saw a television reporter showing the reality of garbage pickers in La Chureca. Their livelihood came from the trash, in which they lived and from which they ate. The children and adults were sick from contact with the garbage; they had only the vultures to accompany them. At that moment, in front of her small black and white TV set, Magdalena experienced an undeniable call. From that moment on, she decided to dedicate her life to a Christian ministry to the service of those victims of marginalization in every imaginable aspect, those whose humanity was being denied by society.

However, this project began with large number of obvious difficulties and inconveniences, such as Magdalena's own personal situation as well as the enormous quantity of social resources and energy that is needed to bring dignity to a context that is the result of historic and structural processes of exclusion, exploitation and marginalization. Magdalena had to learn many unexpected lessons. Some were very disheartening, such as being left to her own devices by her congregation, abandoned and mistrusted by openly chauvinistic patriarchal authority. Another disheartening struggle came from fighting bureaucratic structures and government ministries. She learned that many see helping the poor as a business, an exchange for prestige, an attempt to claim the laurels of altruism in public spaces. She also learned that sincere help comes from the most unexpected places and that the most important allies are often in the same local community context, where those who have been affected organize themselves.

The spark of radical and unconditional love that Magdalena unleashed opened a process of community revitalization, one that today is supported by a network of local autonomous churches. In so doing, one of the more problematic urban spaces of Managua has been transformed in a way not reducible to simple sociological analysis. Nevertheless, a significant part of the lessons learned, both of the revitalization of the church and of the society itself, can more intelligible through an analysis of the context, strategies developed, and creative processes. This text attempts to provide such an analysis.

Religion and Marginality: Context

The experience of revitalization in Villa Guadalupe—the name of the neighborhood created when the garbage workers were relocated to one-room concrete block homes near La Chureca—is best placed within the spectrum of evangelization strategies that characterizes evangelical Christianity[9] in Nicaragua and Central America. In sociological jargon, this involves a consideration of the religious field together with the ideologies and practices that dominate the dynamics of the religious actors, be they individuals, ministries, or complete denominations. On the other hand, La Chureca is not only a marginalized urban space; it is also a space of political contention. The public policies directed at the most destitute population are not just a means to fight poverty and create social justice, but also become a means to acquire political prestige and ultimately power. Differences over the politics of assistance and even over who has the right to help thus become political disputes as well as a religious imperative. Finally, the storage and recycling of garbage can itself offer an opportunity for a highly profitable business models in which private and state economic interests play an important role.

Itinerant pastors and entrepreneurial ministries

Today, Nicaragua, along with other Central American countries, has some of the highest proportions of non-Catholic Christians in Latin America. (Pew Research Center 2014) As is the case in the rest of the continent, the growth in other Christian traditions is almost entirely within evangelical or pentecostal expressions. Despite its diversity and complexity, two strategies of evangelization dominate this segment of the religious field. On the one hand, there is the traditional method of opening new mission fields and church planting through the use of itinerant preachers. This method dominated for many years and is associated with traditional denominational structures. On the other hand, we

---

9 The definition of evangelical used here draws on that offered by Paul Freston (1998, 2004) together with its extension through the "Renewalist" category proposed by Pew (2006). But these categories are extremely fluid and their content depends on a varied and complex interrelation between self-affiliations, historical traditions, denominational structures, and statistical observations.

find strategies of evangelization based on doctrines of church growth under a logic of territorial expansion, centralized institutional structures and a web of cells, family groups, and other units of expansion. This group of methods is considered by many the new form of evangelization par excellence, given how effective it appears from a numerical point of view. Such methods originate and are found frequently post-denominational or interdenominational structures such as megachurches and independent ministries that operate in metropolitan zones. These structures often have episcopal forms of church polity in that they tend to be highly hierarchical, hardly transparent, and profoundly dependent on the charismatic leadership of the pastor in charge. This contrasts with more presbyterial polities, whose historical origin emerged in opposition to the Roman model, in which decisions are taken collectively by the ministers assembled across a denomination or network of churches. One can observe in all this a certain correspondence between forms of church polity and evangelization strategies. Each strategy corresponds to moments and institutional structures that can be corroborated, at least partially, through empirical observation. Reality, however, is always more complex.

The new methods of evangelization enjoy more popularity among the large denominations, which have both traditional polities and new ministries that apply methods of church growth to the enthusiasm of many and the skepticism of others. The Assemblies of God in Nicaragua are a great example of this. There is a lively internal discussion among its leadership over the form and degree to which they should welcome these new forms of evangelizing, but in general the tendency is to incorporate them into denominational structures. This phenomenon, albeit underwritten by the success of certain pastoral leaders, presents certain aspects worthy of critical reflection.

One cannot fail to notice the managerial character of many churches and ministries that are managed in word and deed like businesses. This includes an obsession for the efficiency of the organizational structures, growth in numbers, territorial expansion, the massive mobilization of the faithful in showy megaevents, and the mobilization of resources in a competition for the construction of massive places of worship. These efforts are expressed in familiar discourse: to win souls for Christ, to win territories for Christ, or to bring to fruition visions and prophesies of the pastor. In this logic of territorial expansion, many ministries have confronted the problem of a mutual cannibalization as believers seek to identify with the level of success of the church to which they belong. Small congregations that have worked locally for years do not stand a chance to survive when the buses of megachurches start coming to their neighborhood to transport people to their spectacular services.

Yet the reality is far more complex. As evident as these challenges are, the new forms of churches cannot be reduced to them. These new actors also create structures of support and help for their faithful that go well beyond the spiritual, including day care, financial advice, psychological assistance to families, soup kitchens, and other social projects.[10] Likewise, some larger churches have become aware of these problems and cooperate with small churches without trying to absorb them. Many Christians also attend both megachurches and their local congregations. Nevertheless, there is a question that remains relevant. Why had none of these successful new ministries or churches come to La Chureca, where the needs were so evident? We believe that many ministries, helping the poor and marginalized continues to be subordinated to strategic questions shaped by managerialism.

---

10 From 1990 to 2007 the Interior Ministry registered 643 evangelical churches and institution. It is striking the number of evangelical institutions that are dedicated to social work. Of the 643 institutions registered until 2007, 80 are described as social organizations with community projects; family services; work with children, adolescents, youth and women; programs in human rights; economic development; and rehabilitation efforts for people at risk or addicted to liquor or drugs. Of this number, 72 women serve as legal representatives of these churches and institutions. In the majority of organizations directed by women there are social initiatives in favor of children, adolescents and youth. During this same period, 123 Catholic institutions were registered with religious goals and charitable actions. An additional 172 Christian organizations offering social, educational or community services were registered. A total of 938 religious institutions were registered during this period, which leads us to think that this type of institution is becoming increasingly relevant in Nicaraguan society. (Aguirre 2012, 1-6).

Not even the traditional denominations had reached La Chureca.[11] No one. Nothing. Magdalena herself belonged to one of those traditional denominations. Ironically, the same service where she was anointed as a pastor was also when she was effectively dismissed from her congregation. Her church wished her the best in her new ministry, but they neither understood nor supported her. As a woman in the midst of a divorce, a series of accusations and suspicions even arose regarding her moral integrity as well as her mental health. Today, after her successful ministry, she is celebrated in evangelical circles. Though we don't want to examine at length the complexity of gender issues in evangelical churches, it is clear that her story illustrates major challenges women face in taking on leadership roles in Christian revitalization.

Magdalena's departure from her congregation followed inevitably from her instinctive suspension of all traditional methods of evangelization and church planting. She would not "open up a field" or "win souls for Christ," or "gain territory" nor "fight a spiritual war." Her ministerial focus was simply the intolerable level of human suffering and extreme marginalization.

On one of the first occasions Magdalena preached in La Chureca, she was without any audience apparent at all, as a lone voice in the middle of the desert of garbage. When night fell, small lights began to appear. The people who lived among the garbage, who heard her preaching about God's vision for the community,

11 According to data from the Directorio de las Iglesias Protestante en Nicaragua 1996 – 1997 published by INDEF, from the 1960s to the 1990s, in the sectors of Acahualinca and Los Martínez that surround the La Chureca dump, the following churches were present: International Church of the Foursquare Gospel (1957), The Primitive Evangelical Mission of Nicaragua (1962), Christian Mission (1970), Association of Churches of Christ of Nicaragua (1972), Apostolic Church of the Faith in Jesus Christ (1990), Ebenezer Church of the Assemblies of God (1990), Free Apostolic Church (1991), Apostolic Church the Palms of Jesus (1995), A Voice Alert for Jesus Christ Ministry (1996) and the Second Cathedral Christian Church of the Assemblies of God (1995). Since the first decade of the 21st century there has been a presence of new Pentecostal churches and cell groups from megachurches with tendencies toward accelerated growth.

actually told her what her former church had said. "What are you doing here? Go away, this place will hurt you." Her answer said it all. "No, you are the ones who have been hurt."

Politics of urban marginalization

La Chureca is no longer the horror it once was. Pastor Magdalena's initiative galvanized other efforts from religious actors—both evangelicals and non-evangelicals—as well as secular agencies such as NGOs, the government, and others. Given the urgency to combat the horrors suffered by the inhabitants of this bleak landscape, one might imagine that alliances would come about easily. But that was not the case at all. What did help was the emergence of a local web of cooperation between independent churches. In the midst of that, however, was a tense interaction between a religious initiative "from the ground up" and the policies of poverty reduction implemented "from above", that is to say the political dimension of revitalization.

In 2007, Managua's city government worked with the Spanish Agency of International Cooperation for Development to design a project to improve living conditions in La Chureca. It was implemented between 2009 and 2012 for a total cost of 30 million Euros.[12] This project enclosed the massive city dump and restricted access, relocating the inhabitants of La Chureca to nearby newly build housing with spaces for recreation, health care, and education. Most importantly, it funded the construction of a recycling plant along with job training and employment for many, but not all, of the former garbage pickers. Literacy and education programs were implemented in the community. Clearly, this project brought great relief to a considerable number of people in terms of health, living conditions, and stable employment. Moreover, there was an environmental benefit for the rest of the city. Nevertheless, these types of projects are not exempt from contradictions. The massive investment of the Spanish development agency also brought great profits for the private (Spanish) companies involved in the project. Trash recycling can

---

12 See http://www.laprensa.com.ni/2013/02/20/nacionales/135365-llego-el-final-de-la-chureca.

be a booming business. Problems arise when the profits of these types of investments engender new processes of exclusion.

Not all the former inhabitants who made a living from the garbage received housing or employment at the recycling plant. Those who were left out continue to live from garbage but now in even more difficult conditions since it is now illegal to enter the dump, effectively criminalizing their work. It is beyond the scope of this study to detail these aspects, but it is evident that the political function of these projects leaves scarce space for critique. These projects exclude those aspects now considered a public nuisance, including precisely the grassroots work carried out for several years by Pastor Magdalena and the church called "New Jerusalem." Those responsible for the redevelopment project at first approached her, offering appreciation for work and a new space in the housing project for the church. Then at the last minute, she and the church were suddenly excluded from planning, unbeknownst to her, neutralizing her ability to react. Things eventually worked out only because the financial support of donor churches in North America[13] facilitated acquisition of a nearby lot and the empathy of a decision maker in the mayor's office who prevented the building of an access street across the church property, something that would have effectively expropriated the church lot.

We cannot offer a detailed political analysis here. The way power is exercised by small ministries "from below" is clearly very different from the way large denominations and megachurches use their power. It suffices to say these are two distinct ways of being political. To construct our argument, we turn briefly to a discussion of this dimension in the evangelical religious field.

Consider how social scientists, among others, criticize the apolitical character of evangelical Christianity—especially Pentecostalism—in Latin America.[14] This debate has come to be

13 Latin American and Caribbean missionaries living in the US provide support. These same missionaries now invite pastor Magdalena to share her testimony in different countries.

14 Although the work of Schäfer (2009) in Guatemala had already demonstrated in the 1990s the relationship between high social class, theologies of spiritual war and domination, and strategies of direct political influence, on the one hand, and a low social class, apocalyptic theologies

a topic of reflection in evangelical institutions. As a result, today it is hard to find evangelicals that preach a radical detachment from the world and reject political participation. The pertinent question today is rather how evangelicals participate or ought to participate in the political process. The position most frequent among Nicaraguan evangelicals[15] is a kind of secular and republican separation that underscores the duties of a good Christian (such as voting and obeying the laws) as a matter of conscience, private and separate from the church. Others advocate the establishment of an explicitly Christian order where the design of public policies is guided by the Bible and candidates are elected based of their Christian values, thus denying a clear separation between faith and politics. Such postures have been adopted at different leadership levels and have led to the founding of explicitly evangelical political parties to compete in elections. In general, these options quickly fail since the evangelical electorate is more complex than what their own leaders assume and have a perspective that differentiates between their faith and their political preferences. "Evangelical citizens vote for evangelical political parties" has turned out to be a false claim for Central America in the majority of cases and in particular for Nicaragua. In cases where evangelicals do take power, they have often become "blinded by power." In Nicaragua, a sector of the Assemblies of God is trying a new model of this kind, inspired by so-called dominion theology. We shall see what the future brings. However, there is still another approach evangelicals might take to political participation that is currently being discussed by social scientists and which is what can be seen in the case of La Chureca. Are not all these forms of congregational life that lead to the creation of local churches, schools. clinics, and community kitchens, that transform urban spaces and organize people, precisely people who have been excluded from or who have become disillusioned with political participation, forms of citizen action as well as religious participation? Is this not an alternative

---

and detachment from the world, and strategies of avoidance of political participation.

15 In order to analyze the political participation of evangelicals in Nicaragua, we are drawing upon 150 interviews conducted with the leadership of different evangelical denominations, institutions and organizations in the country.

form of citizenship, organized from below, according to a religious logic that by rejecting official politics becomes political in the best sense of the word?

This question and the answer—complex as it is—surely corresponds to the process of revitalization in "New Jerusalem." Humanitarian commitment and religious faith came together and mobilized many. Consider a member of the church who had ample experience and training in social work through a feminist NGO. She was devastated when her coworkers in the NGO tried to coerce her to have an abortion so she could continue devoting her time to the organization. Now she devotes that same passionate level of energy to social needs as a leader within the New Jerusalem Church in La Chureca. Is her former activity political but her present activity merely religious? The same could be said of the trained educator who left a stable job with a good salary to direct the church school, thus giving families a better educational option for their children.

However, it may well be that the most important of the political effects of this church and the most revitalizing one, as well as the one that most forcefully questions formal and established political actors, is the radical politics of inclusion, the politics of Christian love. The unconditional inclusion evident at "New Jerusalem" is not preceded by any negotiation. Everything is directed to lifting up the human dignity of the "Churequeros." Before wanting to make them citizens, voters, employees or consumers, "New Jerusalem" wants to make them children of God. That is, it wants to make them simply and fully human, not in theory, but in practice and experience. It seems to us that reflection on this experience in contrast with other forms of political action by evangelical actors could provide many important lessons, but we will leave that for the theologians rather than to the sociologist and historian who are writing this paper.

When people in La Chureca accepted Christ upon hearing Magdalena preach the first time, Magdalena's original congregation, which had not yet expelled her, exhorted her to bring those people to the church. However, she realized that this would not work. The people of La Chureca had interiorized the exclusion and disgust with which they were treated and were embarrassed to be invited to go to a church. They knew very well that others would not treat them as Magdalena did. So, they constructed their own alternative. The next time she was preaching amidst the trash, an overlooked, elderly garbage picker brought Pastor Magdalena a box he had found among the trash. "Here, Pastor, take this so you won't have to stand on top of garbage and so that people will be better able to hear you." She turned to him and gently said "What 'people'? You are the people! Sit down to hear the Word."

Evangelical churches: Revitalized by emergency

The history of evangelical churches in Nicaragua is inextricably tied to humanitarian initiatives during national emergencies when the most affected have typically been women, children, and the elderly. The earthquake of 1972 devastated the city of Managua, leaving it in ruins and taking thousands of lives. This tragic event marked the start of the main denominations working together in order to find alternatives to address the tragedy that had taken place. In response, the Evangelical Committee to Assist Victims (CEPAD) began[16] with the direct support of the Nicaraguan Baptist Convention. Soon Pentecostal churches were also involved in this effort.

In the wake of that same earthquake, the garbage dump of La Chureca began to form. Its first inhabitants were survivors of the earthquake and floods that affected the coastal zone of Lake Xolotlan. Subsequently, various migrants from the countryside began to pour into the city. By 1998, after Hurricane Mitch, the local population grew dramatically. In the 1970s and 1980s, the place had been invisible to the churches and other social

16 CEPAD was born on December 27, 1972. On March 31, 1973, it changed its name to the Evangelical Pro-Development Committee, taking up different service programs that it began to implement after the earthquake, such as: an educational program, child welfare, urban community development, social promotion and community organizing, agricultural training, clean drinking water, sewage systems, housing, health—expanding their projects to the national territory. CEPAD was the first organization to encourage the evangelical churches to include projects with a social focus in their pastoral agenda, something that is common nowadays.

institutions, but by the 1990s NGOs[17] began to carry out social projects to assist children and families who were subsisting on the garbage.

Church Agenda in the 70s and 80s

- Proclamation of a premillennial eschatology
- Attention to the victims of war
- Promotion of peace in interreligious alliances
- Participation in political action and Sandinista Defense Committees
- Implementation of social and educational projects

Evangelical churches during this period played an important role in responding to the painful consequences of the Contra War, consoling families in grief, participating in groups that pursued peace processes along with various religious and social national and international institutions. They implemented social and educational projects, carried out public projects, and participated in the Sandinista Defense Committees. At the same time, another sector embraced a premillennial eschatology that proclaimed the imminent coming of Christ and cultivated an attitude of indifference toward worldly matters. (Martínez 1989, 137-138.)

The churches also joined together in response to the state of emergency created by Hurricane Joan and later Hurricane Mitch, mobilizing national and international help, including donations in kind, sheltering victims and offering moral support to survivors. The painful situation provoked by the earthquake, the war, and other natural disasters forced churches to expand

17 The 1990s saw a significant expansion of NGOs. In 2011, the Ministry of Interior in Nicaragua reported 4,360 non-profit associations and many more without legal status. The ONG Directory barely reached 322 NGOs in the year 2000. From this limited group, only 6% had been established prior to 1980s. In the 1980s, there was a 22% increase; in the 1990s, there was a demographic explosion: 72% of the NGOs that existed in 2000 were founded in neo-liberal Nicaragua. This scenario gave rise to ecclesiastical NGOs related to evangelical and Pentecostal denominations. Pentecostals also jumped on the NGO bandwagon. For further information on the topic, see Rocha 2011.

their agenda from limited pastoral matters focused only on the spiritual toward an interest in social issues, albeit limited. Thus, by the 1990s, the churches begin to reach out to the surrounding society by combine ecclesiastical initiatives with social projects.

Churches in the 1990s

- Social and educational projects implemented by the churches
- Political participation of the evangelical leadership in confessional parties
- Process of reconciliation in a post-war society
- Contribution to the social integration of the demobilized participants in the war

During this time, evangelical churches experienced astonishing numeric growth. New denominations emerged, primarily Pentecostal, independent of traditional Nicaraguan churches. By 2009, the Ministry of the Interior reported that it has registered 800 denominations.[18] This growth created a celebratory mood among church leaders, encouraging them to implement initiatives[19] to remake the political system of the country.

During the last fifteen years, then, the churches changed enormously. Although the churches continued their social initiatives, new interests arose in theologies that focus on managerial and financial aspects. Congregations expected material prosperity. In that sense, the church's social activities are shaped by strategies of numerical growth. However, the goal is not to promote sustainability in the territories where the

18 The growth of the evangelical population not only happened in terms of number of persons, but also in terms of number of denominations. In the year 2009, close to 800 evangelical denominations were registered in the Ministry of Interior. For Axel Borchgrevinch, "A Study of Civil Society in Nicaragua," in the year 2006, 603 evangelical denominations registered with the Ministry of Interior, the majority of which were of the Pentecostal tradition. Fifteen years ago, one could count with the fingers of one hand the evangelical denominations, whereas now it is an almost impossible task (Aguirre y Araica 2010, 46).

19 A number of studies explore these issues (Zub 2002, 9-12; Bardeguez 1997, 14-15; Bautz, Gonzalez, and Orozco 1994, 8).

congregants that attend megachurches reside. Instead, buses bring people to participate in these religious spectacles where the entrepreneurial pastor dominates.

The focus on numerical growth and prosperity began to substitute for the social projects that churches had undertaken starting in the 1970s. However, some churches resisted these new theologies, seeking alternatives to address the issues affecting more intensely the communities, establishing liaisons with local governments and national and international institutions.

A Church Born in the Landfill

Independent churches occupy a prominent place in the changes to Nicaraguan Protestantism. The first eighty years were defined by the historical denominations and Pentecostal denominations. However, the diversification and growth of the 1990s and the resulting boom during the first decade of the twenty-first century definitively changed the scene. Independent churches began to occupy organizational spaces, giving them social power in the city and countryside, along with a national vision and leadership interested in addressing issues like poverty, sickness, and the overall vulnerability of the members of its congregations.

The New Jerusalem Church is part of these emerging independent and autochthonous churches, largely Pentecostal. The congregation emerged as a response to the issues of the inhabitants who literally lived in the garbage, in stark contrast to the model of church that looks to the center of the city. Instead, this particular church chose to cater to those marginalized in the city, integrating preaching and liturgy with social action.

Children in the dump

La Chureca is located in the Acahualinca neighborhood, in District II of Managua, in the upper northeast of the city on the shore of the Xolotlan Lake.

> It has existed since 1973. More than 30 years later, in December 2007, it won a place among the 'The 20 Horrors of the Current World' in a contest

> organized by the Spanish magazine Interviu. It consists of 42 hectares occupied by mountains of garbage. La Chureca is the largest open-air landfill in Latin America. (Grisby 2008)

Andrea Lobo Araujo named these families "the people of the garbage dump." These approximately 1,500 people survived with the small amount of money they received from sorting and selling recyclables. Of these, 53 percent were under 18 years of age and 92 percent lived in makeshift houses share with at least six people, without drinking water, access to health services, or education. In all, 62 percent had no access to sanitary facilities and one in four adults were illiterate.

Andrea narrates the daily activities of people in La Chureca:

> They pick up plastic, glass, paper, aluminum, and other metals. On "good" days, they might pick up 200 pounds of plastic, some glass, and ten pounds of aluminum. Entire families work all day long, from six in the morning in this inferno, sheltering themselves from the sun or the rain under a cardboard box or under the shade of the "family car" for those lucky enough to have one. Children, even from the age of four, begin their "professional career" helping keep an eye on the collected material, sorting or cleaning. In the beginning, they sort the easiest materials to collect, such as paper and plastic. Sometimes, they even find a toy among the waste. By the age of fourteen, they know everything required of a worker at the landfill. (http://periodismointegracionucm3.blogspot.com/2012/03/el-pueblo-del-basurero-la-chureca.html)

In the interviews carried out with members of the New Jerusalem church, they recounted the hardships endured with their sons and daughters, with whom they worked intense hours from the morning until sunset; first collecting solid waste and later sorting them by category. Likewise, they would collect any leftover food found among the trash. Children would often die under the garbage, crushed by the heavy wheels of trucks, in constant danger as they were of not being seen by the truck drivers.

Among tears and sighs, they recall times marked by loss of loved ones and physical and emotional scars. But they also express a sense of gratitude because their situation changed when an unknown woman came to preach to them, Magdalena Herrera, who they later called "God's Servant" or simply "the Pastor." From the moment she began there, her mission was to form a church within the community to assist the community.

A theology that revitalizes everyday life

A salient feature of the discourse of Pastor Magdalena and the members of the New Jerusalem Church is a Pentecostal testimonial theology that interprets the presence of God in their daily activities. This type of theological understanding is common in small and independent churches, but less so in large Pentecostal denominations, historic churches, and megachurches, where there is more emphasis on motivational rhetoric and the achievement of individual or family prosperity. These new theological emphases often render this older, testimonial style marginal or practically nonexistent. In such churches, there are few spaces where members can share their testimonies. Instead, priority is given to strategic leadership that presents an image of success.

"Rise up and deliver my Word. I will change the lives of these people."

Pastor Magdalena understands her work as responding to God's desire to change the lives of the families that lived in La Chureca. She was propelled by seeing little children eat from the waste in the landfill next to packs of vultures doing the same thing. Her sense of calling, and that of the church in general, is to serve, to bring concrete solutions to the community. The churches located nearby, however, maintained a distant and indifferent attitude to the reality of the "Churequeros." They were cognizant of their existence but did not want to include them.

Pastor Magdalena's decision was different. She nurtured the hope that God had a plan for this population and began a process that today is praised by both Catholic and evangelical leaders as well as government and NGO leaders. Her impact and that of the New Jerusalem Church became even larger when she secured sponsorship for educational initiatives and infant nutrition, goals that had been a priority for her from the start.

"We cooperated without concern for doctrine, focused on people's needs."

Evangelical churches tend to put doctrine at the forefront of their ministries. The first six decades of the history of Nicaraguan Protestantism were accentuated by doctrinal conflicts among various denominations, particularly between the historical churches and the Pentecostal churches. In turn, this strife led to the emergence of new, nationally-based denominations. Over the last thirty years, doctrinal matters have taken a back seat to church growth and the aspiration of having a growing and prosperous church membership. In this context, the churches have gone through a transition from emphasis on doctrine or tradition to a model of church growth focused on prosperous members.

In the context of La Chureca, Pastor Magdalena worked from the beginning with brothers and sisters who came out of church backgrounds with various doctrines, including those who were trinitarian, Oneness Pentecostal or Adventists. They put aside such theoretical matters to work together and build a non-traditional church in the midst of the garbage dump, one open to all persons who live in that place. Testimonial preaching, prayer, guidance, and a community kitchen were the first activities that inspired the growth of the nascent New Jerusalem Church. In due time, a preschool and an elementary school were also founded.

The interpretation of sound doctrine is one that identifies the necessities of people and God's acting among them to provide holistic restoration. The actions of each believer are centered in a constant dedication in solidarity toward those who need help. This goes hand in hand with an ethic regarding moral conduct. Because of the values of solidarity and human dignity, it is important to dress with dignity, preserve one's marriage, use respectful language, and avoid alcohol and drugs.

In addition to fasting, prayer, and fellowship with other Pentecostal churches, the believers are encouraged by Pastor Magdalena to dedicate time and resources to visit families in need, particularly the many suffering from unemployment, illness, or lack of food. The congregation helps feed and support those families. This practice is identifiable in the preaching, conversations, testimonies, and prayers, where they are specifically mentioned in the sermon and in thanksgiving offered to God.

"Now I was focused on serving those in need."

During many years, Pastor Magdalena run a small food stand in a Managua's oriental market. This allowed her the means to bring food to brothers and sisters in La Chureca. Unexpectedly one day she felt a calling to devote herself full time to the care of the families in La Chureca. She decided to leave the business to initiate a new phase of the ministry. She fasted and prayed for forty days with the goal of submitting her plans to divine design.

That decision was underpinned by a theology that animates a profound spirituality, not so much a debilitating of the body through fasting, but rather by a re-focusing on others, fostering a culture of mutual sharing among the members of the community and being aware of others' pain. Pastor Magdalena is seen as an example, as she also left the comfort of her home to live with her small children in the landfill, so as to help model the communal and social restoration of those who opt to follow Christ.

The theological focus is thus rooted in people's needs. It is neither about the growth of the church nor members' prosperity, but rather a real acknowledgment of their needs. This involves visiting the people, listening to them, and involving oneself with them in their daily activities, sharing in their joys and sorrows. The members of the church identify with that focus. When they share their testimonies, they name those who they have helped build up. They see this as their highest achievement: material things are considered secondary. The person is what matters and is regarded as an actual brother or sister, not as a cliché of religious language but instead as Christian practice.

"You, Lord, have arms to help me with these children."

People see a smiling woman walking by, sharing biblical verses with a group of youth who accompany her with a wagon to pick up firewood to help cook a meal for the boys and girls who participate in the children's feeding program. That woman is Pastor Magdalena. People recognize and appreciate her because they see her always surrounded by smiling youth, helping and awaiting the moment they will receive their plate of food.

The New Jerusalem church embraces the boys and girls of La Chureca, and the church building serves as a safe house while the parents work in the garbage. Babies are given milk and treated with tenderness. When they get sick, prayers are offered on their behalf, but they are also taken to the doctor to receive medical attention. The church that has emerged is one centered around children who are accompanied by their parents.

The pastor and the church's leaders read the Bible as emphasizing their mission to assist the children, the "least ones," imparting the message of salvation, ensuring good nutrition, facilitating education, and protecting them from pitfalls that could jeopardize their future such as addiction to drugs and alcohol. The church also keeps them from unwholesome company that could lead them to participation in gangs and street crime.

"The Lord tells me that these children not only need to be fed; they had to be taught how to fish so they could eat when I could no longer provide."

Pastor Magdalena worries about the future of the boys and girls in La Chureca. She is concerned that assistance programs cannot ultimately solve the problem of food scarcity. After a few days of fasting and prayer, she received a vision of setting up a little school, a project she was able to bring to fruition in 2008. She feels that education is the best way to ensure better conditions for children and their families. For that reason, she worked with the Ministry of Education so that the school would be a registered school, fully compliant with Nicaraguan legal requirements.

Her dedication helped change the mindset of the parents, who previously would take their children to work with them. Now, they commit to send them to school. The church began to make a difference in the La Chureca community by encouraging education for different members of the families. The church entered an alliance with the Ministry of Education to train Christian young people to teach as part of their practice of Christian service to a community in need not only of food, but also of didactic methods supported by Biblical texts that respond to the topics presented in the classes.

A year later, she started a Bible institute to train church leadership with a theology of service based not in theory but in daily practice. The principal focus is on missionary preparation to care for those in need, where children are the primary beneficiaries. The children are invited into the congregation, and in this way the church gains new members. The school and the Bible institute both help families realize that education is a critical factor for their personal and spiritual development. Today, young people in La Chureca share this same dream to prepare themselves as professionals to serve their community.

"I had said that God would give new houses, transform the dump, and I see the vision came true."

While she was building the church in La Chureca, Pastor Magdalena proclaimed a new vision that she had received from a visiting North American pastor who declared: "I will liberate the settlement of La Chureca from slavery." Starting from that vision, Pastor Magdalena imagined the people inhabiting new houses, the complete opposite of the reality in which they were living, housed as they were at the time in huts made of bits of plastic, sacks, cartons, aluminum, and wood, among other materials. But the pastor and the people believed in that revelation, and they waited on God's design. They did not know how it would come to be, but kept faith in that promise from God. There arose a feeling of hopefulness among the congregation, and five new preaching stations were started.

In August of 2007, the Vice-President of Spain, Maria Teresa Fernandez de la Vega, visited La Chureca and left "shocked by the drama," whereupon she pursued a project to provide funding to close the open-air mountain of garbage and construct a subterranean landfill with recycling technologies. The plan included houses for all the resident families, with sewage lines, potable water and electricity, as well as educational programs for all, from the children to illiterate adults. (http://archive.elnuevodiario.com.ni/nacional/233567-ultimos-dias-chureca/)

Fernandez's visit and the implementation of the project were interpreted as the manifestation of these prophecies coming true. The leadership and members of the New Jerusalem church theologized this event, as did the community in general. As a young female worker at the processing plant said, "Thanks be to God and to the project promoted by the government of President Ortega and our comrade Rosario Murillo and the Spanish Agency for Cooperation, now there is work for my husband and me, and my family benefited…now we have a roof over our heads, a place where I can do work where I don't have to walk from place to place. I'm indoors, not under the sun anymore, and I am only sorting one material. I am protected by gloves and a face mask. And the most important thing is that I have a stable income that gives stability to my children." (http://www.el19digital.com/articulos/ver/titulo:9911-del-antiguo-botadero-de-basura-de-managua-a-una-vida-digna)

To be able to live in new dignified houses, to work and live in a place with better public health conditions is considered a special blessing from God, a liberation. That is why one of the church leaders expressively spoke: "God took us out of that place the same way he took the Hebrew slaves out of Egypt." This analogy is frequently heard among members of the church.

There is an attitude of gratitude toward God because their situations have improved, but they also face new challenges now. Struggles continue against the influence of social ills that imperil youth such as alcoholism, drug addiction, delinquency, domestic violence, unemployment and the indifference that comes from forgetting from where they have come.

Coming Out into another World

Many generations passed through the landfill of La Chureca and many families populated the place. They came from the northern and western areas of the country, especially those affected by natural disasters. During various decades, a population grew that developed a negative attitude toward the world around them. They built their own world, away from urban Managua, mainly due to the rejection of the surrounding society, marked by stereotypes that damaged the self-esteem of the residents deemed "dangerous" and "filthy" people. As a result, parents decided that their little boys and girls should not go to the outside world so as to avoid ridicule and rejection from other children living in better conditions. Parents even prevented their children from attending school. It is not uncommon to hear people say that during their childhood they had never been to other parts of Managua and that their only playgrounds were the bales of garbage that surrounded them. There they invented their own games. Finding broken toys among the garbage brought moments of great joy. At dusk, they passed the time among piles of garbage that also emitted fumes, dust, fetid odors and worse. There they laughed and there they cried, without ever knowing what was happening in the loud and dangerous city by which they were rejected because of the way they were forced to survive.

The term "Churequeros" came to be used by people in Managua with just this connotation. It was an expression of derision and sarcasm that referred to those families who sorted garbage. This was the great challenge that the Pastor Magdalena faced when she arrived. Contrary to the deprecating terminology used to label this population, she would say to them, "You are people."

Improving their self-esteem was her first task. She worked to convince them of their own worth and importance to God. She emphasized that they had a transformative mission for the rest of society. From La Chureca, she said, a miraculous event would take place that would affect not only Nicaragua, but other countries as well. She chose leaders and began empowering believers with a positive attitude, trusting in the change they would bring about in that place. And indeed, it happened.

The first-time members of the church received an invitation to participate in a special worship outside the landfill at a church in a nearby neighborhood, they were hesitant. They were afraid of rejection and discrimination by their fellow believers due to their humble clothing, sunburned faces, and hands battered by the hard work of picking through garbage for recyclable objects. Likewise, they had internalized low self-esteem due to the atmosphere of rejection they had experienced for various decades and even generations. After hearing several sermons from Pastor Magdalena, they relented and left La Chureca to discover welcoming fellowship. Over time, church leadership began to coordinate alliances among local churches for the implementation of joint initiatives with the goal of more effectively serving those in dire need. Currently, the mission of the church has grown and families have taken on the challenge of pastoral work and opened missionary fields where they create meeting places and offer services for children. Similarly, they offer guidance for at-risk youth, including visits to hospitals and jails where they provide prayer and material or financial help to those who require it.

Starting in the 1990s, NGOs and the local government had gotten families from La Chureca accustomed to seeing themselves as victims. They were considered "poor things," objects of pity for whom decent people should feel compassion. Government officials arrived with donations of food, clothing and personal hygiene items. Help came but there was no evidence that their situation was improving at all. On the contrary, a culture of dependence developed. This represented an obstacle for the work of the New Jerusalem Church. Even its first endeavors assumed a patronizing character. All this changed, however, when grassroots leadership emerged from within the community. They were not outsiders; they and their pastor realized that they could utilize their own resources to address issues affecting the community. They formulated strategies to develop alliances with outside churches and Christian ministries as well as state agencies, but they insisted that the members of the church could contribute material, financial, and human resources. Thus they build the children's feeding center, preschool, and elementary school with the contributions of time, energy, and food items from the people themselves put to the service of the community.

These initiatives did not come about through financing by national or international institutions. Instead, a network of Christian women from the oriental market and the parents of the children gave what they could toward activities to benefit the children. The teachers who belong to the church and live there are a source of inspiration for the youth, who have seen their efforts to better themselves and contribute to the welfare of the community. Recently, support from international ministries has allowed for an expansion of the child population that is being served in different areas of Managua.

Picture the following scenario. A young woman smiles as she walks to her school, comes in and greets the teacher, who happens to be her mother. She greets warmly those who accompany her mother. She has a backpack filled with books and notebooks. At mid-day, mother and daughter say goodbye with a kiss. After the young woman leaves, her mother says excitedly, "She is going to university, and soon will have a good job." The young university student helps with church activities. The church accompanied their family when they were in La Chureca and it continues to accompany them now that they are living in Villa Guadalupe. It was the church that inspired the dreams of the new generation: the desire to learn, serve, and find more dignified job opportunities to make a living. This is noticeable in the congregation's youth and in the community in general.

The members of the church share a bond of having lived the same situation in the trash and having had similar origins as survivors of natural disasters and war, confined to a place outside the city, forgotten and used on many occasions by institutions that claim to exist to help them. In the center of the place the work of the church began and a new reality was constructed. People began to get involved and to dream of a different future.

Today, the leadership of the church not only gets involved religious matters, it also has earned recognition from the Mayor's Office, with which it maintains direct communication. It participates in meetings of the Cabinet of Citizen Action, where decisions about communal projects are made. Through these public spaces, the church received a lot for the construction of an office, an orphanage for children, a children's feeding center, a vocational school, and a recreational space for the community.

This model of Christian action, as seen in the practice of Pastor Magdalena and other church leaders, goes beyond the walls of the church building because it is necessary to be directly involved in people's lives, their families, and local context. This same perspective has been adopted by the community's youth, as is the case with the neighborhood's coordinator, who in addition to belonging to a neo-pentecostal church, works with the political leaders, representatives from state institutions and NGOs to survey more than three hundred families to get to know their needs and design initiatives to address local problems. Although the churches' participation in such activities is not strongly felt, the work of the New Jerusalem Church is valued. There is a clear contrast between the outreach of the megachurches that send their buses to bring children to the big churches on the central avenues of the city, but which do not respond to local needs, and the more prevalent small independent churches who come to the New Jerusalem Church to participate in social projects.

The church has organized leaders who take on pastoral and social duties, with a strong focus on solidarity. Pastor Magdalena is regularly invited to various countries to share her testimony and the results achieved collectively by the church and the community together with international ministries and the city government. Her plans for the future include organizing a network of churches with installations for community kitchens, preschools, clinics, vocational centers and recreational spaces where children and youth, together with their families, can be served in a holistic way and receive the spiritual edification that will make them better persons. For this reason, when she introduces a child to the church she says, "Here is a future professional who will serve God and nation."

References:

Aguirre Salinas, Carlos.
2012. Instituciones religiosas inscritas en el Ministerio de Gobernación en el período de 1990 al 2007, Managua: Procuraduría de Participación Ciudadana.

Aguirre Salinas, Carlos y Alberto Araica.
2010. Pentecostalismo en transición y globalización en Nicaragua. Influencia de las nuevas corrientes religiosas en la praxis social y política de las iglesias pentecostales. Managua: CEI.

Bardeguez, Jorge.
1997. "Nuevos escenarios políticos en la pastoral evangélica nicaragüense." Misión Evangélica Hoy 8-9.

Bautz, Wolfgang, Noel González, y Javier Orozco.
1994. Política y religión. Estudio de caso: Los evangélicos en Nicaragua, Managua. Managua: Friedrich Ebert Stiftung-CIEETS.

Freston, Paul.
1998. "Pentecostalism in Latin America: Characteristics and Controversies." Social Compass 45/3: 335-358.

2004. Evangelicals and Politics in Asia, Africa, and Latin America. Cambridge: Cambridge University Press.

Freston, Paul, ed.
2008. Evangelical Christianity and Democracy in Latin America. Oxford; New York: Oxford University Press.

Grigsby Vergara, William.
2008. "Nicaragua: La "nueva" Chureca: de la basura a la dignidad humana". Revista Envío 313. http://www.envio.org.ni/articulo/3736

Martínez, Abelino.
1989. Las sectas en Nicaragua: Oferta y demanda de salvación. San José: DEI.

Pew Research Center.
2006. Spirit and Power. Washington, DC: The PEW Forum on Religion and Public Life.

2014. Religion in Latin America: Widespread Change in a Historically Catholic Region. https://www.pewforum.org/2014/11/13/religion-in-latin-america.

Rocha, José Luis.
2011. "Los jinetes del desarrollo en tiempos neoliberales. Segundo jinete: las ONG". Revista Envío 30/354: 46-55.

Schäfer, Heinrich.
2003. Zur Theorie von kollektiver Identität und Habitus am Beispiel sozialer Bewegungen. Berlin: Humboldt Universität.

2009a. "La generación del sentido religioso - observaciones acerca de la diversidad pentecostal en América Latina." In Voces del pentecostalismo Latinoamericano (III): Identidad, teología, historia, Daniel Chiquete and Luis Orellana, eds. Concepción: RELEP.

2009b. "The Praxeological Square as a Method for the Intercultural Study of Religious Movements." In Cultures in Process: Encounter and Experience, Stephan Gramley and Ralph Schneider, eds. Bielefeld: Aisthesis.

Zub K., Roberto.
2002. Protestantismo y participación política en Nicaragua. Managua: CIEETS-UENIC-MLK.

CHAPTER 3: BUILDING BRIDGES TOWARDS INCLUSION AND DIGNITY

Belice Bridge Labor and Educational Project

America Gabriela Ochoa and Robert Brenneman

In the middle of a reality of fear and mistrust, when walking around poor neighborhoods, one realizes that these young people have much merit, because it is a very dehumanizing situation. Affection and tenderness were guiding principles for this project in the middle of that dehumanization. – Francisco Iznardo, SJ

A Church with closed doors betrays herself and her mission, and, instead of being a bridge, becomes a roadblock. – Pope Francis[20]

Francisco Iznardo (Padre Paco), general coordinator of the Belice Bridge Labor and Educational Project, describes in the above paragraph why he works with youth in this project. The Belice Bridge Labor and Educational Project is a project of the Society of Jesus in Guatemala. The project works with young people in a marginalized area of the city. Like many other young people who live in marginalized areas, these young people are trapped in a context of poverty and violence that denies them real opportunities to improve their situation. It is a good example of a movement of Evangelical churches and Catholic parishes who have decided to work in favor of an ever growing young and marginalized population in Central America. The goal of the project is to pursue the transformation of the current situation and the future of these young people and that of their communities. As described by its leaders, the project seeks to break the poverty and violence cycle in which these young people live, through education, work opportunities and attention to their individual development and emotional health. The goals of the project are to reconstruct youths' self-esteem, create a sense of belonging and offer them a space and a viable opportunity to learn and to transform their situation. The other part of the project's vision is to turn the young people into agents of change in their own communities and to involve them in the leadership of the project.

20 "Francis opens synod calling for church that is bridge, not roadblock." The National Catholic Reporter. October 4, 2015. http://ncronline.org/news/vatican/francis-opens-synod-calling-church-bridge-not-roadblock.

The project began in year 2002 through the vision of a Spanish Jesuit named Father Manolo Maqueira, who sought to create an alternative for youth within the context of violence, poverty and marginalization of "poor neighborhoods and settlements" of Guatemala City, where educational opportunities and dignified jobs do not exist. Most of the marginalized youth see themselves forced to opt out of education or to abandon their studies due to lack of resources. Consequently, they do not have access to competitive jobs that would help them generate a dignified income. The project's vision is to train professional and qualified young people who believe in themselves and who will be able to contribute to the improvement of their situation for their families and communities. The project builds bridges in Guatemalan society, bridges that connect groups of different social status that nevertheless have something to offer each other.

In a society of glaring contrasts that is so divided by social class as the Guatemalan society, young people in marginalized areas need bridges to connect them to the opportunities and new social networks to assist them in breaking the poverty cycle in which they live. The purpose of the project is to train young people, believe in them and then connect them with the opportunities they need. The project is crucial because it is transformative for the lives of the youth who belong to the project and also has an impact in their communities. The Belice Bridge Project intends to generate a change in the marginalized communities' situation through their own young people. Breaking the cycle of poverty and violence is not such a distant dream when opportunities are real and there are bridges to reach them. This case is important 1) because it reveals the depth of the obstacles to human dignity in a country that is so divided and that has so many young people, and 2) because it provides an instructive example of the capability of individuals motivated by their faith, who are serving as "bridges" between very distant populations, and who are succeeding in providing entrance to a more dignified world for young people who would have no other way of entering. In other words, the "bridge" concept is not merely part of this project name (due to the community's location which is literally under a bridge), but serves as a metaphor for the work of the project, and symbolizes the work of other churches, parishes and projects that are also serving as "bridges" between very isolated groups.

Context

From the very beginning of the Belice Bridge Labor and Educational Project, the leadership has taken the local and national context very seriously. The small country of Guatemala conceals a large cultural and social diversity. It possesses a surprising variety of climates and ecology given its small footprint of only 108,000 square kilometers. By the same token, Guatemala shows a religious dynamism and diversity that is not seen elsewhere in the western hemisphere.

Social and economic contrasts

According to the promotional billboards put up by the Tourism Institute, ethnic diversity in Guatemala is mainly experienced through smiling faces and clothing of many colors. In fact, access to social power is still not attainable for the indigenous peoples, who account for 40% of the country's population. Political parties, the military, the great majority of congressional seats and, of course, the presidency, are in the hands of the "Ladino" mestizo population, who have held power since the "criollo" class left power at the end of the 19th century (Pelaez 1998 [1970]). This Ladino population dominates in urban spaces, especially the capital city.

Nevertheless, this does not mean that exclusion only impacts the indigenous people. A second division in the country is the economic division, which may be as great as the division between ethnic groups. Guatemala, due to its geographic location, its natural resources and because of its large and growing population, represents the largest economy in Central America with a GDP of US$118 billion in 2014, which comes to a per capita income of $7,500. However, historical inequality continues in force and it is this reality that creates a situation in which over 50% of Guatemalans live in poverty and 13% live in extreme poverty (CIA 2015).There are many factors which cause and preserve this situation of economic inequality but, undoubtedly, one of the main factors is the lack of social investment. With only 13% of GDP, Guatemala has one of the lowest tax collection rates in all Latin America (ICEFI 2012). And with minimal funds, little is accomplished. The education budget of Guatemala is the lowest in the region, in the range of 2.8% of GDP, as compared to 5.8% invested by Mexico, its northern neighbor, with 4.66% invested in Nicaragua or with 3.46% in El Salvador; this figure demonstrates the low priority given to education and youth in Guatemala (Malik 2014). Public school principals are placed in very difficult limitations of having to look for a way to offer an education with minimum resources for the thousands of children and teenagers whose families do not have the economic capacity to send them to private schools.

More evidence of inequality can be seen in the massively unequal access to security. In the two last decades, Guatemala has seen a "transformation" in the levels of violence and insecurity experienced by the population (Restrepo and Tobon Garcia 2011). Insecurity and risk, which in past decades had a political connotation and impacted Leftist intellectuals or well-organized, reform-minded indigenous populations, nowadays have expanded, especially in urban spaces. In contrast with the political violence of the seventies and eighties, today's violence is economic in nature and is based on identity, with urban youth as the primary targets, especially those live in marginalized areas (Brenneman Forthcoming). Coupled to this, the proliferation of small arms has turned daily life into a dangerous race for millions of people living in the capital. Scarce investment in public security structures (through national police and the Public Prosecutor's Office) has led to a proliferation of private security companies and agents. In a country with six private security agents for every national police officer (Florquin 2011), there is little political will on the part of the middle class to invest more in public security structures. In this manner, security in Guatemala is for sale, meaning that it is a distant and inaccessible luxury for impoverished citizens.

One answer to the scarcity of educational opportunities and public security has been the proliferation and professionalization of urban gangs. Even though there have always been local bands of youth who gathered to socialize and participate in rituals of violence and petty crime, in the 1990's and 2000's, these local street gangs went through a transformation or "evolution" in their organizational style and in their capacity to squeeze money from their own neighbors (Levenson 2013, Loudis et al. 2006). This is how they do it, taking advantage of scarce or sporadic police presence and corruption in public justice structures. The impact of this "evolution" in the gangs has been to add another barrier to the difficulties these young people face in marginalized areas. And it explains why the San Antonio neighborhood, where Belice Bridge Project was founded, is a good example of what sociologists refer to as "concentrated disadvantage" (Wodtke, Harding, and Elwert 2011).

Faith contrasts

Guatemala is a country with a diverse and dynamic religious context. Most Guatemalans practice the Christian faith and families can be seen on any given Sunday walking to the church services or mass. In the last forty years, a strong growth has been observed among Protestants, especially Pentecostals and Charismatic groups (Holland 2010). Even though it is still considered a Roman Catholic country, merely 50% of the Guatemalan population self-identifies as such and 30% self-identifies as Protestant. Within the Catholic church in Guatemala there is also very strong Catholic charismatic movement (or charismatic renewal) (Pew 2006).

The recent history of churches in Guatemala, and especially regarding their relationship with political violence, on the one hand is characterized as a struggle for justice on the part of the Catholic church, and up to relatively recently, as an attempt to keep distance from political matters, social justice or violence topics on the part of Protestant churches with very few exceptions (Garrard-Burnett 1998, 2010). However, since 2000 and with the end of civil war in 1996, some have observed a new energy in some churches and parishes to get involved in the life of young people from the poorest, most dangerous and marginalized neighborhoods of Central America. Even though this energy does not characterize all churches or parishes, a small movement of Christian workers has emerged, many of them pastors and priests, who have undertaken the challenge to search for opportunities and legitimate careers for young people who are, have been or could be attracted to gangs. The Belice Bridge Educational and Labor Project is a very instructive example of this movement that gives us an idea of the creativity and dedication of these small yet important projects.

Development

The organizational structure of the Belice Bridge Project is very clear. The project is divided into five operating area. Nevertheless, one of the principles by which the project operates is the principle of cooperative work and testimony through personal integrity in one's actions. Hence, everybody supports everyone else's work although there are defined tasks that divide the responsibilities but are not hierarchically arranged.

There are five operating areas in the project:

- Administrative
- Academic
- Labor or productivity
- Human education
- Social outreach

Every project area has a coordinator and Father Iznardo serves as general coordinator for all project areas. Father Iznardo's work, as he describes it, is to make sure all areas are coordinated with each other, and to encourage and support the team in its daily work. In addition to serving as project general coordinator, Father Iznardo also organizes weekly masses in the chapel of the Jesus of the Good Hope community where he lives.

Administrative

The administrative area is small, basically made up of Father Iznardo, an administrative secretary and the director of the project's academic area. However, each of the area coordinators coordinates their work with the general coordinator. The administrative area is in charge of all administrative and logistical details, as well as assessing the project's sustainability, implementation of new workshops and maintaining contact with associated companies and the general public.

Academic

One of the main problems that youth in the marginalized areas face is the lack of opportunity and resources to get an education. Without education, young people are destined to find poorly remunerated jobs, to suffer exploitation and to be unable to break out of the poverty circle experienced in their communities. The academic program is focused on supporting young people to complete their studies at the high school level and, in this way, be able to continue to advance towards a college degree. This area offers elementary, junior high school and high school levels. The objective is to provide high-quality education to allow the young people to compete in the labor market and to have access to the tools necessary to develop as professionals. For students to be academically successful, it is necessary to take into account the social context of the youth in this zone. Many of them did not have access to education during their childhood. For this reason, the project offers elementary-level education in an accelerated program that allows teenagers to complete the elementary level of education in three years.

Production

The San Antonio neighborhood and the surrounding areas are characterized by a deep concentration of social and economic disadvantages. In many homes, the economic need is so acute that, even for children but especially for older youth, the idea of attending classes every day seems to be a distant dream. Survival demands that every young person be involved in procuring funds for their own meals and, in many cases, for other members of their household. For this reason, project leaders have tried from the beginning to incorporate job opportunities and income generation together with the merely educational experience. All young students work half-time and take classes half-time. The production area is focused on offering a half-time work position to each young person in one of the companies that supports the project. These jobs are deemed "work scholarships". Young people can generate an economic income for themselves and their families while completing their studies. In many cases, the income generated by the young people in the project is the only fixed and significant income their families have. This income motivates continuity and perseverance among the students and it is very important, because for young people who lack role models to follow in their families, it is very difficult to make an effort and work for a better future through education and work, because in most cases they are not "following their parents' footsteps". Many of the young participants will be the first in their families to complete junior high school studies.

However, it is not only about generating an income in the short term. Through the work scholarships, in addition to receiving an economic income, the students in the project also gain work experience and social networks which prove to be invaluable when they decide to look for work upon completing their high school studies. Many of the young people working with these work scholarships are formally hired as employees by the same companies when they complete their studies.

Human Development

The Belice Bridge Project, like many other projects with a Catholic background, intends to regard people as whole persons. For this reason, there is the human development area, which is focused on young people's human development and aims to accompany them in their personal situation and also in the collective experience of the group as part of the project. The youth involved in the project live in dehumanizing situations of deep poverty and violence. In the midst of a context of fear and mistrust, affection and tenderness, as explained by the general coordinator, "are the guiding principles in this project". Programs in the area of human development are intended to strengthen students' confidence and self-esteem as well as to develop a sense of belonging and to provide a sense of the responsibility they have as agents of change in their communities. The program conducts workshops on leadership and encourages reflection about personal and service history. In addition, the project offers optional retreats for the young people. During these retreats, the young people have time to reflect on the mission of the project and the vision of the project's founder. Even though the retreats touch on biblical and spiritual topics, like for example Jesus' life of service, the leadership does not intend to evangelize through the program. As Padre Paco puts it, "Young people need to feel loved and lovable."

In fact, despite its Roman Catholic background and despite the fact that it is led by a priest, the Belice Bridge Project does not promote Christian faith, let alone Roman Catholicism, in a very explicit manner. This is due not only to the intent of avoiding the promotion of one group over another, but also because many students' faith experience of has not been that of a God that is near or of a supportive community, according to Father Iznardo. Many young people have had the experience of a very ritualistic faith and a punishing and heavy-handed God. Leaders try to communicate the love, service, companionship and the responsibility to generate change through personal example or "testimony", as practical values of a faith that produces change and that liberates. This reticence to promote openly Catholic faith is in agreement with other studies carried out in Central America. For example, Wolseth (2011) in his ethnographic study of a Jesuit ministry directed at young people in a neighborhood in El Progreso, Honduras, found that the priests in that context promoted social justice for the community and tried to avoid topics related to faith that they feared would provoke division in the community. Likewise, Brenneman (2012) compared Pentecostal and evangelical ministries directed toward gang members with similar ministries run by Roman Catholic churches. He found that, in general, Catholic ministries tend to promote a very open concept of "human development" instead of a Christian or Catholic spirituality. In this sense, the Belice Bridge Project is in keeping with the communitarian tradition of the majority of parish ministries directed at young people.

Social Outreach

The social outreach area targets the work of students participating in the Belice Bridge Project by supporting and helping them to be role models for the children of their communities.

Students who participate in social outreach projects are young people who have completed the human development workshops and who have shown they have maturity and self-esteem. These students lead academic re-enforcement classes and provide English and traditional dance classes for the children of their communities. These same (older teen) students also organize recreational activities for the children as a way of supporting and accompanying them within the very harsh context in which they are being brought up. The vision behind the social outreach project is that these older teens represent an option that is different from the model children observe in their communities, where social role models are mostly gang members and where success in life is associated with violence and crime. According to Rolando Gutierrez, a project former student who is now working in the project as a teacher, the positive example of persons not involved in gangs or crime is very important to change children's and young people's vision for their future. The teenagers receive training and workshops before they begin to recruit children with whom to work. Every activity they carry out with children takes place in neighborhood parish halls or Jesuit-related spaces.

Project History

The Belice Bridge Labor and Educational Project (BBLEP) is a Society of Jesus project that started with the pastoral and accompaniment work Father Manolo Maqueira began in San Antonio Parish, Zone 6 of Guatemala City. When he was assigned to the San Antonio Parish in 1996, Father Manolo decided to live with the people of the Jesus of the Good Hope community, located under the Belice Bridge. Living with the people, feeling their pain and observing the hopelessness in which they lived, led Fr. Manolo to seek solutions. The priest realized that working with adults and trying to transform their lives was very difficult, because many were already involved in gangs or had lived in very harsh situations which had marked their lives in an irreversible manner. To wait until people reached adulthood was not an option that would break the cycles of violence and poverty in the marginalized areas. The need was to work with young people who were not yet involved in criminal or violent acts and offer them viable opportunities that would allow them to participate actively in changing their situation and their future.

The Belice Bridge Project was initiated in the year 2002 with thirty youth in a small rented house in Zone 1 of Guatemala City near the poor San Antonio neighborhood. Father Manolo's vision was to offer young people in contexts of violence, poverty and marginality an opportunity to train to be professionals with values, to strengthen their self-esteem and to serve as agents of change in their communities. Fr. Manolo created a program in which young people could work and complete their studies at the same time. Education was fundamental, but building new social networks, creating different role models and working on their human development were also important. Marginalized, hopeless young people were at the center of Father Manolo's efforts, and he connected them with other members of Guatemalan society and with the opportunities to change their situation. Father Manolo passed away in 2006, dedicated to the end to the parish and project work. The Society of Jesus then appointed Father Francisco Iznardo (Padre Paco) to coordinate the Project. Padre Paco had already been supporting Father Manolo with the project work. However, he was working at the Ixcan diocese in rural Guatemala with returned refugees and communities in resistance since the end of the Guatemala's civil war in 1994.

Padre Paco took over the project. He believed in Father Manolo's vision and recognized that it was important and necessary to work and support young people to change their situation and that of their communities. Padre Paco comments that after living in the Jesus of the Good Hope community, "Manolo's intuition to put together work and studies to rebuild a person was fundamental. That intuition meant accompanying the young person during three or five years and accompanying them emotionally. To reconstruct the person so that he or she will have an influence and a testimony in his or her neighborhood is something that will change structures."

Project work with young people is holistic and goes beyond the academic education or providing an income through work scholarships. The project works with students' self-esteem and with their personal life histories. Padre Paco explains that when he arrived at the project, he realized that although he had come from living and working in a jungle, the reality of marginalized communities in which the young people live had elements similar to the "jungle" in which he had worked previously.

> It is a jungle that is much harsher, more hostile and dehumanizing, but it is worth betting on since in fact the people were not responsible for this situation. That is, we are really looking at the margins of what this system of predation and hoarding in which we are living causes.

Padre Paco has dedicated himself completely to the program. Currently the program has 315 students and continues to grow. The project currently operates on land donated by the Rafael Landivar Jesuit University, with facilities built with funding from the Spanish Agency for International Cooperation. The campus has open outdoor areas that offer a different environment to young people who normally do not have access to such spaces. Padre Paco explains they are now "in excellent surroundings". However, they also use the premises to show young people they are worthwhile and deserve a dignified place to study and work. The Belice Bridge Project had to move away from its original location due to gang fights over territory. Two of their students were killed because even though they did not belong to gangs, they would arrive to the Project from different marginalized zones that were considered to belong to rival gangs.

Among the greatest challenges faced by the project are the killing of these two students and the shutting down of one of the companies that had provided a significant number of work positions when the project started. These events generated uncertainty regarding the project's future. Nevertheless, doors continue to open and many young people depend on the project. They have no one else to support them or to cover their basic needs. Students at the project are motivated to work hard and to prove they are valuable participants in the companies where they work. In fact, another constant challenge has been to find companies willing to participate by offering young people work positions. Ensuring work positions is a significant challenge for the project. However, up to the present, the young people's performance in the companies has managed to keep the doors open and serves as a reference to build new relationships with other companies.

Another great challenge faced by the project on a daily basis is competing with the attractive offer of joining the gangs or the fear gangs create among young people who resist joining them. Guatemalan youth from marginalized areas often enter gangs because they have no other choice. A recent example that has shaken the homes of the neighborhood should suffice to illustrate the fear gangs inspire. A twelve-year-old child, a resident of the poor Jesus de la Buena Esperanza neighborhood, was thrown from the Belice Bridge in June 2015 by gang members because he refused to kill a bus driver who did not want to pay extortions. Although the boy survived the fall, he suffered internal injuries that caused his death in the hospital some days later. When remembering this sad story, Padre Paco wonders, "How many children have said yes, and are being hired assassins at twelve or thirteen years of age? What are we doing that keeps us from being more successful or to whom should we report, because this in fact is not our duty, but the state's duty?" Coupled with this challenge are the poverty and marginality of these young people and children that make them invisible and disposable in society. Project challenges are many. However, the greatest challenge, according to project leaders, is to succeed in providing crucial support to these youth in need.

Lessons Learned

At the Belice Bridge Project, something is learned every day. Father Iznardo and his team have learned to accompany young people and encourage them to change their situation. One of the major challenges is to succeed in providing human support. "How far to be demanding and how far to show tenderness?" These are Father Iznardo's words when describing his challenges and his experiences when working with these young people. To listen to the young students at the school and observe their enthusiasm for participating in leadership workshops and preparing material to work with children in their communities, make it clear that the "affection and tenderness" that Father Iznardo describes as strong needs in the lives of these young people, have been applied successfully by the program. In any case, every day one learns more about responding to the needs of young people who come from contexts not only of poverty but also of violence and physical and mental abuse.

It is a learning experience merely to listen to the experiences shared by the Belice Bridge Project students and graduates. The project is doing work that seems impossible to imagine for most Guatemalans. How to change the situation of outcast youth? How is the gap between social classes in Guatemala to be overcome and how are spaces created so that the great human potential of young people from marginalized neighborhoods is not lost? Exclusion and misery will always be accompanied by violence and there is growing social-scientific evidence of the connection between inequality and violence (Wilkinson and Pickett 2009). In Father Iznardo's own words, "In a society with so much consumerism and so much inequality, you are shown all the possibilities but they are denied to you." Father Manolo's vision, together with Father Iznardo and his team's commitment, has led to implementing a program that is succeeding in changing the situation of outcast youth and it is also closing the gap between social sectors. While it is true that this change represents a very small percentage because the project cannot work in all the marginalized areas where there are young people, the work is nonetheless effective and is making a difference in the lives of hundreds of young people in an area of great need.

To listen to the students' histories challenges the faith of those of us who thought that hope in situations and contexts so harsh and dehumanizing could not exist. However, life and hope are present. The young people have dreams and struggle to improve their situation and that of their families. As to the answer to the question regarding the role of faith in his ministry, Father Iznardo shared that "in the midst of such a death-dealing system, the visible faith of the people calls for reflection, and it helps me very much . . . in the middle of pain and suffering, [I saw that] there was life, there was much life; so for me, rather than saying what role does faith play (in my work), the reality is that my work helps me keep my faith." Hope and faith in tomorrow challenges us to recognize that there is much to do. Young people need to be accompanied and what Father Iznardo does, living with the people who suffer and struggling with them to alleviate pain, must shake us up and motivate us to think about what we are doing to accompany the people who suffer, or what we are doing to alleviate their suffering. The pressure of consumerism and hoarding plays a very important role in perpetuating the poverty and violence in marginalized communities such as those supported by Belice Bridge Project. However, this type of community is not found only in Guatemala. It is necessary to recognize the connection that exists between the way each one of us choses to live and the poverty and misery of others. The poor must not be invisible nor should we leave the responsibility to others.

When reflecting on this case, the story of Jesus came to our minds and hearts. In that story from the Gospel of Luke 8: 43-48, Jesus heals a woman with chronic bleeding. In the Palestinian context of the first century, a woman with this type of illness would have been rejected and isolated by her society, in much the same way that young people from poor neighborhoods are rejected for bearing the stigma of coming from "red zones" without formal education and "suspected" of being gang members or thieves. Yet when the woman touches Jesus, she receives not only physical healing but also social healing. When Jesus pronounces her "healed" in an open and public manner, he restores her dignity and her place of belonging within society. He gives her his attention and his time, restoring her integrity in the presence of onlookers. In other words, Jesus uses his position and capacity to offer a "bridge" to overcome the gap which separated her from the rest of society.

As the authors of this case study, we know that the Belice Bridge Project is not unique, let alone perfect. However, it is instructive since it exhibits two key elements for the success of socio-religious ministries, accompaniment and creativity.

The priests live in the community where they work and do not enjoy luxuries that other residents of the sector do not have. Nevertheless, they have used their contacts as Jesuits to create "bridges" between the young people, work opportunities and school. The creativity to build a school that combines work and study serves not only to provide an income, but also to provide the opportunity to acquire social competencies and "cultural capital" (Bourdieu 1984) for finding a job (or enrolling in a college) after graduation. Finally, the requirement to work and study at the same time has the additional effect of reducing youths' free time, which minimizes their contact with gangs and reduces the probability of early pregnancies. All this contributes to graduates' success. According to a study conducted by the Association for the Advance of Social Sciences in Guatemala, from the founding of the project until year 2010, of sixty young graduates, twenty five had continued their studies in college and none had gotten involved with gangs (Colussi and Orantes 2010). Others were working and very few graduates had had their own children despite the culture of very young parents that is typical in this sector. In short, the impact of the project is tangible.

Nevertheless, we were surprised by the minimal reference to the teaching of Christian spirituality. Despite the great tradition of deep Ignatian spirituality—a spirituality that is lived and practiced—the concern not to create divisions among the young people outweighs the desire to present them with an alternative to the ritualistic faith in a punishing God. In fact, it seems to us that presenting opportunities for young people to approach a liberating God through a spirituality of service, as exemplified in the Jesuit tradition, would not be an imposition. In contrast, it would be a gift of great value for them. In fact, even though young people who are successful—perhaps especially those who are successful—are going to enter an adult world that is not very forgiving or very liberating and that absorbs time and offers false dreams of success and consumerism even to professionals. However, we offer this observation as outside observers who recognize that the leaders and the graduates are the ones who best understand the needs of these young people.

The Future

In June 2014, the authors (Robert and America) became acquainted with the Belice Bridge Project for the first time when we visited the Jesus de la Buena Esperanza neighborhood, where the project premises, the chapel and Father Iznardo's small apartment are located. We travelled with a group of eight sociology students from Saint Michael's College where we teach. After we visited the project, one of the graduates, who is now a teacher in the school, guided us on a tour through the community, passing under the bridge to see the social situation in which project students live. It was a very new, even striking experience for our students, most of whom came from very safe and solid, upper-middle class New England homes. They had never seen such harsh living conditions with so much deprivation. By chance, we had scheduled a visit in the afternoon to the new facilities of a very well-known megachurch in Guatemala. The congregation's new campus was built at a cost of over US$50 million and has an ample parking lot, 24-hour security, and state-of-the-art technology for producing television programs. The experience of visiting these two places, these two realities in one single day, made the impact of the tour through the Belice Bridge community even stronger. Students realized that Guatemala is not a country submerged in pure poverty; rather it is a country with a deeply divided society that is full of economic inequality. In addition, Guatemala has a church just as divided and unequal. The division is not purely of a theological nature between Protestants and Catholics, rather it lies in an obvious disagreement over how to be people of God and how to communicate the good news of the gospel.

I (Roberto) discovered during my research work regarding gang members' exit from gangs (Brenneman 2012), that there are a considerable number of pastors and priests that work in their own communities with young people who have abandoned a gang or who are at risk of joining one. These pastors and priests do not have a formal movement, let alone an official association. However, their work on behalf of poor and outcast young people, many times with the direct support of a local congregation located in the same neighborhood, mark them as a ray of hope and it is evidence of a vibrant and dynamic church, sensitive to the context in which it is located. Urban violence and socio-economic inequality are the most prominent characteristics of the Central America of today, and in these marginalized neighborhoods, pastors and priests as Father Iznardo or Father Maqueira tend to serve as "bridges" or "brokers" for young people whose circumstances, location or associations have isolated and stigmatized them, denying them their entrance to the formal labor market. This denial and exclusion creates alienation in marginalized youth and as a result, in many cases, it makes them reject formal society and opens a path to crime and despair. On several occasions, Pope Francis has emphasized the role of the Christian church as a bridge—a bridge that should open up communication not only between God and human beings, but also between all peoples. In fact, he has demonstrated with his words and actions his special role as a bridge (the meaning of pontiff) at the service of a God who is full of mercy. It seems to us that the practice and mission of the Belice Bridge Project is a good example of this charism that is present in the Roman Catholic Church around the world.

In conclusion, we believe that in the future both Catholic and evangelical churches in Central America will have to recognize, confront and prioritize work in this divided social reality. They will have to develop the sensitivity to understand how to "speak the language" of marginalized youth and get closer to them without offering charades about easy success or "shortcuts" to wealth and status. We believe that faith-based projects for outcast young people offer hope and challenge, not only to marginalized youth but also to the churches themselves. Congregations and their leaders need to act from a concrete vision of working for justice, bringing news of hope and peace for all members of society.

References:

Bourdieu, Pierre.

1984. Distinction: A Social Critique of the Judgment of Taste. Cambridge: Harvard University Press.

Brenneman, Robert.

2012. Homies and Hermanos: God and Gangs in Central America. New York: Oxford University Press.

2015. "Violencia, religión y legitimidad institucional al norte de Centroamérica." En Las iglesias ante la violencia en América Latina: Los derechos humanos en el pasado y el presente, ed. Alexander Wilde, 381-404. México, D.F.: FLACSO-México.

Colussi, Marcelo, and María del Carmen Orantes.

2010. Sistematización crítica. Guatemala: AVANCSO.

Florquin, Nicolas.

2011. "A Booming Business: Private Security and Small Arms." In Small Arms Survey 2011: States of Security, ed. Robert Muggah. Cambridge: Cambridge University Press.

Garrard-Burnett, Virginia.

1998. Protestantism in Guatemala: Living in the New Jerusalem. Austin: University of Texas.

2010. Terror in the Land of the Spirit: Guatemala under General Efraín Ríos Montt 1982-1983. New York: Oxford University Press.

Holland, Clifton.

2010. Enciclopedia de grupos religiosos en las Americas y la Peninsula Iberica: Religión en Guatemala. San Pedro, Costa Rica: PROLADES.

ICEFI.
2012. "Lente fiscal centroamericano". En Investigación de coyuntura. Ciudad de Guatemala: Instituto Centroamericano de Estudios Fiscales.

Levenson, Deborah T.
2013. Adiós Niño: The Gangs of Guatemala City and the Politics of Death. Durham, NC: Duke University Press.

Loudis, Richard, Christina del Castillo, Anu Rajaraman, and Marco Castillo.
2006. Annex 2: Guatemala Profile. edited by USAID.

Malik, Khalid.
2014. 2014 Human Development Report. New York: United Nations Development Programme.

Pelaez, Severo.
1998 [1970]. La patria del criollo. México, D.F.: Universidad Autónoma de México.

Pew.
2006. Spirit and Power: A 10-Country Survey of Pentecostals. Washington D.C.: The Pew Forum on Religion and Public Life.

Restrepo, Jorge A., y Alonso Tobón García.
2011. Guatemala en la encrucijada: Panorama de una violencia transformada. Ginebra: Secretariado de la Declaración de Ginebra.

Wilkinson, Richard, and Kate Pickett.
2009. The Spirit Level: Why Equality Makes Us Stronger. New York: Bloomsbury Press.

Wodtke, Geoffrey T., David J. Harding, and Felix Elwert.
2011. "Neighborhood Effects in Temporal Perspective: The Impact of Long-Term Exposure to Concentrated Disadvantage on High School Graduation." American Sociological Review 76 (5):23.

Wolseth, Jon.
2011. Jesus and the Gang: Youth Violence and Christianity in Urban Honduras. Tucson, AZ: University of Arizona Press.

CHAPTER 4: DYING TO RISING

Revitalization and the Catholic Church in Cuba

Ondina Cortes, rmi and
Laura Maria Fernandez Gomez

The Catholic Church of Cuba, after centuries of journeying through light and shadow, today stands at a significant moment in history. Despite ongoing challenges, a church renewal, an awakening of faith within the people, is evident today. A lengthy process of resurgence and revitalization has brought it to this point. The characteristics of this revitalization within the Catholic Church in Cuba as a whole can best be seen at the grassroots. The Diocese of Santa Clara, one of the most active of the eleven dioceses, illustrates this process well.

A full understanding of the contemporary revitalization of the Catholic Church in Cuba requires consideration of the current situation of the county as well as that of the Catholic Church, including the long history of Catholicism in Cuba. The response of the Catholic Church in Cuba to the 1959 revolution and key moments in the ensuing process of ecclesial revitalization are vital parts of the story. Considered broadly, the journey of the Catholic Church in Cuba, with all its challenges, possibilities, and successes, offers an opportunity to shed light on and inspire revitalization in similar contexts.

The Current Situation of Cuba

Cuba today faces many challenges. Its population is declining due to a low birth rate and increasing migration abroad, especially by young people. The average age has been increasing dramatically (Oficina Nacional de Estadísticas 2008-2011). Broad sectors of the population suffer from "material poverty, due to wages that are not enough to maintain a decent family standard of living" (Plan Pastoral, 18). Everyday problems of housing, transportation, clothing, and food cause notable stress and exhaustion, because they have been endured for many years.

The authorities have announced changes to respond to this situation, including the elimination of subsidies, the elimination of unnecessary jobs, new regulations for increasing self-employment (including opening family businesses) as a means of reducing unemployment, and laws to encourage foreign investment, while preserving the jobs of Cubans through state enterprises with wages assigned according to recently enacted laws (Gaceta Oficial No. 20 Extraordinaria de 16 de abril de 2014).[21]

The quality of health care, education, and sports programs is declining. But notable changes have taken place: loosening of migration measures, free access to hotels, permission to sell and buy properties and vehicles, and internet access, albeit limited (Plan Pastoral, 23).

Situations of corruption abound. To survive amid widespread scarcity, people have become accustomed to stealing, lying, and cheating. The state is still the largest and most secure employer. However, morale is low in this sector, as is the work ethic (Plan Pastoral, 26). Large sectors of the population, especially young people, are waiting for deeper reforms such as greater economic, social, and political autonomy where the common good can be sought without having to wait for "top down" solutions.

Many would like to see a transformation of the state model to one that is "less bureaucratic and more participatory, less paternalistic and more fostering, less authoritarian and more democratic" (Plan Pastoral, 27). Others, although ever fewer, still defend the system, in part because commitment to the nation is seen as the same as commitment to an ideology or party.

There is a general desire to modernize national legislation in the political sphere (La Esperanza no defrauda, 31). People yearn to live in a country "that combines justice and freedom, prosperity and solidarity, well-being and moral and spiritual values" (Plan Pastoral, 30). Today, Cubans hope that advances and talks between Cuba and the United States will take place, and that the many years of conflict will be resolved. The Catholic Church in the Diocese of Santa Clara exists within this broader context.

The Diocese of Santa Clara

The diocese was created by John Paul II on April 1, 1995 from territory of the former Diocese of Cienfuegos-Santa Clara. It covers approximately 5,000 square miles, encompassing the

21 Law 118, passed by the National Assembly of People's Power, April 2014.

provinces of Villa Clara and Sancti Spiritus with the exception of the municipalities of Jatibonico and Trinidad. The population is approximately 1.5 million people. Some of the first European settlements in Cuba are located there. The oldest are the towns of Remedios and Sancti Spiritus, both settled over 500 years ago. This large stretch of territory and population presently is served by its bishop together with 33 priests, 15 deacons, and 55 nuns. Thirty-four parish churches exist together with an additional 63 chapels and just over 250 mission houses.

This local church is characterized by a strong missionary drive and pastoral work that aims to engage culture within its context. The mission teams have more than 150 members, most of them young people. Since 2000, a Diocesan Mission is held in the summer. Two training centers help resource these teams. The center in Santa Clara is the Dr. Felicia Pérez Hall and the center in Sancti Spiritus is Father Noya Hall. Both offer courses and degrees from institutes and universities from various countries in the Americas and Europe.

Several parishes have their own publications and there are two diocesan-wide publications: the magazine Amanecer, which has been published for twenty years, and the less formal Amanecer Informativo. The Manuel García Garofalo Diocesan Library opened in 2007 and has since become a major cultural center. As a means of further advancing this work, the Diocesan Culture Commission organizes symposiums, concerts, exhibitions, workshops and cultural events.

The Catholic Church in Cuba from the Colonial Period to 1959

As with elsewhere in the Americas, Christianity took root in Cuba through the colonization process, which for the Spanish monarchy had the twofold aim of extending the territories of the crown and spreading the Catholic faith. During the sixteenth and seventeenth century, the work of evangelization was carried out primarily by religious communities and a poorly educated Spanish secular clergy. Religious communities also set up hospitals and educational institutions. The island, along with Jamaica and Florida, was set up as a separate diocese in 1517 or 1518 under the Archdiocese of Santo Domingo in the present-day Dominican Republic (Suárez Polcari 2003, 47-48). At first, the bishop was located in Baracoa, but four years later the seat of the diocese was transferred to Santiago de Cuba.

However, most bishops preferred to live in Havana, which was established as the capital of the colony in 1607 and was more favored both geographically and financially (Suárez Polcari 2003, 71). The ecclesiastical census of 1689 shows the vitality of the church at that time, reporting 225 diocesan priests, 205 men religious, and 100 women religious (CRECED, 14). Most diocesan clergy were native, but most of the religious (both women and men) tended to be from Spain. In 1789, the island was divided between newly-established Diocese of San Cristóbal de la Habana and the Archdiocese of Santiago de Cuba. During this time, the church in Cuba continued to be closely related to the Spanish territories of Louisiana, Florida, and even part of what is today South Carolina.

Throughout this time, the proportion of native clergy continued to increase, replacing the Spanish missionaries (ENEC, 32). According to a census carried out in the second half of the eighteenth century, there were 700 priests in Cuba and Havana alone had 33 churches (CRECED, 20). The Seminary of San Carlos y San Ambrosio was founded in Havana in 1774 (Suárez Polcari 2003, 236). The seminary, which offered degrees in philosophy, theology, law, and mathematics, became a major center of Cuban intellectual life.

During the first decades of the nineteenth century, the Diocese of Havana flourished under the outstanding leadership of Bishop Juan J. Díaz de Espada (1802-1832). A sense of Cuban identity and the desire for independence arose among the educated classes. The Catholic Church played a significant role in the development of national identity through men like Father José Agustín Caballero (Suarez Polcari 2003, 342-345) and especially Father Felix Varela (Estevez 1989). They developed and shared their ideas within the classrooms of the seminary and the salons of the colonial capital. The patronato regio, whereby colonial Spain provided the equivalent of the tithe to the church and infrastructural support in return for the power to name local bishops and authorize the work of the religious orders, had produced a generally prosperous church and relatively flourishing faith life during these early centuries.

However, by mid-nineteenth century, Spain had lost its colonies throughout the Americas and the airs of independence in its remaining Caribbean colonies were a clear threat to continued Spanish rule there as well. As a result, Spain exercised its power over naming bishops and funding the Catholic Church so as to ensure loyalty to the colonial regime (Suarez Polcari 2003, 45). A decline of native clergy followed, bringing in its wake a new wave of Spanish priests, who often lacked both zeal and resources to carry out pastoral work. There were notable exceptions, particularly the renowned bishop-missionary of Santiago de Cuba, Saint Anthony Mary Claret (1850-1857).[22] In general, however, the Catholic Church in Cuba was in a state of pastoral and financial abandonment, dependent on the Spanish government for its livelihood. In the 1880's, a number of Cuban immigrants to the United States, who had converted to Protestantism, began to return to Cuba to develop various Protestant churches despite the prohibition of the colonial government. Many of these missionaries became leaders in the struggle for independence against Spain.

The devotion to the image of Our Lady of Charity, found on the northeast coast of Cuba in 1612, had gradually spread to the rest of the island by the nineteenth century (Portuondo Zúñiga 2011). The independence movement led by Carlos Manuel de Céspedes dedicated itself at the feet of the image of Our Lady of Charity in its shrine church in El Cobre. Céspedes went there with the mambises (rebels) "to render a patriotic tribute to the Virgin" because "he believed that devotion to the Virgin of Cobre was a powerful source of union among Cubans" (Portuondo Zúñiga 2011, 220-221). This is best understood as an act of personal and collective religious devotion, as suggested all the more by Céspedes' use of the canopy of the family altar honoring the image of Our Lady of Charity to create the first flag of Cuba (Campistrous 1998, 18).

---

22 See Claret's missionary action in Lebroc Martínez y Bermejo, 1992.

Devotion to Our Lady of Charity took increasingly firm hold throughout Cuba during the independence struggle. Since that time, Our Lady of Charity has often been called "La Virgen Mambisa," meaning that she was herself a rebel, on the side of the rebels, supporting Cuban freedom (Portuondo Zúñiga 2011, 218). A few years after the war was over, it was the mambises who asked the pope to name Our Lady of Charity as patroness of Cuba in 1915, and that request was granted in 1916 (Portuondo Zúñiga 2011, 236). Thus, not surprisingly, one of the oldest replicas of the image of Our Lady of Charity, venerated in the parish of Santo Tomas in Santiago, is known simply as the Mambisa. This image is the one that was carried around the country on a national procession throughout 1951 and 1952 (Portuondo Zúñiga 2011, 261) as well as in 2010-2011, on the occasion of the four hundredth anniversary of the finding of the image. The song "Virgen Mambisa," composed by Rogelio Zelada, has further cemented popular understanding of her place within Cuban history and culture in general.

After three years of military occupation by the United States, Cuba's republican experience began with the election of the first President, Tomás Estrada Palma (Sweig 2009, 11-12). The half-century that followed included short periods of political stability and constitutional advances, alternating with military dictatorships and U.S. interventions (Pérez 1999, 375). Even after the 1934 abrogation of the Platt Amendment, which had given the United States an unlimited legal right to intervene in Cuban political life, North American presence and influence continued in a variety of ways. The Constitution adopted in 1901 was based on the U.S. Constitution and hence granted freedom of religion (Article 26). It was during this time that a wide variety of other Christian churches grew in Cuba, particularly as a result of the U.S. political and economic presence.

Methodism first arrived in Cuba in 1883, as Cubans who migrated to Florida returned home with their new found faith (Wright 2015). The first Convention of Evangelical Churches took place in 1902, one year after the Constitution and three years after the U.S. military had first occupied Cuba (www.ecured.cu). Methodists, Presbyterian, Episcopal, and Baptist churches, as well as the Quakers, had developed a strong and growing presence in Cuba, with the Adventists, Lutherans, and Salvation Army coming soon after. Initially, most missionaries and church leaders were foreigners. The founding of an ecumenical theological seminary in the early 1900s helped educate native leadership. Pentecostalism first took root around 1930 (www.ecured.cu). The Methodist, Presbyterian, and Episcopal Churches founded the Evangelical Seminary at Matanzas, Cuba, on October 1, 1946. This is the only ecumenical seminary in Cuba. Since 2006, Methodists have had their own seminary (www.setcuba.org). In 1946 as well, the Second International Congress of Evangelical Youth in the Americas was held. (Fernández Santalices 2001, 110).

During the first generation of independence, leadership of the Catholic Church remained pro-Spanish and stayed on the margins of national life. New developments did occur, however, in the wake of national independence and the U.S. occupation. Within the first ten years, new dioceses were created, named now by the Pope rather than Spain, and the new bishops were therefore Cuban. The Knights of Columbus was a Catholic fraternal order developed in the United States as a response to societies, such as the Masons, that took root in Cuba. A national level Catholic magazine, called San Antonio, began to be published as well (Andújar 2009, 1). The Federation of Catholic Action was formed in the late 1920s. Under the pastoral guidance of bishops such as Manuel Arteaga y Betancourt of Havana (1942-1963), the first Cuban to be made cardinal (1946), Enrique Pérez Serantes,[23] Alberto Martin Villaverde,[24] Valentín Zubizarreta[25] and others, the Catholic Church became increasingly embodied in the twentieth century Cuban context. By the mid-twentieth century, the Cuban Catholic Church had once again come to play a vigorous and constructive role in the life of the nation.

In 1960, self-identified Catholics constituted some 72.5 per cent of the total population. At the same time, the Catholic Church in Cuba remained among the weakest expression

23 Archbishop of Santiago de Cuba, see Uría Rodríguez 2012.

24 Bishop of Matanzas from 1938 to 1960. http://www.catholic-hierarchy.org/diocese/lad.html.

25 Bishop of Camagüey (1914-1925) and then of Santiago (1925-1948). http://www.catholic-hierarchy.org/diocese/lad.html.

of Catholicism in Latin America vis-à-vis church attendance (Crahan 1985, 321). Regular church attendance by ordinary people had become much reduced during the nineteenth century and continued at low levels. Popular commitment to Catholicism was instead expressed by devotional practices within families. In any case, institutional installed capacity outside the major cities remained weak. The major development in the mid-twentieth century was that the growing middle classes in the cities, most of whom received their education from Catholic religious orders, attended church at much higher levels. In addition, Cuba's strong transnational professional class remained deeply Catholic and reflected the latest ideas in Europe and United States, as well as in Latin America. As a result, the Catholic Church in Cuba was among the most advanced in Latin America in terms of progressive social thought and concern for the poor (Trujillo Lemes 2011, 60). There was considerable support for many of the social changes proposed by the revolutionaries in the 1950s. At this level of Catholic life and leadership, though a relatively small fraction of the larger population, there was a great deal of commitment for social change and democratization during the dictatorship of Fulgencio Batista in the 1950s.

On January 1, 1959, as a result of several years of armed struggle, the dictator fled the country. The revolution triumphed under the leadership of Fidel Castro and others, many of whom soon disappeared from the political scene for various reasons or took up secondary positions. Over the following decades, the Catholic Church and religion in general on the island went through three major periods, each marking a different sort of relationship with the Cuban state: confrontation, silence, and resurgence.

Responses to the 1959 Revolution

Institutional Confrontation

The Cuban revolution began with the full support of the Catholic Church, most especially its younger members organized through the Federation of Catholic Action, the University Catholic Group, and other lay movements and groups with a strong social commitment. However, relations changed dramatically as the socialist, Marxist, and Leninist character of the revolution was revealed. The Catholic bishops stated forcefully that Christianity was incompatible with atheistic communism.[26] Some see this strong reaction as reflecting the experience of the Catholic Church under the leftist forces during the Spanish Civil War in the 1930s and under European Communist regimes in the 1950s (Andújar 2009, 1). However, the bishops also reacted because of what they saw happening before their eyes: executions, surveillance structures in neighborhoods, orchestrated mob beatings of priests and lay leaders, takeovers of Catholic schools, and the exclusion of Christian voices from the press, radio, and television.

These actions against human rights and freedom of religion and "not the social and economic programs, became the primary issue of the Church" (Super 2003). Through a Collective Circular Letter that was disseminated through church channels, the Catholic bishops declared that "The Church has no fear of the deepest social reforms provided that they are based on justice and charity, because it seeks the well-being of the people... but that is precisely why ... it can only condemn Communist doctrines" (Bishops of Cuba, August 7, 1960). Some Catholic leaders joined the struggle against the new regime, and this led some to suspect anyone who went to church of counter-revolutionary activity (Crahan 1999, 95). From a different perspective, others consider that the conflict between the Church and the new government was related to the "Church's commitment to the social classes affected by the revolutionary process and the economic power linked to these groups" (Trujillo Lemes 2011, 139).

During the 1961 CIA-sponsored Bay of Pigs invasion by Cuban exiles, the Archbishop of Havana and one of his auxiliary bishops were arrested. Cardinal Arteaga and Manuel Pedro Rodríguez, the bishop of Pinar del Río, avoided arrest by taking refuge on embassy premises. Numerous priests, religious, and lay people were arrested as well (Fernández Santalices 2000, 124). Religious groups and church activities became progressively more limited. On September 17, 1961, Bishop Boza Masvidal

26 In a pastoral letter titled "For God and for Cuba," Archbishop Pérez Serantes of Santiago explained the incompatibility between communism and Christianity (Pérez Serantes 1960).

and 131 priests were expelled and exiled to Spain (Clark 1985, 11). The Cuban Government banned processions and all other religious activities outside of church buildings on the claim that these religious expressions were actually anti-government demonstrations (Crahan 1999, 95). Of the 800 Catholic priests who had been in Cuba before 1959, approximately 600 went in exile during the tumultuous first years of the revolution. The effect on Catholic religious orders, notably women religious, was even more severe: only 200 out of approximately 2,000 nuns, or sisters, remained in the country after the first years of the revolution (ENEC 1987, 25). Their near disappearance was not only because their schools and charities were taken over by the government, thereby eliminating their area of mission and livelihood all at once. It was also because their religious superiors outside the country remembered what had happened in Spain and Eastern Europe, when so many religious were killed and subjected to torture and imprisonment. Their departures were final: once they had left the country, they did not receive permission to return.

The political, economic, and social changes triggered a mass emigration that deprived the church of Cuba of much of its lay leadership and committed laity in general. Cuban Catholic Action, which had been such a strong Catholic movement in Cuba in the 1950s, underwent a rapid disintegration as many of its leaders and members went into exile or were jailed. Others, whether out of opportunism or conviction, left Catholic Action to join the revolutionary process. They were not allowed to continue in both. To be active in the revolution meant to abandon the Church. By 1965, Catholic Action was nearly defunct and the bishops formally dissolved it in 1967, since the government had already applied a law to limit its activities (Rodríguez 1998). In its place, the bishops created something they called the Organized Lay Apostolate (Fernandez Santalices 2001, 128), but it was all a pale shadow of what had once been among the strongest Catholic Action movements in Latin America.

The Church of Silence

After this period of confrontation, the Catholic Church in Cuba, now much diminished and even dismantled, "struck down but not destroyed" (2 Cor 4:8-9), began a quiet phase of internal consolidation. Rita Petrirena Hernández, a leader serving for some sixteen years in the Secretariat of Pastoral Activity of the Conference of Bishops of Cuba, calls this a time of contemplative silence in which the Church reflected on what God was asking (Interview, Miami, June 12, 2015). Rev. Eugenio Castellanos, rector of the sanctuary of Our Lady of Charity in El Cobre, recalls those times as similar to those of the first Christian communities just after the Resurrection of the Lord, when few people followed the Way, yet those who did formed a true family where faith was lived and love shared deeply and joyfully (Interview, El Cobre, April 8, 2015). As Bishop Arturo González of Santa Clara put it, the Lord allowed "the church to be pruned" for its own eventual full revitalization (Interview, Miami, June 15, 2015).

With the church reduced to silence, and atheism officially imposed by the state,[27] many Cubans came to see religion as a thing of the past. Some couples, wanting what was best for their children in a difficult situation, even decided to not raise their children with religious ideas so that they could live without being persecuted in school. Others had to choose between faith and their futures. People active in the church could not aspire to certain careers or jobs. In 1965, UMAP (Military Units to Aid Production) were created. These were military-like labor camps to which virtually all young active Catholics, including seminarians, were sent, along with homosexuals, malcontents, and other political undesirables (Pedraza 2007, 123). These quasi-concentration camps lasted until 1968. Many of those sent to UMAP later became key figures in the Catholic Church, such as Cardinal Jaime Ortega and his auxiliary Bishop Alfredo Petit.

---

27 The 1976 Constitution defines Cuba as an atheistic state. In July 1992, the Constitution was amended and Article 42 was added, prohibiting discrimination on the basis of religious beliefs and allowing Christians to belong to the Communist Party. From this point on, Cuba was defined as a secular state.

Thus, camps designed to punish and control ironically became a kind of training and proving ground for future church leadership and contemporary Catholic revitalization.

Throughout these difficult times, there was a "faithful remnant" (Bishop Arturo González, interview, Miami, June 15, 2015) that kept churches open and the faith alive. Committed Catholics who remained in the country devoted themselves more to work within the church than social, cultural, economic, and political work, given the enormous restrictions on witnessing outside the confines of the church building. Instead, they put emphasis on silent witness, on giving a good and faithful example in their studies, work, and lives in general. They visited the sick and the elderly and cared for fellow believers, supporting and serving the community.

During this time, the Cuban hierarchy did not publish any documents or pastoral letters of any kind. However, some dispute the notion that the Church was totally silent, since there were priests who expressed their views and sought to enter into a dialogue with the revolutionary process, such as Ignacio Biaín and Carlos Manuel de Céspedes (Trujillo Lemes 2011).

This was the setting in which developments within the global Catholic Church as a result of the Second Vatican Council (1963-1965) were received. Efforts were made to implement the Council insofar as possible. Though adult education and catechesis of children declined precipitously, the level of depth did not. The real leaders often became grandparents, retirees who could not be threatened with a loss of their job. They taught the faith and took children to receive the sacraments and participate in regular church life. This experience shaped a kind of disciple, firm in the faith, and tested in suffering and persecution (Rita Petrirena, interview, Miami, June 12, 2015).

By 1969, the Cuban state had abolished any public celebration of Christmas outside the walls of a church, which were themselves under surveillance. As a result, faith disappeared even more from the Cuban cultural horizon. With the decline and suppression of the Catholic Church from the public square, God came to be increasingly seen as absent from social structures and even from family life. Calendars no longer mentioned any religious dates or celebrations of any kind.

Given the suppression of the public expression of organized religion, particularly the Catholic Church, the search for God within popular culture during these years was channeled through popular religiosity. In Cuba, popular religiosity often blends with forms of syncretism such as Santeria and spiritism, religious expressions that had long been private, secretive, and organized at a larger level. These forms of religiosity were all the more attractive—and less threatening to the state—precisely because they make no overarching moral demands, but rather offer magical elements which provide a sense of tranquility or security, even as they might also create fears and anxieties. Rev. René David, a French theologian who taught for more than thirty years at San Carlos Seminary, claims that "more or less syncretistic religion had saved the religious faith of Cubans in the most difficult moments, and he went so far as to say that it was owed gratitude" (Cardinal Ortega 2012). In this way, the wider culture continued to have an experience of faith even as organized religion was legally suppressed and under surveillance.

Over the course of the 1970s, the Church in Cuba had learned to believe in the manifest presence of God's love in its midst despite its dramatic reduction in size and strength. It was a Church that lived its dispossession joyfully. Like Christians in the catacombs, they celebrated Easter faith in the midst of opposition.[28] When the time came to prepare for participation in the 1979 continent-wide conference of Latin America bishops in Puebla, Mexico, the now-reshaped Catholic Church in Cuba was ready to think deeply about its mission and relationship with the culture surrounding it.

---

28 The "pact of the catacombs" has recently re-emerged in public discussion and is reminiscent of some aspects of the revitalization experience of the Catholic Church in Cuba. This so-called pact was a commitment made by various bishops at the end of Vatican II to promote a church with no pretension of power and a clear option for the poor in simple fidelity to the Gospel. See http://www.religionnews.com/2015/11/03/the-catacombs-pact-emerges-after-50-years-and-pope-francis-gives-it-new-life/.

A Church in resurgence

A process of accelerated revitalization began in the second half of the 1980s. At this time, various other Christian communities, particularly the evangelical and Pentecostal churches, also experienced a strengthening. The publication Fidel and Religion, a book-length interview with the Dominican Frei Betto of Brazil, helped remove people's fear of the topic of religion (Pedraza 2007, 242). Although the truth of Fidel's responses to various questions was widely debated (Montenegro Gonzalez 2010), the book opened the doors to a greater acceptance of religious matters on the part of the government (Bishop Arturo González, interview, Miami, June 15, 2015).

Cuban National Ecclesial Encounter

At Puebla, the Bishops of Cuba experienced a sense of being from a social, economic, political and religious context very different from that of the rest of Latin America (Márquez, 2005, 10). Bishop Fernando Azcárate, SJ, proposed "a Puebla in Cuba," to "take into account the Cuban reality, which was not reflected in the conclusions of the Puebla final document" (Céspedes 2005, 23). In 1982, national commissions and diocesan organizations began to work together with the rest of the Church in a process called the Cuban Ecclesial Reflection (REC) as a preparation for the 1986 Cuban National Ecclesial Encounter (ENEC).

The starting point for ENEC was a clear-eyed reading of the situation of the Church in Cuba: "we Catholics experience in Cuba a socialist state which proposes an exclusively scientific and materialistic conception of the world, a vision of human beings, history, the future, and existence as a whole that is different from the Christian vision of human beings and the world" (ENEC Documento Final, 150). Faced with this situation, Catholics have "tried to find paths that lead to a situation of dialogue between Catholics and Marxists" (ENEC Documento Final, 161). Far from a stance of confrontation, the church—pastors and lay people—seeks to be present "in the midst of its people as servant and teacher of truth and of justice in love" (ENEC Documento Final, 182). ENEC catalyzed a dialogical vision of the relationship of the church with the reality of Cuba and its mission within it. ENEC was the choice of the church "to journey together in the renewal of the Cuban church" (ENEC Documento Final, 19).

The process used in ENEC was even more critically defining for the Catholic Church in Cuba than its conclusions. ENEC "was the most important ecclesial and ecclesiological event of the whole Church in Cuba... it was the model of the most participatory, reflective, and hope-filled meeting that has [ever] taken place" (Rodriguez Díaz 2005, 15). The Holy See followed this process closely and gave its full support, and was present with an emissary of the Holy Father, Cardinal Eduardo Pironio (Céspedes 2005, 24). The model of church chosen in ENEC was a praying, missionary, and incarnate church. ENEC is the point at which the definitive process of revitalization begins for the Catholic Church in Cuba. Through this reflection, it now found new strength and new light to reorganize itself in terms of its mission. The ensuing pastoral plans all sprang from this starting point.

Re-evangelizing: The pilgrim journey

On the occasion of the celebration of the 500 years of evangelization of the Americas in 1992, the pope gave a cross to the bishops' conference in each country of the Americas on October 12, 1984. Cuba's cross was received by the president of the bishops' conference, Bishop Adolfo Rodriguez of Camagüey. This cross traveled throughout all the dioceses of Cuba as if on pilgrimage from the Church universal, representing solidarity, unity, and new hope. The cross became the occasion for door-to-door visiting to invite people to church, share reading material, and initiate conversations. It was the first formally organized evangelization work of the Catholic Church outside church doors since 1959. This pilgrimage of the cross began in the far west of the island, in Pinar del Rio, on February 24, 1985 (one year before ENEC) and concluded on October 27, 1991 in the cathedral of Santiago de Cuba at the eastern edge of the island (Rodriguez 2005, 15). Many people went to church, often for the first time in many years, to greet the pilgrim cross publicly.

In October 1989, a pilgrimage with an image of Our Lady of Charity began in Havana to prepare for the visit of John Paul II that was being planned for late 1991 at the invitation of the Cuban government. So great was the public response that processions were organized without government authorization. In May, however, these manifestations of piety were prohibited in Havana and the pope's visit was postponed. The first Houses of Prayer also began at this time in 1989 (Rodriguez 2005). Revitalization had begun in full swing.

The 1990s: Initiatives in the midst of crisis

After the dissolution of the Soviet Union and the loss of the old Soviet subsidy of its economy, Cuba experienced its worst economic crisis since the revolution. Official speeches and documents refer to this traumatic time as "the special period."

From a socio-cultural perspective, these conditions help explain the religious revival that took place during the 1990s. In this view, faith became an important factor in dealing with the crisis by offering strength, hope, and an alternative source of meaning for life (Perera and Perez 2009, 144). The softening of government penalization of religious practice and new church initiatives also played an important role in the revitalization. However, socio-economic and legal conditions alone cannot explain the "religious boom" that occurred in all religious groups (Ramírez Calzadilla 2001).

Caritas Cuba, the charitable agency of the Catholic Church, was founded in 1991, and began its work in the midst of growing social difficulties. In 1994, the country experienced an outbreak of neuropathy, a result of famine and the shortage of foodstuffs. This left many with motor or visual impairments and marked a particularly difficult year. This desperate situation led to a new mass exodus from the island, known as the "balsero crisis." The balseros left the country on rafts or other improvised vessels for Florida, a tide of departures that began with the sinking of the tugboat 13 de Marzo in Havana Bay.[29] It will never be fully known

29 This incident took place on July 13, 1994. Forty-one of the 72 passengers died, including 10 children. To this day no one has been made responsible for these deaths (Inter-American Commission on Human Rights 1996).

how many died in the attempt to leave the country, but estimates are that one of every four died in the attempt. About 40,000 people arrived in South Florida. Throughout this period, Cardinal Ortega in Havana and the Conference of Bishops overall issued various public statements, including reflections, messages, and declarations on the situation of the country, including the exodus by sea and its cost in human lives.

In the 1990s, long after all non-governmental publications in Cuba had been eliminated, Catholic publications began to re-emerge within the dioceses of Cuba. Some have kept going against all odds. Still others have gone through various stages, changing names and the regularity of their publication, but nonetheless continuing a presence within the world of communications. They represent a new point of view and a growing voice within the social, economic, and political situation in Cuba. During the same time, just as these new forms of communication were developing, dioceses also took on more of a role in formation and education, having been allowed to receive donations of books for adult faith and leadership formation in the late 1980s. Beginning in 1995, pastoral agencies of the Conference of Catholic Bishops of Cuba undertook new initiatives. They began to conduct consultations, examine the national situation in light of the Gospel and the social teaching of the Church, prioritize new pastoral objectives, identify goals to be achieved, and propose specific actions in order to bring them to fruition. National pastoral planning began to mature at a new level. That work continues and by 2015 the Catholic Church in Cuba has moved forward with its Fifth Pastoral Plan.

Protestant churches also experienced an awakening and witness a proliferation of "religious offers that make the Cuban religious reality more heterogeneous, plural, and complex" (Pérez Cruz et al. 2013, 26). Charismatic worship became popular within older denominations such as Methodists and Baptists. Many independent churches, movements, and ministries, began to spring up throughout the island (Pérez Cruz, et al. 213, 32).

"Love Hopes All Things", 1993

After a long silence, the 1993 pastoral letter of the Cuban bishops, Love Hopes All Things, echoed the feelings of the people and expressed solidarity with the anguish, achievements, and failures of the country. Written in the midst of the great economic hardships people were facing, the letter spoke of the need to "... eradicate some irritating policies" and denounced "the exclusive and omnipresent nature of the official ideology... the restrictions on the exercise of certain freedoms... fear... the high number of prisoners... discrimination by reason of philosophical and political ideas or religious creeds" (46-50). It also denounced the economic embargo by the United States (32-33). "The bishops claim no advantages, privilege, or special concession for the Church; they simply propose that a frank, amicable, and free dialogue in which each express their feelings verbally and cordially is possible" (Montenegro Gonzalez 2010, 337). The letter was well received within the church, but prompted harsh criticism from the government, which accused the bishops of treason.

The Visit of John Paul II

Pope John Paul II finally did arrive in Cuba in 1998 after additional skirmishes with the government. In contrast to the previously planned papal visit, this visit was prepared and led by the church, not the government. The first mass was celebrated in Santa Clara and dedicated to the theme of the family. In preparation for this, and for the first time in the history of the Diocese of Santa Clara, missions were carried out systematically, door to door, in every parish, with a particularly strong outreach to youth.

The papal mass overflowed with people who wanted to hear the voice of the pope, whether or not they were believers. After the visit, the diocesan magazine devoted a special issue collecting all of John Paul's homilies and speeches in Cuba. The vast outpouring for the papal mass, together with related media coverage, made the church more visible. People began to increasingly come to the churches and church activities. The visit unquestionably opened new horizons. Its first result was a notable increase in the number of people, both young people and adults, who came asking for baptism. It also strengthened the Church's confidence in its organizing ability, and its power to draw people together. It had organized the visit of a pope!

At the same time, a transformation began in the communities due to the arrival of new members from the wider society. The newcomers usually had a weak doctrinal preparation and were not very committed. A positive outcome was the evident less fear and reluctance in talking about faith. However, many lifelong laypeople continued to leave the country for different reasons, including pressure from their children, as the economy continued to deteriorate.

After the visit of John Paul II, the Diocese of Santa Clara began efforts to evangelize the culture in ways not possible before, including libraries, cultural centers, and schools of professional formation. A space for a library has been built in the diocesan office building to house donated books and this has become an important cultural venue in the city. Symposiums, contests, conferences, and art expositions are held there. It is also a center for the Winter Festival of the Cubanacán Film Club and venue for launching books in the International Book Fair held every year. The goal is to attract people who might not otherwise connect with the church to evangelize and sow deeper seeds of faith. For the same reason, concerts and music festivals are held in the cathedral, which has an uncommonly good size and acoustics for the city. Some classes of the Diocesan Training Center also operate in the cathedral.

The Diocesan Training Center opened in 2001 and has eight branches throughout the diocese. The courses are deeply appreciated in student and professional circles because of the diversity of options, the quality of the teachers who teach them, and the foreign church-related universities that accredit them. Reflecting the goal of reaching well beyond the church's present flock, sixty percent of those who take these courses are not religiously observant.

Charitable activities are found throughout the diocese as a manifestation of Christian compassion and outreach, and are organized by the diocesan organization for charitable activities,

Caritas. Services include soup kitchens (35 in the diocese), laundries for the elderly and the sick (16 in the diocese), support groups serving families of persons with Down Syndrome (2 in the diocese), and groups to promote cultural activities, recreation, and spirituality for the elderly (38 in the diocese).

The Pilgrimage of Our Lady of Charity

The national pilgrimage of the Virgen Mambisa image of Our Lady of Charity began in late 2010. It traveled across Cuba in preparation for the celebration of 400 years of the discovery of the image of Our Lady of Charity to take place in 2012.

The pilgrimage was preceded by a mission announcing the date of the arrival in each city, town, village, hamlet, or rural district. But the real mission was in the pilgrimage itself, in the ability of the image of the Virgin to draw people. During the image's pilgrimage in the Diocese of Santa Clara, the bishop accompanied the image practically everywhere. He prayed with those assembled, encouraged them, passed out holy cards, and did some basis catechesis, depending on the occasion. At the foot of the image, divided families were reconciled. Those who came were prisoners and police officers, dissidents and strong supporters of the government, believers and professed atheists, Catholics and those of other religions. There was palpable delight and a sense of blessing when the image passed by people in their homes, neighborhoods, and work places.

In the Diocese of Santa Clara, the itinerary included hospitals, prisons, a police station, as well as all the chapels, churches, parishes and mission houses. Poems, songs, and concerts were dedicated to the image during this pilgrimage. In the city of Santa Clara, a concert was held to honor the image at the emblematic Our Lady of Charity Theater. The passage of the Virgin left blessings, but also challenges. Clearly, there was a need to both purify the simple faith of the majority of Cubans as well as to give substance to the feeling aroused by the passage of the image. This required training missionaries, catechists, and educators to serve above all as witnesses. The goal was to first welcome all those who came forward, not looking down on anyone for their ignorance of doctrine or practice of syncretic religion, yet to look for ways to help people's faith grow and become purer.

The changes in the last fifty years have made Cubans a people who need to rediscover their roots. An important task, therefore, is getting to know the history of Cuba. Cubans have experienced conflict within and among themselves as a result of the political polarization and the measures imposed by the government to carry out the revolution. Regardless of their role in this process, everyone has felt the impact of these changes. The Catholic Church in Cuba recognizes that part of its mission in Cuba today is to help all Cubans discover the roots and sources of hope. This involves growing in faith, forgiveness, and reconciliation, in turn strengthening the family and the family's role in personal growth.

To bring all this about, the church needs to continually discover and strengthen its identity as church, to recover lay witness, and to spiritually strengthen the Christian community. At the same time, the church aims to help educate people for life in freedom, to "lose fear" not merely for individual freedom but also as freedom to nourish the common good, to struggle to be free of everything that hinders human and spiritual growth. This involves training for consensus-building, initiative, responsibility, and respect for self and others. Ultimately, it is about making efforts to gain more spaces of true gospel freedom. In the Cuban context, this will mean continued work toward reconciliation among all Cubans through an examination of conscience that not only forgives but asks for forgiveness.

"Hope Does Not Disappoint"

In this 2013 document, the bishops once again invite the Cuban people and especially the Catholic faithful to dialogue and to reconciliation, emphasizing the participation of all and the search for unity in diversity, respecting the plurality of viewpoints. The letter courageously takes up the issue of freedom, urges a "strong and responsible social autonomy" (19), and criticizes the state for its paternalistic posture. It names the hopes of Cubans: overcoming poverty, personal fulfillment, a new political order, dialogue, the concert of nations, the family, and youth.

Preliminary Analysis of the Impact of the Visit of Francis

Everyone was pleased by the visit of the Pope Francis. His simple language could be understood by everyone, and his words were reconciling. While some might have wished that in some contexts those words had been more prophetic, they did not arouse mistrust or suspicion. His spontaneous gestures caused great joy, although some regretted that he did not visit a prison, a marginal neighborhood, or a home for the elderly, because all three exist in Cuba, and that is where the most forgotten and those most in need of mercy are.

This is a preliminary analysis; his speeches need to be studied better, his gestures re-examined, and the testimonies of those who saw him up close and conversed with him need to be heard. It is especially necessary to try to live the mercy that he spoke about so frequently.

The visit made the church visible in Cuba. The public testimonies of the nun, the young university student, and the family in Santiago were all simple, real, and direct. Just as important was the presence of two priests on TV, one commenting on the news and the other explaining the celebrations; the communicative ability of the Catholic Church was a discovery for everyone. The visit may be an opportunity to take steps in this terrain.

Revitalization Lessons Learned

Challenges

The most serious problem currently facing the Church in Cuba—and the country itself—is the temporary and permanent emigration of its leaders, parishioners, and people in general. There is an exodus of Cuban priests, leaving pastoral work in the hands of foreign clergy. For example, in 2015 there was only one Cuban priest in the entire Diocese of Guantanamo-Baracoa.

Many lay people who stayed in the 1960s, 1970s, and 1980s, are now leaving because their children and grandchildren want to emigrate or have already done so. Since restoration of relations between Cuba and the United States, emigration has increased, with most Cuban emigrants entering through South America (Venezuela or Ecuador) or through Central America and then crossing into Mexico to reach the U.S. border.[30] This increasing emigration is due to the fear that the laws granting Cubans political asylum upon their arrival in the United States will change.[31]

The Church must continuously train new pastoral agents because the exodus is ongoing. Consider an example from a communications course held at the national level. This course enrolled forty of the most promising type of young lay leaders—those with at least a pre-university schooling level, under age of forty, known and encouraged by their bishops. Of that number, only twenty remained in Cuba. Of the five students from Santa Clara, only two stayed in Cuba. Only three of the ten lay people who began working on the first issue of the magazine Amanecer are still in Cuba.

Temporary emigration also takes place when Cubans are sent to provide health services or education in other countries for two or three years, which are called "international missions." This has had a negative impact on the family, because "children stay with their grandparents or with one of the parents ... and many divorces ensue, the family breaks up" (Interview Rosy Lopez, El Cobre, April 7, 2014).

30 From October 2014 to August 2015 at least 27,413 Cubans crossed the border with Mexico; another 9,000 came to Miami by air without a visa, while others arrived by sea or entered with a visa and stayed (San Martin 2015).

31 The fear is that the United States will eliminate the Cuban Adjustment Act of 1966. However, this law simply allows the Cubans who are in the United States to adjust their status to resident after being in the country for year without having to leave. See Bustamante 2105.

New Possibilities

The new Pastoral Plan prepared for 2014-2020[32] refers to the encounter with Christ on the road to Emmaus. It proposes a journey of conversion and action, stressing basic training for Christian life and ongoing training for discipleship, with special attention to the family and the Christian community. Given the fact of mobility in Cuba, the Plan is aimed at a church in mission, always beginning, utilizing fundamental elements such as the testimony of joy and fraternity, austerity and solidarity.

The rapprochement between the United States and Cuba opens up paths of communication and exchange between Cubans on the island and those outside. This offers the church fruitful terrain for fostering reconciliation between Catholics on the island and Catholic Cubans in the diaspora. The need for reconciliation is the result of multiple factors. Travel restrictions imposed by the Cuban government and the U.S. embargo, plus very limited access to phone and mail communication, created a profound distance between the people of the island and the diaspora. People both within and outside the island felt the impact of family breakup and the loss of friendships. However, decades of living in very different social contexts have shaped Cubans of the island and of the diaspora differently.[33] This contributes to their different if not opposing perspectives on many issues surrounding the reality of Cuba.

Successes

Having explored the situation through written material, church documents, and interviews, the following successes or key elements in the revitalization of the Catholic Church in Cuba may be identified.

---

32 Since 1995 the Cuban Church has been promoting a "way of participatory planning to stimulate and carry out its evangelizing action" (Plan Pastoral, 60).

33 For a deeper understanding the need for reconciliation among Cubans see Communion in Diversity? Exploring a Practical Theology of Reconciliation among Cuban Exiles (Cortés, 2013).

Faith in the Power of the Small

The Church in Cuba interpreted the experience of the decline in number of personnel and institutions and its limited public presence in society from a faith perspective. This led the Church to appreciate the power of the small scale, the mustard seed, in gospel terms. The Church learned to evangelize without great resources, without access to spaces in education or media. The small number of faithful favored personal contact between ministers and people. The witness of simplicity has had a significant gospel impact. The Church was able to "strengthen the faith in situations that were heading toward despair in a land that apparently was going to separate itself from God" (Dionisio García Ibánez, Archbishop of Santiago de Cuba, interview, El Cobre, April 6, 2015).

Bishop Emilio Aranguren summed it up in his words to Pope Francis: "Over the decades, this church, in the silence of the everyday, has been strengthening its own pastoral spirituality in four keys of the Kingdom: the value of 'the little', 'the small', 'the anonymous' and 'the gradual'" (Holguin September 21, 2015). Ultimately, all religious revitalization is the result of "God's life-giving action" and the "faithful response of the Church to God's loving action which leads it to express its faith creatively in different circumstances that the journey through history presents to it" (Céspedes 2004, 255).

Participation of the Laity

As the Church lost priests due to the lack of vocations and emigration, the laity assumed greater responsibility in evangelization. Many churches remained open thanks to the constancy of lay people, sometimes elderly women, who sustained the faith. Mission houses began to be set up in the 1980s,[34] giving lay people an important leadership role in the development of small communities. Many laypeople were trained in the Church's

34 "The greatest difficulties faced by these mission houses . . . lack of sites, the lack of leaders in the same locality, difficulty of transport, the mix of popular religiosity with syncretism and spiritism, the advanced age of some of the leaders, few visits from the priest and the mobility of pastoral agents" (Plan Pastoral, 47).

social doctrine, pastoral ministry, and catechesis. The emigration of many committed laity and the arrival of people with little religious formation has challenged this form of presence. New Catholics generally have little awareness of their mission as lay people (Plan Pastoral, 53). This needs to be continually fostered.

Missionary Church

The Church has emphasized a missionary spirituality based on the practice of going to people where they are, instead of waiting for them to come to the Church. In different dioceses adults and youth carry the Scriptures and Eucharist each week to areas where not even mission houses exist, out of the conviction that "the Church must reach everyone" (Archbishop Dionisio García Ibánez of Santiago de Cuba, interview, El Cobre, April 6, 2015). Cuba now has 2,300 mission houses (Plan Pastoral, 46). This has allowed the Church reach remote locations and become inserted in the countryside and cities to be close to the people.

Unity in the Church

Because there were few Catholics in the early years, a great union was forged between laity, religious, priests, and bishops (Bishop Dionisio García Ibáñez, interview, El Cobre, April 6, 2015). In an environment hostile towards believers, unity had to be supported and maintained. This is a value that the Catholic Church in Cuba does not want to lose at the same time it opens itself to greater participation which will generate diversity. The Church must to combine communion and participation to avoid a vertical and clerical model of church.

A Church at the service of those most in need

The charity work of the Catholic Church in Cuba in health ministries, prisons, and care for the elderly has been the greatest testimony of its faith. When the Church lost its health and charity institutions, it assumed a simple ministry of presence, but with the ENEC it began to organize services. Since the founding of Caritas Cuba, an organized network has been developed to serve the people in their ordinary needs (soup kitchens and centers for the elderly, the sick, and the disabled) and when natural disasters occur. Thus, the church presents "another discourse, not of resentment or hatred, but of love and forgiveness . . . the battered Church is still the one that is committed, but it has not taken advantage of these services to win followers, or to proselytize" (Bishop Arturo González, interview, Miami, June 15, 2015).

A Church willing to engage in dialogue with all in the pursuit of the common good

Since ENEC, the Catholic Church in Cuba has intentionally situated itself within society and "has made an explicit decision to evangelize the culture, the latter being understood in its broadest and simultaneously most exact meaning, by means of positive presence and dialogue" (Céspedes 2004, 263). This dialogue between the government and the church, proposed for decades by the church, began to take place after 1985 (Céspedes 2004, 259), but it became especially active in preparation for the visit of John Paul II and subsequent papal visits.

Collaboration between government and church has also taken place in response to natural catastrophes like hurricanes. Such dialogue and collaboration in humanitarian efforts respond to the Church's mission to serve human flourishing and should not be seen as an alignment with the political system (Márquez 2012, 83). In addition to engaging the government for common purposes, the Catholic Church has fostered dialogue with the culture by creating spaces for artistic expression and exchange in different fields of knowledge, especially the social sciences and the humanities.

A Church open to all

The Catholic Church in Cuba has been able to open its arms to those who after several decades of estrangement from the church, and even in opposition to the church, began to return or to come to the churches for the first time. No one was asked, "Where were you? What did you or didn't you do?" (Bishop Arturo Gonzalez, interview, Miami, June 15, 2015). The Church has sought to be reconciling, healing the wounds left by personal and national history. It seeks to unite the people in order to build the future. There is a deep relationship between reconciliation and revitalization.

The new life of the Church arises from the healing of people, from building communities of faith, from the drawing power to unite people in the midst of diversity. The issue of reconciliation has been and is central in the ministry of the Catholic Church in Cuba. Reconciliation is the revitalization to which the Church aspires and in which it is pastorally engaged. The revitalization of the Church is measured not by institutional growth, but by the quality of Christian life and communion, resulting from reconciliation in its human and spiritual, personal and social dimensions.

La Caridad

From the standpoint of reconciliation, La Virgen de la Caridad, "symbol of Cubanicity" (Portuando Zúñiga 2011) plays a particularly important role as a path to encountering Jesus and to encountering brothers and sisters. Devotion to this symbol since its origins has united the Cuban people. People feel her "as intercessor of impossible things. . . She has kept the Cuban Church present" (Alina de La Caridad López Suárez, interview, El Cobre, April 4, 2015). The history and meaning of the story and symbol of La Caridad represents the very possibility of reconciliation amid the diversity of races, visions, and ideologies existing within the Cuban people.

Conclusion

The Catholic Church in Cuba, rooted in the Paschal mystery, has experienced a long Way of the Cross, passion, and death, which has blossomed in new life. This church, stripped of its institutions and forced to withdraw into its church buildings, lost its ability to influence public and social life. Instead, it learned to carry out its mission without economic resources, sustained by a "faithful remnant" of grandmothers and a few courageous laypeople and priests, testimony to what was said of the early Christian community: "See how they love one another" (Acts 4:32-37).

Out of the ashes a renewed church was reborn, poor, service-oriented and fraternal, close to the gospel, living the joy of the gospel. The Catholic Church in Cuba redirected the entirety of its mission toward proclaiming Jesus Christ, converting people without seeking to change what could not be changed within the regime, doing what was possible while living and witnessing faithfully. Having lost the superfluous, it concentrated on the essential: being God's presence in the midst of the people.

The Catholic Church in Cuba has striven to be a church incarnate in its people and culture. Its closeness to the suffering and strivings of this people has enabled it to be relevant. Thus, it has quite intentionally incorporated signs, rituals, and Cuban music into evangelization, opening doors into the Cuban heart and soul. Our Lady of Charity, at one and the same time a national and religious symbol, is a sign of what the faith continues to contribute to Cuban life. Once she became part of the life and history of this people, no one has been able to wrench her out of its soul. The task of the church is to accompany and nourish this faith so that it may lead to Jesus and commitment to his Reign.

As the Church has gained space and better conditions for dialogue with the government have developed, the church must remain on alert so as not to lose its identity forged on the cross. The temptation of power and of possession always beset the Church on its pilgrim journey on this earth, in Cuba and everywhere. That is why it must keep seeking the "spaces that are properly its own for carrying out its mission and not positions of power or political influence" (Andújar 2009, 8). In a stance of dialogue, the Church must keep strengthening its prophetic vocation, offering relevant proposals for the common good and not silencing the necessary critique of what is not just or constructive. As a bridge of communion, the church must keep helping to heal wounds, creating spaces where the people may express themselves through art, learn to think and to respect the thinking of others, and dream of the possible.

The current moment calls for a church which, faced with disappointment and frustration, offers a message of hope. Faced with the loss of the horizon of transcendence, the church reaffirms the faith that grounds the value of human dignity. Faced with discourse that fuels aggression and exclusion, the church speaks of reconciliation and participation to build the future "with all and for the sake of all" (José Marti).

References:

Andújar, Gustavo.
2009. "Iglesia y sociedad en Cuba a los 15 años del Amor Todo lo Espera." Vitral, XV, n. 89.

Anonymous.
1987. Encuentro Nacional Eclesial Cubano (ENEC). Documento Final. Roma: Tipografía Don Bosco.

2014. Gaceta Oficial de Cuba. No. 20 Extraordinaria de 16 de abril de 2014. http://www.cubadebate.cu/wp-content/uploads/2014/04/GO_X_20_2014_gaceta-ley-de-inversion-extranjera.pdf. Accessed October 30, 2015.

Aranguren, Monseñor Emilio, Obispo de Holguin.
2015. Saludo al Papa Francisco. Holguín, September 21.

Bustamante, Michael J.
2015. "Is the Cuban Adjustment Act in Trouble?" Cuba Counterpoints, June 4. http://cubacounterpoints.com/features/is-the-cuban-adjustment-act-in-trouble/#more-1069. Accessed October 20, 2015.

Campistrous Pérez, María C.
1998. "El Cobre: altar mayor de Cuba," Verdad y Esperanza. Publicación de la Unión Católica de Prensa de Cuba, enero: 18.

Céspedes, Carlos Manuel.
2005. "Una cierta nostalgia de futuridad a los veinte años del ENEC." Verdad y Esperanza. Publicación de la Unión de Prensa de Cuba, 3-24.

2004. "Reanimación Católica en Cuba." En Globalización religiosa y neoliberalismo. Espiritualidad, política y economía en un mundo en crisis. III Encuentro Internacional de Estudios Socio-Religiosos. Naucalpan, Mexico: CIPS, Department of Religious Studies.

Clark, John.
1985. Religious Repression in Cuba. Miami: University of Miami Press.

Conferencia de Obispos Católicos de Cuba.
1960. "Circular Colectiva del Episcopado Cubano, agosto 7, 1960". En La Voz de la Iglesia en Cuba. 100 Documentos Episcopales. Mexico, D.F.: Obra Nacional de la Buena Prensa.

1993. "El Amor todo lo espera". En La Voz de la Iglesia en Cuba. 100 Documentos Episcopales. México D.F.: Obra Nacional de la Buena Prensa.

1995. "Promulgación del Documento Final del ENEC." En La Voz de la Iglesia en Cuba. 100 Documentos Episcopales. Mexico: Obra Nacional de la Buena Prensa.

2013. "La Esperanza no defrauda." Carta Circular del Episcopado de Cuba. http://www.diocesisdesantaclara.com/noticias/item/778-obispos-de-cuba-hacen-p%C3%BAblica-la-nueva-carta-pastoral-%E2%80%9Cla-esperanza-no-defrauda%E2%80%9D.html. Accessed October 20, 2015.

2014. Plan Pastoral de la Iglesia Católica en Cuba. 2014-2020.

Constitución de Cuba de 1901. https://www.hicuba.com/constitucion-1901.htm.

Cortés, Ondina.

2013. "Communion in Diversity? Exploring a Practical Theology of Reconciliation Among Cuban Exiles," PhD diss, St. Thomas University. ProQuest (3589421).

Crahan, Margaret E.

1985. "Cuba: Religion and Revolutionary Institutionalization." Journal of Latin American Studies 17 (2): 319-340. Cambridge University Press. http://www.jstor.org/stable/156825. Accessed: December 20, 2012.

1999. "Cuba." In Religious Freedom and Evangelization in Latin America. The Challenge of Religious Pluralism, edited by Paul Sigmund, 87-112. Maryknoll: Orbis.

CRECED.

1996. Comunidades de Reflexión Eclesial Cubana en la Diáspora: Final Document. Miami: Graphic Ideas Corporation.

Estévez, Felipe J.

1989. El perfil pastoral de Félix Varela. Miami.: Ediciones Universal.

Fernández Santalices, Manuel.

2001. Cronología Histórica de Cuba. 1492-2000. Miami: Ediciones Universal.

Inter-American Commission on Human Rights.

1996. Report Number 47/96 CASE 11.436 Victims of the Tugboat "13 de Marzo" vs. Cuba, October 16. http://www2.fiu.edu/~fcf/13mem71398.htm. Accessed September 25, 2012.

Lebroc Martínez, Reinerio y Jesús Bermejo.
1992. San Antonio María Claret: Arzobispo Misionero de Cuba. Madrid: Misioneros Hijos del Inmaculado Corazón de María.

Márquez, Orlando.
2005. "El ENEC era lo que la Iglesia necesitaba." Verdad y Esperanza. Publicación de la Unión de Prensa de Cuba, 9-12.

2012. "La Iglesia como puente de acercamiento," Espacio Laical. 3:79-86

Montenegro González, Augusto.
2010. "Historia de la Iglesia en Cuba (1977-1994)". Anuario de Historia de la Iglesia 19: 293-338.

Oficina Nacional de Estadísticas e Información de la Republica de Cuba. http://www.one.cu/.

Ortega, Cardenal Jaime.
2012. Conferencia impartida en Eischtätt, Alemania. Espacio Laical. 217 (novembre).

Pedraza, Silvia.
2007. Political Disaffection in Cuba's Revolution and Exodus. Cambridge: Cambridge University Press.

Perera, Ana Celia y Ofelia Pérez Cruz.
2009. "Crisis social y reavivamiento religioso: una mirada desde lo sociocultural." Cuicuilco 46:136-157.

Pérez, Louis A.
1999. "Incurring a Debt of Gratitude: 1898 and the Moral Sources of United States Hegemony in Cuba." American Historical Review 104 (2): 356-398.

Pérez Cruz, Ofelia, Ana Celia Perera Pintado, Sonia Jiménez Berrios, Aurora Aguilar Núñez, Lisette Fabelo Pérez, Ileana Hodge Limonta, et al.

2013. Nuevos movimientos religiosos en Cuba. La Habana: Centro de Investigaciones Psicológicas y Sociológicas.

Pérez Serantes, Enrique, Arzobispo de Santiago de Cuba.

1960. "Por Dios y por Cuba." In La voz de Iglesia en Cuba: 100 documentos episcopales, 107-114. México, D.F.: Obra Nacional de la Buena Prensa.

Portuondo Zúñiga, Olga.

2011. La Virgen de la Caridad del Cobre. Símbolo de Cubanía. Santiago de Cuba: Editorial Oriente.

Ramírez Calzadilla, Jorge.

2001. "Intervención en la Mesa Redonda," Cuba: Reanimación Religiosa en los '90, III Encuentro Internacional de Estudios Sociorreligiosos, La Habana.

Rodríguez Díaz, P. Antonio.

1998. "A los 70 años de la Acción Católica en Cuba," Vitral 24 (marzo-abril). http://www.vitral.org/vitral/vitral24/nhist.htm.

2005. "El ENEC, Una Llamada a la Encarnación." Verdad y Esperanza. Publicación de la Unión de Prensa de Cuba, 15-17.

San Martin, Nancy.

2015. "Interminable éxodo de cubanos por la frontera con México," El Nuevo Herald, 31 de octubre.

Suárez Polcari, Ramón.

2003. Historia de la Iglesia Católica en Cuba, Vol. I. Miami: Ed. Universal.

Super, John.
2003. "Interpretations of Church and State in Cuba, 1959-1961." The Catholic Historical Review 89 (3): 511+. World Scholar: Latin America & the Caribbean. Accessed February 25, 2013. http://proxy.stu.edu:2377/tinyurl/5.

Sweig, Julia.
2009. Cuba: What Everyone Needs to Know. Oxford: Oxford University Press.

Trujillo Lemes, Maximiliano Francisco.
2011. El pensamiento social católico en Cuba en la década de los 60. Santiago de Cuba: Editorial Oriente.

Uría Rodríguez, Ignacio.
2012. Iglesia y Revolución en Cuba: Enrique Pérez Serantes (1883-1968), el obispo que salvó a Fidel Castro. Madrid: Editorial Encuentro.

Wright, Elliott.
2015. "Cuba's Vibrant, Growing Methodist Church." New World Outlook, May-June. Accessed on March 7,2016.http://www.umcmission.org/Find-Resources/New-World-Outlook-Magazine/New-World-Outlook-Archives/2015/May/June/0616cubasvibrantchurch.

CHAPTER 5: ABUNDANT LIFE

An Evangelical Megachurch in Costa Rica[35]

Clifton L. Holland and Jordan Dobrowski

Programa Latinoamericano de Estudios Sociorreligiosos (PROLADES)

35 A longer version of this case study report is available from PROLADES, prolades@ice.co.cr.

The appearance of evangelical megachurches in Costa Rica and the other countries of Central America in the mid-1990s has become an important element in evangelical church growth in the region. In the case of Costa Rica, the megachurches (those that have attendance of more than 2,000 people in their weekend worship services from Saturday evening through Sunday) form part of the 36 largest denominations or associations of churches in the country as of May 30, 2014, according to the latest national study of evangelical work in Costa Rica carried out by PROLADES (2013-2014). In visits during 2011 and 2012 to the majority of the mega-churches (51) in the major cities of Central America, including Panama, the PROLADES team discovered that the mega-church phenomenon is a strong indication that a revitalization movement is taking place in this region within the Protestant Christian orbit and is attracting large numbers of formerly inactive members of the majority Roman Catholic population to the worship services and activities in the search for a spiritual experience that is relevant for their daily lives. In this paper, we are taking as a case study the megachurch Abundant Life Christian Community of Coronado (VAC), located in a suburb of San Jose, the capital of Costa Rica. The research team from the Latin American Program for Socio-religious Studies (PROLADES) included Clifton L. Holland, Director (B.A., M.A. with doctoral studies in cultural anthropology, missiology and church history); Roger Vargas (Lic. in psychology and a Costa Rica Christian educator); and Jordan Dobrowski (B.A. in anthropology from Augustana University in South Dakota, USA).

History

According to Senior Pastor Ricardo Salazar (a university graduate who was a professional soccer player in Costa Rica for a few years), VAC is designed to be "a seeker church" where people can participate in a non-formal atmosphere of contemporary music and worship, with a strong emphasis on the family (inspired by the leadership style and ministry of Willow Creek Community Church near Chicago), where broken lives can be restored, new beginnings can be made, and a deeper spiritual life can be developed in a neo-Pentecostal context. The impressive growth of Vida Abundante in Coronado has produced a mother church with 10 daughter congregations in Costa Rica (with an average total attendance of about 8,360), as well as associated churches in Ecuador, Chile, Cuba and the USA (New York City metro area). All of these churches form part of the Federation of Abundant Life Churches (FAVA), a fraternal organization of sister churches. All of these established churches are part of the missionary vision of VAC.

FEDERATION OF VIDA ABUNDANTE CHURCHES IN COSTA RICA

Information provided by Pastor Miguel Sánchez - May 19, 2015

San José Metro Area

Vida Abundante de Coronado (VAC) – 3550 average attendance
Vida Abundante de Cariari – 800-900 average attendance
Vida Abundante de Pavas Oeste –300-400 average attendance
Vida Abundante de Desamparados Sur – 700-800 average attendance
Vida Abundante de Curridabat –500-600 average attendance

Outside the San José Metro Area

Vida Abundante de Cartago – 350 average attendance
Vida Abundante de Heredia – 900-1000 average attendance
Vida Abundante de San Carlos – 120 average attendance
Vida Abundante de Liberia – 110 average attendance
Vida Abundante de Grecia – 230 average attendance
Vida Abundante de San Vito – 300 average attendance

TOTAL AVERAGE WEEKEND ATTENDANCE NATIONALLY = 8,360

This megachurch was selected for a scientific case study that was carried out during the first half of 2015 on two levels: with the pastoral team and with members of the community. Financial support was received from the Center for the Study of World Christian Revitalization Movements. Later in this report we will identify the expulsion and attraction factors at play in the progressive growth of VAC. The more than 400 people interviewed in April and May of 2015 expressed that their personal lives as well as their family life had been spiritually revitalized through their participation in the multifaceted ministries of this megachurch.

VAC is characterized as being "neo-Pentecostal" with a "Finished Work of Christ" theological perspective (similar to the Assemblies of God). Its church polity is based on a governing board of directors (council of elders) who are chosen by consensus among the Pastoral Team rather than by a vote of the congregation. VAC's style of leadership is PASTORAL among a team of equal partners, and not authoritarian. The political perspective of VAC is apolitical (it doesn't favor any particular political party) but it is conservative socially in its general orientation but proactive in reaching out to those with special needs in society (abandoned children, women who are victims of domestic or sexual violence, families in crisis, the elderly, drug addicts, etc.).

It is no surprise that VAC has grown in membership and physical size since its humble beginning in mid-1993 because of the quality of its leadership; its vision, mission and message, "Making each member of the family a disciple of Jesus Christ"); and its congregational life-style that has attracted large numbers of people to this church that reached "mega" status in 2001.

Context

A series of public opinion polls revealed that those who identify as "Roman Catholics" declined in Costa Rica from 85% in 1983 to 67% in 2015 (a loss of 18%), whereas those who identified as "Evangelical Christians" increased from 8.6% in 1983 to 25% in 2015 (an increase of 16.4%), which is a span of 32 years. In 2015, 86% of the Costa Rican population sample stated they were born in Catholic homes, and only 12% of the sample stated they were born in Evangelical homes (CID Gallup public opinion poll, January 2015).

The rise of Evangelical mega-churches (predominantly Pentecostal or neo-Pentecostal) in Costa Rica since the late 1990s has provided many Christians with an attractive alternative to formal, traditional worship services, whether Catholic or Protestant, because of their contemporary music, worship and preaching/teaching style, large pastoral staff, large auditoriums and multifaceted ministries. Worship services tend to last two hours or longer, rather than the traditional one-hour format of most non-Pentecostal churches, and are led by "worship teams" of high-quality singers and musicians, with numerous large video monitors so that everyone can see what is happening on the platform while participating in exuberant congregational singing and worshipful activities -- hand-clapping, raising of arms, praying out loud, individuals dancing in rhythm to the music (which we call "the Evangelical two-step"), some speaking and "praying in tongues" (glossolalia), some expressing a great deal of emotion (weeping, shouting "amen" and "hallelujah, etc.), warm greetings and hugs among fellow church members, etc.

These expressions tend to produce a strong sense of "community" among the congregants, so that they feel part of a large family of believers and not just isolated individuals in a crowd of people. Overall, their continued participation in an Evangelical mega-church tends to improve the quality of their personal and family lives because they enjoy the excitement of being part of a massive worship and praise celebration with fellow believers, their self-esteem improves as well as their general sense of happiness and contentment with their own spiritual lives that have been renewed and revitalized as a result of their confession of sin, repentance and a new commitment to God. This is a context that is very favorable to attracting many discontent people from other churches, especially nominal Catholics and Protestants from churches that are not satisfying their spiritual needs.

In 2000, the PROLADES team discovered the existence of only one Evangelical mega-church in the San José Metropolitan Area (SJMA), whereas now there are about a dozen. Many of these churches were founded during the 1990s as house churches, whereas others were organized churches with their own buildings prior to 1990. All of these mega-churches are Pentecostal, Charismatic or Neo-Pentecostal but with different theological and liturgical orientations, as well as different growth patterns.

Two of these megachurches are affiliated with the Assemblies of God (Oasis de Esperanza and Centro Evangelístico de Zapote), which identifies with the Finished Work of Christ Pentecostal Family of Churches, according to the system of classification for the Protestant movement developed by

PROLADES; three are independent Pentecostal churches (La Rosa de Sarón, Pasión por las Almas, and Maná-KingdomTakers); and two are Charismatic and affiliated with traditionally non-Pentecostal denominations (La Ciudad de Dios, Brethren in Christ—Anabaptist-Mennonite Family of Churches; and Templo Bíblico, Association of Costa Rican Bible Churches [AIBC], founded by missionaries and pastors related to the independent Latin American Mission [MLA]). In the case of Templo Bíblico, this church became identified with the Charismatic Renewal Movement in the early 1970s and today is more like many other neo-Pentecostal churches than the traditional AIBC church. La Rose of Sharon Church was the first Evangelical mega-church in Costa Rica that emerged during the 1990s and reported over 12,000 members in 2000, but it is now in decline with its Sunday attendance at only about 5,000; it identifies with the Faith Healing and Deliverance Family of Pentecostal Churches. Passion for Souls and Maná-KingdomTakers both identify with the New Apostolic Reformation Family of Pentecostal Churches. Some of these megachurches preach "the gospel of prosperity" to differing degrees.

One of the eight mega-churches in the greater metropolitan area of San Jose is Abundant Life Christian Community of Coronado (VAC), which identifies as being neo-Pentecostal and caters to those Christians who are seeking to experience a deeper walk with God based on discipleship and service to others, and without the liturgical and cultural baggage associated with traditional Pentecostal churches. VAC is one such place where congregants are not afraid or embarrassed to invite others (family members, friends, neighbors, working associates, fellow students, etc.) to attend worship services and small group meetings, which provide a friendly, appealing and non-threatening environment that is conducive to spiritual growth based on the solid teaching of the Word of God and its practical application to their daily lives.

Development

Description of Abundant Life Christian Community

The origins of Vida Abundante Coronado (VAC) date to May 1993 when a house church of about 50 people began a house church in the Tibas District, a suburb to the north of San Jose, under the leadership of four pastors and elders of the Christian Center in Guadalupe (CCG, affiliated with Transworld Missions, an independent Pentecostal organization): Sixto Porras, Milton Rosales, Ricardo Salazar and Miguel Sánchez, together with their wives. Sixto Porras was one of the founders of Christian Students United (ECU), a group of university students affiliated with the International Fellowship of Evangelical Students (IFES) at the University of Costa Rica (UCR). Later he became the senior pastor at CCG. While studying at the UCR, Ricardo Salazar became a professional soccer player and was acquired by the first division team Saprissa; he retired from professional soccer in 1982 at age 21. Milton Rosales graduated with a Licentiate in Human Development and Psychology. Miguel Sánchez received a Licentiate in Financial Administration.

By 1998, VACs pastoral staff and its 160 members began to think about purchasing property and building their own facilities to house a larger congregation. Today, VAC owns 17 adjoining lots totaling about 40,200 square meters where all of its current church and school facilities have been built. Pastor Miguel Sánchez estimated the total value of VAC's land and properties at about $14 million. VAC's current monthly operational budget is about $113,208 and its yearly budget about $1,358,490. VAC's monthly income covers the church's operational budget and its reserve for future expenses.

Currently, VAC has a pastoral staff of 12 full-time paid members: Ricardo Salazar (Senior Pastor), Guizelle Quesada (Pastor of Counselling and Group Support, and Salazar's wife), Silvia Zúñiga Flores (Coordinator of Family Ministries), Miguel Sánchez (Pastor for Social Action), Jason Cordero (Pastor for Discipleship Training as well as Youth Pastor), Victoria Chavarría (Pastor of Children's Ministries), Jaime Álvarez (Pastor of

Musical Arts), Samuel Pérez (Pastor of Discipleship and Small Group Ministries), Danny Segura (Coordinator of Pastoral and Production Services), Cinthia Bermúdez (Director of Costa Rican Christian School – primary and secondary education), Hazel Cedeño (Pastor for Abandoned Children – administers several child welfare centers with foster parents), and Fabio Quirόz (Pastor for Discipleship and Spiritual Growth).

VAC is administered by a Council of Elders (which functions as a Board of Directors) which is not elected by the members of the congregation because VAC does not maintain an official membership list. Instead, this council is chosen by Pastor Salazar after consultation with the Pastoral Team and the current Council of Elders. None of the pastoral staff have had much formal theological training, but most of them are university graduates and have other specialized leadership training for their respective areas of responsibility with a strong emphasis on discipleship and the family. However, some have studied in Bible institutes or theological seminaries and others are currently studying in formal programs.

VAC places a strong emphasis on discipleship and the formation of healthy Christian families. Several times a year, VAC holds conferences on family issues. Each member of the 12-person pastoral team, with their respective groups of trained leaders, offer a multitude of ministries and services for VAC members and the wider community. In addition, VAC has a variety of small groups (more than 100) directed by lay people that meet in homes and offer training during the week for prayer, Bible study, discipleship, fellowship, etc. Special groups meet in the VAC buildings during the week and on Saturdays to address issues for women, men, couples, single adults, divorced personas, those in codependent relationships, etc. In addition, orientation classes are offered every two months for newcomers and prebaptismal classes (three sessions called "First Steps") for new Christians. Baptism services are held periodically, with approximately 400 baptisms each year.

In addition to the professional team of 12 full-time pastors (men and women) and their assistants, VAC has a 40-member leadership team and over 800 trained volunteers. VAC's motto is "every church member a disciple of Jesus Christ." Quiroz stated that "discipleship training leads to more active participation in church activities, to more active voluntarism, to greater service in the community, and to higher levels of leadership responsibility." All the leaders of these discipleship and small groups have received specialized training by rising through the ranks from student, to assistant leader, and then to group leader (of which there are more than 100 currently). The goal of discipleship is to produce a Christ-centered lifestyle in service to others.

Outside of the auditorium, which seats 1,200 people, there is a bookstore with Christian literature and music. Special attention is provided for infants and preschoolers in a children's worship service. VAC doesn't offer Sunday school classes for groups of any age. Instead, they offer a variety of educational and recreational activities for children and youth during weekends. VAC maintains a website (www.vida.cr) where there is information about all of the ministries, activities, worship services and sermons. Worship services are transmitted live from the auditorium on VAC's video channel (http://vida.churchonline.org/).

VAC operates the Costa Rican Christian School (CRCS), which provides preschool, primary and secondary education in the VAC installations in Coronado, where the school makes use of the buildings, parking lots and recreational areas. Currently, the CRCS is considered one of the best ten private schools in the country because of their educational excellence and the high quality of their installations.

Research Questions

In our case study of VAC, we sought answers to the following questions:

- What combination of socio-religious factors in the national and urban context of Costa Rica has contributed to the accelerated attendance growth in this mega-church during the period 1993 to 2015?

- Where are the new participants coming from in terms of their spiritual journeys: from other Evangelical churches (interchurch migration), from nominal Roman Catholics, from other religious groups (marginal Christian and non-Christian religions), or from the secularized non-religious population?

- What were the socio-religious variables involved in their individual religious experiences that motivated them to leave their former churches or religious group (expulsion factors) and to join this new megachurch (attraction factors)?

- How many of those who are currently active attendees of this mega-church were previously active in churches of other Evangelical denominations or independent churches compared to those who had a religious conversion experience after they started attending this megachurch or one of its ministry activities (such as a home bible study or prayer group, fellowship group, discipleship group, seminars/workshops, youth groups, camping program, etc.?

- How long have the current attendees been involved in this megachurch?

- What is their level of personal and familial satisfaction in this megachurch?

- How has their participation in this megachurch influenced their personal spiritual growth as a follower of Jesus Christ?

- Has there been an ideological or worldview shift in the lives of those who are currently attending this megachurch because of its influence on them?

- How has participation in this megachurch influenced their individual and family lives and their social and/ or political involvement in their local community or civil society in general?

- Based on the fieldwork evidence in the survey of VAC attendees, can we expect that the megachurch phenomena will continue to grow in membership and expand geographically during the next decade in Costal Rica, or will the current trend decrease due to extenuating circumstances?

To obtain answers to our research questions, we made audio and video recordings of interviews with selected members of the pastoral team to listen to them describe in their own words their personal spiritual journeys, the impact that their participation in VAC has had on their personal and family life, and general information on their area of ministerial responsibility. In addition, people who attended VAC between April 25 and May 24 of 2015 filled out 402 questionnaires during or after the worship services and special activities for high school and university students. The goal was to reach 10% of the regular weekly attendance, which averages 3,325 adults and youth. A careful analysis of the results of the interviews with the 12 members of the pastoral team and 402 questionnaires provided the following tentative answers to our research questions.

"What religion were your parents when you were a child?" We found that 62% of the mothers were Roman Catholic compared to 67% of the fathers, while 36% of the mothers were evangelicals compared to only 27% of the fathers. 63.4% of those interviews had changed their religion from Roman Catholic (or another) to evangelical during their youth or before they turned 30.

In terms of marital status, the percentage of married persons in VAC is higher than the national average, as well as the number of divorced persons; the percentage of separated persons in VAC is lower than the national average, as well as persons in common law marriages and widowers; the percentage of single people (never married) is statistically about the same in VAC as the national average. The fact that divorced people in the Roman Catholic Church are marginalized (are not authorized to participate in Holy Communion), as well as those who are divorced and remarried, might give Evangelical megachurches (such as VAC) an advantage because everyone who attends worship services at VAC can participate in the Lord's Supper (Holy Communion) once a month with no questions asked about their marital status. There is a high degree of anonymity among VAC attendees because of the size of the congregation, between 500 and 1,200 in the various worship services on weekends.

We asked a series of questions to determine where the new participants had come from. In response to the question, "Do you currently attend a religious group that is different from the one in which your parents raised you?" 72% of the respondents answered "yes" and 28% said "no" (total responses 239 = 100%). When we asked, "Why did you stop attending your parent's church?", 34% cited lack of interest or indifference and 26% stated their needs were not being met. We can suppose that the "parent's church" for the majority of respondents was the Roman Catholic Church (62% of the mothers and 67% of the fathers), even though a minority had been born in evangelical homes (24% of the mothers and 19% of the fathers). The majority of reasons offered by respondents are negative, but there was a positive response: spiritual conversion/coming closer to God. The negative reasons are "rejection factors" that motivated people to leave the church of their parents and to look for better opportunities and answers for their spiritual needs in other churches. Few respondents reported being affiliated with other Christian sects or with non-Christian religions before attending VAC.

In order to measure whether interviewees had been active in other evangelical churches before coming to VAC, we asked, "Did you attend another church (or other churches) before coming to VAC?" 80% said "yes" and 20% said "no" (total responses were 388 = 100%). We also asked, "How long did you attend the other churches prior to coming to VAC?" 63% of the respondents who previously attended other churches attended them less than 10 years prior to coming to VAC, and 37% attended other churches more than 10 years prior to switching to VAC. How many Evangelical churches have you attended since 2000 before coming to VAC? Between 2000 and 2014, 141 people interviewed reported that they had attended one or more other Evangelical churches prior to attending VAC; those interviewed indicated that during 2000-2006 they attended more churches (403) prior to coming to VAC than during 2007-2014 (253).

So, where did the current VAC attendees come from? Most of them (141 people) came from other Pentecostal churches (452 multiple responses = 74%), mainly from the Assemblies of God (including Oasis of Hope and the Evangelistic Center of Zapote, which are both megachurches), as well as from a few of the Christian Centers of Transworld Missions, the Church of God (Cleveland, TN), and other Abundant Life daughter churches; moreover, it appears that a large number of the current VAC attendees came from independent Pentecostal churches (several of which are megachurches, such as The Rose of Sharon, MANA-KingdomTakers, and Passion for Souls) or small Pentecostal denominations. Also, smaller numbers of current VAC attendees came from non-Pentecostal churches, such as Baptist churches, Bible churches, Central American churches, Mennonite, Methodist or Nazarene churches (111 = 18%). A total of 48 respondents (8%) came from independent Evangelical churches that we have been unable to classify. Only 11 respondents in our sample indicated that they had participated previously in Christian sects or non-Christian religions or groups; the most frequently mentioned were Jehovah's Witnesses and Transcendental Meditation (4 mentions each).

We also sought to identify variables in individuals' religious experience that motivated the decision to change churches. We asked, "What was the quality of your spiritual life before you began attending VAC?" The total count of negative factors stated by respondents was 46%, the positive factors totaled 51%, and neutral factors were 3%. The negative factors included "poor / bad / non-existent" (25.4%), "mediocre" or "very bad" (13.2%) and "lacking / doubting / searching" (7.3%). The positive responses were "good / active" (24.3%), "acceptable / growing" (21.6%), "very good" (4.9%). The neutral factors (3%) included "was worse than now," "same as now" and "I don't remember."

Prior to attending VAC, the respondents may have attended a variety of other churches including Roman Catholic, Evangelical-Christian, Christian sects (principally Jehovah's Witnesses and Mormons) and/or non-Christian religions. We asked the respondents, "What was the principal reason you left the previous religious groups?", and, "What was the principal reason for attending VAC?" Two of the principal reasons given were positive factors: "change of home address / longer distance to church" (27.2%) and "accompany my spouse / children / family members" (9.8%), for a total of 37%. The remaining four principal reasons given were negative factors, which totaled 33.7% ("Disagreement with doctrine / principles / theology," "Dissatisfied spiritually / lack of spiritual growth," "Disliked leadership style" and "Internal changes and problems in the church").

Some of the principal reasons given for attending VAC were the positive, attractive appeal of VAC ("I like VAC's lifestyle, vision and mission," "Preaching and teaching / doctrine / theology," "Preaching of the Word of God and the worship experience," and "Sound doctrine, vision and mission" = 25.9%); the family and friendships ("accompany my spouse / children / family members / friends" = 16.4%); a personal need to grow spiritually ("To get closer to God / Jesus - to change my life," "I needed a change in my personal life," and "Need to grow spiritually / get closer to God / Jesus" = 13.6%); church shopping ("I was invited to attend and liked this church and decided to stay," "Someone recommended VAC to me," and "I came for a visit and I liked the church and decided to stay" = 13.6%); and the convenient location ("I live nearby / it's convenient location" = 4.8%). These responses equaled 280 (74.3%) out of a total of 377 responses (100%).

In section V of our questionnaire, we asked: "What were the three principal reasons why you decided to leave your previous churches?", which included all churches where they attended between 2000 and 2014; this mainly applied to their involvement with other Evangelical churches. Almost 55% of the reasons given for leaving the previous churches were negative factors (moral or doctrinal conflicts, conflicts with pastors / abuse of authority, displeasure / felt uncomfortable, boring / monotonous worship services, lack of support by pastor, lack of ministries / opportunities for ministry), whereas some were the result of positive factors (13.9% = desire for more spiritual growth, need for personal change); some of the reasons were due to extenuating circumstances (24.9% = change of address / travel distance, accompany spouse / family member, changes in the church, work schedule conflicted with church meeting schedule). In addition, there were a variety of other reasons that were not identified (6.5%).

We also asked, "What were the principal reasons why you began attending VAC?" The stated principal reasons for attending VAC were: "Searching for spiritual guidance / personal improvement" (32.6%); "Searching for more personal relationship with Jesus / God" (18.2%); "I was unhappy with my previous church experience" (17%); "I was experiencing a crisis and needed immediate help" (5.9%); "To alleviate guilt / anxiety / depression / conflicts" (5.7%); "I began attending my spouse's church / married a church member" (5.0%); "My concern for the religious education of my children" (4.7%); "I previously felt alone, disoriented, without love and unaccepted" (4.5%); and, "At VAC I experienced signs and wonders / supernatural miracles" (3.4%).

Most of these factors involved a quest by the individual for spiritual renewal and revitalization (87.3%), whereas two of the other factors were related to family matters: "I began attending my spouse's church / married a church member" (5.0%), and "I was concerned about the religious education of my children" (4.7%).

We asked the interviewees to describe their relationship with VAC. We asked, "Do you consider yourself a "member" of VAC?" Yes (330 = 94%); No (52 = 6%); total responses = 352 (100%). "How many years have you attended VAC?" One year or less (39 = 10.2%); 1-5 years (158 = 41.5%); 6-10 years (103 = 27.0%); 11-15 years (58 = 15.2%); 16-20 years (17 = 4.5%); total responses = 381 (100%). This means that 197 respondents have attended VAC for less than 5 years (52%), and that 184 have attended VAC for more than 5 years (48%). "What is the frequency of your attendance at VAC?" Very active, more than once a week (106 = 27.1%); active, once a week (242 = 61.9%); nominal, one or two times a month (37 = 9.4%); inactive, occasionally (6 = 1.5%); total = 391 responses (100%). This means that 89% of those interviewed (348) are active or very active at VAC, whereas only 11% are nominal or inactive in their attendance (42).

When we measured the respondents' "level of satisfaction" at VAC regarding 15 areas of their personal lives, we found that "I want to be more obedient and fruitful in my Christian life" received the highest ranking (4.1 on a scale of 1 to 5, with 5 being the highest ranking) and their concern for others and for the social, economic and political situation of Costa Rica received a high ranking also. The respondents acknowledged that there were three areas that needed the most improvement: daily devotional life, serve with spiritual gifts, and provide spiritual help, which were ranked 2.79, 2.58 and 2.29 respectively. In this ranking system, 1 = poor; 2 = mediocre; 3 = good; 4 = very good; and 5 = excellent. Therefore, the overall ranking of 3.42 given by respondents shows that there is still room for improvement. This is also seen in their responses to the questions about the level of personal satisfaction with their spiritual growth and about the leadership and direction of VAC, which received an overall average level of satisfaction of 3.62, which is lower than what we expected the responses would be. There may have been some confusion on the part of some of those surveyed regarding the ranking system for this section by thinking that 1 = highest and 5 = lowest, which is the opposite of what the instructions stated. We do not know for sure to what degree this may have happened.

The people interviewed were asked to "name the five most important FACTORS that have influenced your spiritual growth and development at VAC." The majority (53.4%) of the responses (62 mentions or more) were the following: "To know the Word of God / To study the Bible" (10.5%), "Meet together with the Christian community" (9.1%), "To walk closer to God / communion with God / Jesus" (7.6%), "Prayer / intercession" (7.5%), "Attend worship services at church" (5.0%), "Preaching / Teaching" (4.7%), "Christian service / helping others" (4.6%) and "Family support" (4.4%). These factors have had the greatest impact of the spiritual growth and development of the respondents.

Our survey of attendees at VAC revealed the following regarding their political affiliation or preference: the largest number reported "no political preference" (93 = 41.2%), followed by Left-Liberal (77 = 34.1%), Center-Moderate (21 = 9.3%) and Right-Conservative (15 = 6.6%). A smaller minority of respondents gave a variety of answers that we categorized as "other" (10 = 4.4%) or "apolitical" (7 = 3.1%). The total number of responses was 226 (100%) out of 402 questionnaires, which means that 176 people didn't bother to answer the question; the latter may be among those with "no political preference" or simply did not want to make their political affiliation known.

In the context of Costa Rica, we have classified the various responses as follows: Center-Moderate (center and democratic), Left-Liberal (National Liberation Party-PLN, Social Democrat, Citizen's Action Party-PAC and Broad Front-FA), Right-Conservative (Christian Democrat, Social Christian Unity Party-PUSC, Libertarian Party-PL, center-right and right). None of the respondents indicated their support for either of the two Evangelical political parties (currently with three deputies in the National Legislature), which are Center-Right.

At least 34.1% of VAC respondents support Left-Liberal political parties and 9.3% support Center-Moderate parties (for a total of 43.4%), which may mean that they do not support the position of the two Evangelical political parties on these "controversial social issues." However, if we add the statistics of those with "no political preference" (None, 93 = 41.1%) to those who claim to be apolitical (only 7 or 3.1% of respondents), we might assume that about 44.2% of the respondents may not have taken a firm position on these issues possibly due to their personal bias that "Evangelicals should not be involved in politics," which is a position that was strongly advocated by many Evangelical pastors prior to the 1990s.

So what is VAC's official leadership position on these "controversial social issues"? If the elders, pastoral staff and the majority of lay leaders are opposed to the legalization of abortion, to homosexual couples' right to a marriage license, and to in-vitro fertilization (IVF), then this position should be reflected in the political orientation of the attendees if VAC's leadership is pushing this agenda. When we consulted with Pastor Miguel Sánchez about these issues on November 12th, he confirmed that the leadership of VAC had discussed them and were opposed to them based on their Evangelical convictions. Prior to the previous national elections, held in February 2014, representatives of all the major political parties and of the two minority Evangelical parties were invited to VAC to share their views about these and other national issues at a special mid-week congregational meeting. Although VAC's leadership team remained politically neutral during this discussion and did not endorse any of the presidential candidates, they did state their opposition to these "controversial social issues." Had we included a specific question in our questionnaire about these issues, Pastor Miguel assured us that the responses that would have been given by those interviewed would have reflected VAC's opposition to them.

Learnings

VAC seems to appeal to people in the middle-income bracket who are upwardly mobile socially and economically. More than 60% of those interviewed have had some university or technical school training. The average monthly income of VAC attendees (based on 295 responses) was $1,827; for married couples it was $1,957; for divorcees $2,005; for separated $591; for singles $1,764; for common law $895; and for widowers $2,000. The average per capita income in Costa Rica was $6,810 annually (February 2013), compared to $28,645 per capita in the USA; the average annual income for VAC attendees was $21,924 ($1,827 monthly X 12) or 3.2 times the national average. Further evidence to support the "upward social mobility" of members of VAC is revealed in the occupations of the respondents and their spouses), and the extreme low level of unemployment (only 1.7% of the spouses and none for the respondents).

The income, educational and occupational levels of VAC attendees means that this congregation should be financially solid and have the human resources to provide adequate leadership for the present and future if the church administration is well managed and maintains a balanced budget (its monthly income covers its operational expenses plus funds needed for future budgeted expenses) under the leadership of the Board of Elders and Pastoral Staff who must maintain their credibility (morally, spiritually and financially) and be strongly supported by the majority of the church's constituency. Currently, 89% of the interviewees are "active" or "very active" in congregational life, compared to 11% was are "inactive" in the attendance at VAC.

Our overall determination as a team of socio-religious researchers is that VAC is an exceptional megachurch with sustainable growth due to its physical location, excellent facilities, "seeker" orientation, the quality of its leaders, the multiplicity of its ministries, the general overall satisfaction level of those who attend, and its good reputation in the community and among evangelicals in general.

In this context, VAC has become an attractive alternative to Roman Catholics who have lost confidence in the church of their birth and are "seeking" to find an Evangelical church that will help them resolve family conflicts and personal, moral and spiritual struggles; provide them with love and acceptance in support groups for Bible study, prayer and fellowship; offer them a more meaningful worship experience in a large congregation of their peers; and help them grow spiritually in their daily walk with God. This is truly a "revitalization" process for these former Catholics and for others who were born into Evangelical Christian homes, but who did not have a personal relationship with Jesus Christ. They may have attended other Evangelical churches in which their spiritual growth and development has been hindered by a variety of circumstances, both within the life of those churches as well as within their own personal and family lives.

For some former Catholics and Evangelicals by birth, their search for a more meaningful Christian life is often difficult because of unresolved conflicts (personal, familiar, moral and spiritual) and the lack of an authentic conversion experience, which limits their participation in the multifaceted ministries offered by VAC or other Evangelical churches. Rather than becoming a "disciple" of Jesus Christ, they remain in the crowd of "followers" who lack commitment and wrestle with their own unresolved conflicts.

Some of these "followers" may attend worship services at VAC and may participate in other church-sponsored activities because this makes them feel better about themselves and helps them have a more positive outlook on life. Along the way, some of these "seekers" truly may become "born again" and take a more active role in church life at VAC where there are many opportunities to grow in knowledge of God's Word and obedience to God's will as part of a faith community.

The Future

The future of Vida Abundante de Coronado appears to be very positive and optimistic based on our evaluation of the results of our April-May surveys of 12 members of the pastoral staff and 398 members (attendees) of the congregation. VAC's style of leadership is highly regarded based on the "levels of satisfaction" index, the church administration and finances are well managed, the attendance at all worship services is consistent and growing, and the active participation of many of its members in small groups (more than 100 groups weekly) and its discipleship program (for beginners, intermediate and advanced) is an indication of its spiritual vitality and growth as a megachurch. VAC has contributed in a significant way to the education of 600 children from the community each year through its management of the Costa Rican Christian School (with an English-language curriculum) that involves 77 people, both evangelicals and Roman Catholics who work in the administration, as teachers or in providing services to students and their families. In addition, VAC has developed multifaceted ministries outside of the church buildings in various communities, with leaders and volunteers trained to serve people with special needs.

We should expect that the megachurches that operate Christian schools will continue to grow and impact their communities more than those without Christian schools, because the children and youth in these Christian education programs will tend to develop an "Evangelical lifestyle" along with their parents, which will strengthen the support base of these mega-churches with the incorporation of these young people into the life and ministry of their congregations as they grow into adulthood. The youth of today are the future leaders of the church of tomorrow.

VAC's slogan of "every member a disciple of Jesus Christ" and its mission to reach "seekers" who desire to have a closer walk with God in a contemporary worship setting where the Word of God is taught with practical applications to their daily lives is indicative of its ability to appeal to a broad audience of people in the community who are discontent with their personal and spiritual lives and who are not being properly nurtured in other religious groups, whether Evangelical Christian or Roman Catholic. At VAC, everyone is welcome, and no one is excluded because of their marital status, age, physical appearance, sexual orientation, educational level or the way they dress.

In conclusion, we believe that the experience most people have in attending VAC's worship services and participating in the multifaceted programs that are offered are bringing about a "spiritual revitalization" of their individual, family and social lives, which is a positive benefit to society in general due to the high moral standards of those church members, their improved work ethic and their concern for the well-being of others. If this is happening at VAC, then it is quite possible that the same process is taking place at other Evangelical megachurches in the San Jose Metro Area of Costa Rica as well as in other major metropolitan areas in Central America.

CHAPTER 6: THE REVITALIZING POWER OF TRANSNATIONAL NETWORKS

A-Brazo and the Global Holistic Mission Movement

Stephen Offutt and Hilda Romero

Introduction

It was sweltering in La Perla, a remote El Salvadoran village. Jorge seemed not to notice—after all, it was always this hot—as he diligently tapped away the computer keys. The one-room building he was in had a corrugated tin roof. The resulting microwave effect made it even hotter inside than out. Still, the 17-year-old sat in his plastic chair and focused on the screen, occasionally glancing at the whiteboard or asking his teacher for assistance. Jorge wanted to learn how to use Microsoft Word and Excel; this was his best, and perhaps only, opportunity.

The computers found their way to La Perla through the networks of A-Brazo, a local faith-based organization (FBO). Future Hope, a Seattle-based partner, provided the computers. A nearby evangelical congregation advised A-Brazo of the need in La Perla. It also identified a young man in the community who could serve as a computer teacher, a university student (quite a rarity in this village) and an elder in another local Pentecostal church. A-Brazo, the evangelical church, the Seattle-based group and the computer teacher all believe that the computer classes are an important part of Christian outreach to the community. They also believe the program, which is explicitly connected to the local congregation, pleases God and increases students' life opportunities.

The social networks that connect these groups are part of the holistic mission movement that is changing the identity of global evangelicalism. Fifty years ago, evangelical missions were most known for the verbal proclamation of the gospel. That part of their identity is not likely to disappear soon. But dynamic growth has occurred in the other types of outreach evangelicals do, including care for the homeless, literacy courses, prison ministries, microfinance initiatives, health clinics, ministries to drug and alcohol addicts, disaster response initiatives, creation care, and a multitude of other outreach endeavors. The communities around many evangelical churches have noticed and so too have academics, some of whom are now calling global Pentecostalism the "new face of Christian social engagement" (Miller and Yamamori 2007).

A-Brazo is a humble organization. Although deeply embedded in the global holistic mission community, it neither invented holistic mission principles nor is it one of the movement's leading organizations. Rather, A-Brazo's daily realities are characterized by the simple joys of faithful service and the tireless navigation of financial, programmatic and logistical challenges. A-Brazo is, in other words, typical of hundreds and perhaps thousands of other faith-based grassroots organizations around the globe.

A-Brazo's networks are thus well-suited to serve as a case study of the holistic mission movement. A-Brazo was founded within holistic mission networks in 2001, shortly after El Salvador's devastating earthquakes. Hilda Romero, a civil engineer who had worked for an international evangelical organization in the 1980s, is A-Brazo's founder. After the 2001 earthquakes, she and a gathering of other local and international evangelicals met to plan their disaster response. All present felt the need for a local organizational structure to channel international relief supplies that were sure to come and to help local congregations implement community programs. It was for this reason that A-Brazo was born. Today, A-Brazo continues to integrate faith and social action and to work closely with local church partners and international actors in the global holistic mission movement.

People operating within the holistic mission movement have started organizations like A-Brazo and have improved congregational community outreach projects all over the world. The movement's scope and breadth is considerable, as is its potential for real impact on a range of spiritual and social issues. Its global growth in the last three decades has been exponential. Put simply, the holistic mission movement is among the more important thermals of Christian revitalization in the current era.

And yet not much systematic analysis of the movement has been done. Among the many questions that remain unanswered is the one that motivates this study: how do the movement's social networks enable or inhibit its ability to create religious and social change? We focus on the movement's networks because they are what keeps this diffuse global movement together. There are, after all, many things that could pull it apart: it spans multiple cultures, continents, denominations, and doctrinal positions. The movement houses a multitude of social agendas, strategies, and ideologies. Its membership is informal—some actors (even within A-Brazo's networks) are not overtly aware that they are part of something larger than their own projects. And yet the movement's global connectedness is part of what creates its great potential for revitalization. Its ability to transport material and intellectual resources across borders and to use its global identity to shift religious opinion and motivate people to action is critical to its success.

Our research[36] leads us to argue that within the movement, overlapping but distinct networks exist. These networks perform different functions which include channeling resources, providing theological and technical education, and creating a sense of a transnational faith community. Network members exist in specific contexts that have particular religious and social challenges. We show that in El Salvador, the holistic mission movement's transnational networks equip its members to overcome some kinds of challenges, but are not as helpful to its members in the face of other kinds of challenges.

We lay out our argument in the following way. First, we describe three dimensions of A-Brazo's context: the global holistic mission movement, El Salvador's religious context, and El Salvador's difficult social realities. Second, we present the findings of our research, showing the type, nature, and extent of A-Brazo's holistic mission networks. Finally, we explore different learnings from the study and draw some tentative conclusions.

Context

To understand how holistic mission networks impact their members' (and particularly those of A-Brazo) efforts to create religious and social change, context is needed concerning

36 Research for this project was conducted in May, July and August 2015. It included semi-structured interviews with 11 religious leaders and three project beneficiaries. We also conducted ethnographic research, which included visits to a community project site, attendance of church services, Bible studies, and prayer groups, and simply spending time in communities and with various leaders. Finally, two focus groups were conducted.

the origins and nature of the global evangelical holistic mission movement, El Salvador's religious environment, and the social problems that confront A-Brazo in El Salvador. The present section is dedicated to this task.

The global evangelical holistic mission movement

Principles espoused by the contemporary evangelical holistic mission movement have antecedents in almost every Christian tradition. Catholic social teachings have directed the Church to engage in issues of justice and poverty for centuries.[37] In the Eastern Orthodox Church, Basil of Caesarea (4th century) set the early standard when he oversaw the creation of a complex of orphanages, hospitals, and workhouses. During Britain's Industrial Revolution, John Wesley urged his affluent followers to live in authentic community with the poor and not to isolate themselves from the lower classes. In the early 20th century, classical Pentecostal denominations were mostly poor themselves, and sought to care for the poor within and beyond their congregations. All of these traditions (and many others) have found ample Biblical support for their theology and their praxis. From the Pentateuch to the Epistles, the Scriptures are rife with teachings and examples of concern about poverty. These historical antecedents and Scriptural directives continue to exert influence on their specific faith traditions as well as on global evangelicalism's holistic mission movement.

The rich and complex history of Christian concern for the poor makes it counterproductive to attribute the genesis of the contemporary evangelical holistic mission movement to any one person or event. Even if the conversation is confined to activities within 20th century evangelicalism, multiple starting points can be traced. Poverty alleviation was, for example, part of the new evangelical identity as it sought to distinguish itself from Fundamentalism in the mid-20th century. Harold Ockenga, Carl FH Henry and other founding fathers of the contemporary

---

37 There is some debate on how one might define the body of literature known as Catholic Social Teaching. Some argue that it began as late as 1891 with the writing of Rerum novarum. However, this document was itself grounded in Catholic teachings that run back as far as the 4th century and the writings of St. Augustine of Hippo.

evangelical movement urged their followers to care for the poor. Such calls coincided with two other trends. First, US soldiers who had been exposed to the severity of global poverty during World War II returned home motivated to engage in humanitarian efforts. Second, a relatively new organizational form was taking root: the faith-based Non-Governmental Organization (NGO) (Wuthnow 2009). Evangelicals were early entrepreneurs in this field: World Relief, the social arm of the National Association of Evangelicals, was founded 1944. Other faith-based NGOs quickly followed, including World Vision, Compassion International, and numerous denominationally driven organizations. Such groups were not yet using the term "holistic mission" and some of their faith based poverty alleviation strategies were primitive. Still, white American evangelicals in the 1940s and 1950s expressed a clear willingness to channel energy and resources toward the goal of alleviating poverty (Reynolds and Offutt 2014).

Another starting point for the evangelical holistic mission movement can be traced to a young international group of evangelicals that coalesced in the 1960s. They perceived (with some justification) that the mainstream American evangelical mode of social engagement was only concerned with the verbal proclamation of the gospel. Even discipleship was de-emphasized. The NGOs mentioned above were still relatively small, and in any event made few attempts to address issues of conflict or oppression beyond caring for the widow and the orphan (Swartz 2012). But university students and others personally impacted by violent military dictatorships, which were often allies of the United States in its fight against the Soviet Union, struggled to square this lack of engagement with their reading of the Scriptures and the ministry of Jesus.

Rene Padilla and Samuel Escobar emerged as leaders of this group, which collectively came to be known as the "radical" evangelicals (Tizon 2008). Padilla and Escobar were first generation converts to evangelical Christianity. They rejoiced at their personal conversion and relationship with Jesus and they believed that the gospel had something to say about the oppression being experienced in their Latin American context. Padilla and Escobar were invited to the 1974 Lausanne Congress on World

Evangelization. In alliance with John Stott and delegates from across the Global South (some of whom were previously connected through InterVarsity's global networks), they successfully influenced the crafting of the Lausanne Covenant,[38] perhaps the most important evangelical document of the twentieth century. But the group believed much work still needed to be done, as they felt evangelicals continued to underplay the importance of social action.

The radical evangelicals thus fanned and flamed the fledgling holistic mission movement over the next several decades. Critical actors,[39] conferences,[40] and publications[41] have helped it along. Once viewed with suspicion by main stream evangelicals, it is now formally supported by many of the evangelical world's most important leaders. The Willow Creek church has, for instance, been tremendously strategic in supporting holistic mission principles around the globe. Franklin Graham, the son of Billy Graham, is the head of Samaritan's Purse, a disaster response organization. Average evangelical churches that have never 'signed up' to be directly involved in the movement now use literature and educational curriculum produced by the movement. A more holistic orientation is becoming increasingly evident throughout American evangelicalism and beyond (Steensland andGoff 2014).

---

38 They successfully negotiated the inclusion of Article Five, which outlines Christian social responsibility from an evangelical perspective.

39 Ron Sider, Vinay Samuel, John Stott, David Bosch, John Perkins, Tony Campolo, Rene Padilla, Samuel Escobar, and many others played a key role in the process (Tizon 2008).

40 The conference out of which the "Chicago Declaration" was formed in 1973, and the conference sponsored by World Evangelical Fellowship in Wheaton in 1983 were particularly important. Mission conferences, such as the Urbana conferences held every three years, have also helped to mobilize social action. So do the annual Christian Community Development Association (CCDA) meetings, which began in 1989. In the last decade, the Micah Network conferences have helped churches in the Global South and East to embrace the vision of holistic mission.

41 Most notably Mission as Transformation, edited by Vinay Samuel and Chris Sugden (1999), and Walking with the Poor by Bryant Myers (1999). More recently, popular books such as When Helping Hurts by Steve Corbett and Brian Fikkert (2009) and A Hole in the Gospel by Richard Stearns (2009) have galvanized evangelical churches to faith based social action.

Today, the holistic mission movement has two clear goals. First, it wants to transform global evangelical activity. Although encouraged by the success they have already had, holistic mission actors believe that the evangelical movement is still not sufficiently mobilized to engage the pressing social issues of the day.

They want evangelicals to be a public witness in every social sphere. Second, the holistic mission movement wants to solve social problems. They do not just want to transform a particular religious movement (evangelicalism), they want to transform the societies in which they are embedded. By doing so, they will fulfill Christ's call to be salt and light in the world.

El Salvador's religious context

In order to understand whether the holistic mission movement is accomplishing these goals in El Salvador, the country's religious and social context must be described. El Salvador has two main religious groups, Catholics and evangelicals, and the divide between them is highly contentious. Like the rest of Latin America, El Salvador is historically Catholic. But rapid evangelical growth in recent decades has it on the defensive. Only 59% of Salvadorans continue to self-identify as Catholic. That is low compared to other Latin American countries, but the 61% of Catholics that report practicing their faith at least once a week is among the highest in the region (Hagopian 2009). The decline of the Catholic Church thus must not be overstated. It remains influential in public discourse—more so than any other religious group—and it is overrepresented among the country's elites and decision makers. The country's Catholic heritage is at once celebrated and contested—Monsenor Romero, for instance, was martyred by forces friendly to the state in the civil war. Yet today the national airport is named after him and statues of Romero populate the most prominent public squares around the country. Hagopian (2009) argues that El Salvador's Catholic Church continues to enjoy a relatively high level of religious hegemony in the midst of growing regional religious pluralism.

While the Catholic Church maintains cultural dominance, the evangelical movement in El Salvador has made explosive inroads. Evangelicalism first emerged among the country's poor over 100 years ago, but the movement remained small and marginalized for over half a century. Then, beginning in the 1970s, the movement grew rapidly. In the early 1990s, Coleman, Aguilar, Sandoval, and Steigenga (1993) reported that evangelicals made up 12 percent of the population, but they remained the poorest and most illiterate religious group in the country. A few years later, Williams (1997) estimated evangelicalism's presence to have grown to between 15 and 20 percent, and churches began to emerge in more affluent neighborhoods. Today most observers believe that evangelicals make up more than 35 percent of the country's population (IUDOP 2009). Evangelical denominations and megachurches own radio and television stations which allow them to punch above their weight in the popular media sector.

Certain characteristics help to define the evangelical movement in El Salvador. These include ascetic practices, an effort to avoid religious hierarchy, high levels of lay female participation, low educational requirements for pastors, a commitment to church planting, and strong denominational identities and competition within the movement. Evangelicalism has tended toward separatism from mainstream culture, trying to distinguish itself from corruption, alcoholism, and other seedier parts of Latin culture. It has traditionally done so by limiting the social ties that could ensnare its members in these kinds of practices. Evangelicalism's ever increasing size and social mobility are beginning to erode some of these tendencies (Offutt 2015), but on the whole, they remain true.

The evangelical movement is and always has been highly motivated to transform society. But it has not always felt that social outreach programs help to accomplish that goal. Rather, evangelicals reflexively understand conversion to be the key to resolving social problems (Smilde 1998). They are partially correct—conversion plays a powerful part in transforming goals, values, motivations and behaviors within individuals and communities. Such an approach has also not stopped evangelicals from responding in some way to human need— "cup of cold water" outreach by evangelical churches has always been common.

But evangelicals in El Salvador have not traditionally responded to other significant areas of community or human need. David McGee, a leader in ENLACE, a community development organization founded by missionaries with the Assemblies of God, observed that "church theology does not encourage evangelical churches to serve their community." Rachel Beveridge, director of an NGO called Seeds of New Creation, supported this notion, stating that "people have had an 'escapism Christianity' where they really have thought of the gospel as 'God came to save us so that we can all go to heaven.'" Such an approach can have negative repercussions in church-community relations. In communities where ENLACE has worked, McGee notes that local churches were "considered a parasite in the community. . . [community members think that churches] take away from the community. 'They take our offerings for their programs, their stuff.'" In short, while evangelicals have always thought that their message is intended to save the world, they have not always shaped their interaction with the world in ways that address the felt needs of others. As will become evident in the following pages, this is intended to be a distinguishing feature of "holistic mission evangelicals".

El Salvador's social context

The most prominent social problems in El Salvador include migration, violence, poverty and natural disasters. With respect to migration, an estimated 30%, or 3.2 million of all Salvadorans live outside of El Salvador, 2 million of whom live in the United States.[42] But, like many other migrants today, Salvadorans keep one foot in their country of origin even as they start new lives elsewhere (Levitt 1998). Migration and other forces of globalization thus impact every facet of Salvadoran society. Their impact in the economic sphere is particularly important: Salvadoran migrants sent a record $4.22 billion back home to friends and family in 2014, up from $3.97 billion the previous year (Reserve Bank of El Salvador 2015). Remittances account for 17% of the country's GDP and they outstrip all other Salvadoran exports combined. If remittances were shut off, the national economy would collapse.

42 Other destination countries include Canada, Western Europe, Australia, and other Central American countries.

The economic benefits accrued from Salvadoran migration are embedded in less welcome social dynamics. In La Perla, for example, a recent high school graduate estimates that more than 70% of his classmates have attempted to emigrate: all of them were undocumented. This creates stress on family structures in El Salvador and puts people who travel in vulnerable situations. In many Salvadoran communities, female headed households account for upwards of 70% of homes, this in spite of the fact that women represent an increasing share of migrants. Some who leave never arrive at their intended destination; some who do are quickly deported. Even those who arrive and stay in their new homes must constantly negotiate their undocumented status. Feelings of insecurity often color their new lives.

Violence, El Salvador's second major social problem, has two primary sources: gangs and domestic abuse. El Salvador is now the "murder capital of the world" and the most violent country on earth that is not at war. In the first nine months of 2015, 4, 930 people were murdered (population 6.5 million). The murder rate is currently 20 times that of the United States (Economist 2015). Gangs are the single largest contributor to such statistics; the two primary gangs are the "18" and the "Salvatrucha". Gangs are no longer satisfied with killing people in communities, fighting amongst themselves, charging "rent" to local businesses, keeping those that enter and exit neighborhoods under surveillance, recruiting elementary school students and 'asking' high school students to drop out of school. Gangs now seek political influence. To that end, in July 2015, the gangs forced the national bus system to shut down for three days. Eight bus drivers who continued to provide service were assassinated. But violence against gangs is also on the rise; police killed about 300 gang members in the first seven months of 2015 (Malkin 2015). During the bus system standoff, the government sent army tanks to patrol San Salvador's most gang-infested neighborhoods.

Domestic violence is accentuated by El Salvador's pervasive machismo culture. Official police records showed more than seven sexual attacks per day being reported during the first three months of 2013 (Lakhani 2013). The real numbers are much higher as most cases go unreported. Most attacks occur in the home. Teenage girls are the most frequent victims of sexual attacks; other types of physical abuse are experienced by women (and men) of all ages. In sum, the culture of violence in El Salvador affects the social, psychological, and/or economic well-being of a high percentage of El Salvador's residents.

Poverty[43] can also cripple people and communities in El Salvador. Part of our research was conducted in Puerto de La Libertad, a fairly typical Salvadoran town. There, health indices are low: 24% report experiencing the death of a child and over 80% report some dietary deficiency. Education is also inadequate: 20% of the adult population is illiterate. Only 30% of people have gone to high school, a statistic that dips to 11% in rural areas.[44] Even those who do go to school receive a low quality education. Standard of living indices in urban and rural areas show significant deficiencies in housing, access to water, and transportation. Again using the example of Puerto de la Libertad, some urban neighborhoods were formed by people displaced by the civil war. Twenty-five years later, refugee-type conditions persist. Houses are often one or two room structures of corrugated steel and dirt floors. Access to potable water is a challenge, and the river along which they were placed is polluted.[45] An easy majority (perhaps as much as 70%) of the young adult population in some communities attempts to emigrate. Push factors for emigrants include a dearth of economic opportunities and fear of violence. In short, although El Salvador is considered a "middle income country", many of its citizens struggle to meet their basic human needs.

Poverty spikes when natural disasters strike the country. Unfortunately, this occurs at frequent intervals. Major earthquakes occurred roughly every 15-20 years throughout the

43 We follow the lead of the Oxford Poverty & Development Initiative in defining poverty. They use a multidimensional poverty index, which takes into account health, education, and basic standard of living components. Income level, while important, is not a definitional element of poverty.

44 The data includes several rural communities that surround Puerto.

45 The statistics reported on health, education, and standard of living are from survey data collected in the region by Offutt & Reynolds (2014). The investigators used the Multidimensional Poverty Index (MPI) instrument developed at Oxford University and used in some variation by the UN, the World Bank, and other multilateral organizations.

20th century, wreaking significant damage. The most recent of these occurred in 1986 and 2001, collectively destroying tens of thousands of houses and requiring hundreds of millions of dollars of international disaster assistance. Hurricanes, tropical storms, and floods also inflict damage on the country. Since 1998, Hurricanes Mitch, Ida and Stan have caused fatalities and created significant damage. Most recently, a mini-tsunami was experienced across El Salvador's coastline, created by storms near New Zealand. Poor decisions made in the construction of houses and in national environmental policies make El Salvador even more vulnerable to such natural disasters.

Research Results: A-Brazo's Holistic Mission Networks

As A-Brazo operates in the religious and social contexts just described, it draws on the holistic mission movement's networks. In this section, we create a typology of those networks. A-Brazo's holistic mission networks extend along four primary lines. We examine each in detail, and describe the kind of involvement in which A-Brazo is engaged.

The first set of networks is geared toward disaster policy, education, and training. They include La Roca, a network that runs throughout Central America and consists of faith-based organizations that respond to disasters. La Roca is supported by Tearfund, an evangelical foundation based in the United Kingdom. Tearfund in turn receives considerable support from the Salvation Army in the UK. La Roca is intended to help organizations mutually support each other and increase each other's organizational capacity through sharing best practices and encouraging employees to visit projects of other La Roca partners. A-Brazo has also been active in the Action by Churches Together (ACT) Alliance, a disaster network sponsored by the World Council of Churches. A-Brazo entered this network when it served as an implementing partner for Presbyterian Disaster Assistance (PDA). ACT is based out of Geneva, Switzerland. Romero is a member of the La Roca board and previously served as PDA's representative to the ACT Alliance.

Although these networks exist to generate technical competencies, they also carry explicit evangelical messages. For example, at an October 2015 convening of the Roca network in Honduras, representatives of Asociación Vida de Guatemala, a member organization, put forward a theology of networks. They argued that a network is a "complementary relationship with a common purpose, sustained by the interest in learning and growing together in obedience to God while extending His Kingdom." They further stated that the Bible calls for restored relationships and suggested that flat, mutually supportive networks might approximate the relationships that exist within the Trinity. Finally, Asociación Vida de Guatemala's representatives stated that collaborative networks are a witness to local communities and they strengthen local churches. Such arguments infuse the La Roca with religious meaning and purpose as they improve disaster response efforts of local faith based organizations.

The second set of networks in which A-Brazo participates provides more formal theological training for holistic mission. These networks reveal the close ties the movement maintains with its point of origin; Ruth Padilla DeBorst, daughter of Rene Padilla, has been a central actor in developing these networks in El Salvador. Padilla DeBorst was instrumental in crafting Seeds of New Creation's current set of programs and institutional identity. She also played a critical role in creating El Salvador's Integral Mission Network. A-Brazo is a network member and Romero has served on its board. The Integral Mission Network is intended to generate a community of holistic mission practitioners in El Salvador and to equip them with a biblical and theological basis for approaching their ministries in this way. Pastors, missionaries, lay leaders and NGO employees have attended these meetings.

Such organizations and networks are linked into regional bodies, including the Latin American Theological Fraternity (FTL) and the Community of Interdisciplinary Theological Studies (CETI). The FTL was originally formed by Rene Padilla and his colleagues. It links like-minded theological scholars throughout the Americas and holds a major conference, called the Latin American Congress of Evangelization (CLADE), about every ten years. In 2012, CLADE V was held in Costa Rica. Ruth

Padilla DeBorst was the President of FTL at that time. Romero attended the conference. CETI is a Costa Rica-based degree granting institution that provides education in holistic mission. It is run by the Padilla DeBorst family. CETI training modules are accessible in El Salvador on-line, but they are delivered in face to face settings in conjunction with Seeds of New Creation. Using the latter delivery strategy, CETI has trained most of Elim's[46] pastors. They have also trained pastors in other denominations and employees of faith-based NGOs such as World Vision, Compassion International, and ENLACE. This network content provides the theological motivation and justification for changing evangelical practice in El Salvador. Romero studied with CETI out of a desire to learn more about holistic mission. She received classes on-line that were taught by Victor Rey, a professor in Chile.

The Micah Network has also been an important evangelical theological and educational network for A-Brazo. The Micah Network is "a global Christian community of organizations and individuals committed to integral mission." (http://www.micahnetwork.org/). The Micah Network was established in 1999 and now has over 550 members in more than 80 countries. It is particularly committed to building the capacity of local NGOs in the Global South to pursue holistic mission activities. Romero has served as a representative of the region of Latin America for the Micah Network. As such, she attended board and working meetings in Thailand (2009), Kenya (2012), and Peru (2015). Tearfund also supports the Micah Network, and there are close connections between La Roca and the Micah Network, as well as between the Micah Network and the FTL.

A third group of networks are primarily geared toward funding and projects. This group includes donors and technically competent actors who believe in the integral mission approach. Future Hope, an NGO based out of Seattle, WA, is one example. Future Hope members began their relationship with A-Brazo through a short-term mission trip in 2003. It has since partnered with A-Brazo to implement the church based computer literacy program mentioned in the introduction. Future Hope provides

46 Elim is one of the 5 largest megachurches in the world. It was roughly 130,000 members and is located in San Salvador.

funding for the project as well as the salary for a local teacher. In a second example, A-Brazo has been contracted by Compassion International to help with some of its projects. Romero and other members of A-Brazo's team were extensively involved in Haiti from 2010-2015, collaborating with Compassion to reconstruct 23 of Compassion's schools that were destroyed in Haiti's 2010 earthquake. A-Brazo has taken on similar types of collaborative projects with Catholic Relief Services, a Presbyterian church in Port Townsend, WA and a group of medical volunteers called CHIMPS. Likewise, A-Brazo works with numerous other local faith-based organizations, including the Stephen Foundation and ENLACE, two organizations rooted in the Assemblies of God networks. All of these churches and organizations are motivated by holistic mission principles.

A-Brazo's fourth set of relationships exist with local congregations. These are critical for A-Brazo's involvement in local communities. The Central American Mission (now called Camino Global) is the denomination in which A-Brazo operates most effectively. Romero has served on the denomination's disaster relief committee and she and other A-Brazo personnel have developed close ties to CAM pastors around the country. Such ties allow local pastors to initiate contact with A-Brazo when communities are impacted by disasters; A-Brazo then works closely with the church when implementing projects. A-Brazo is also linked to congregations in most other evangelical denominations, including the Assemblies of God, several Baptist denominations, the Church of God, the Nazarenes, and several smaller Pentecostal denominations. These congregational networks allow A-Brazo to maintain its embeddedness in impoverished communities around the country.

When taking into account all four network types, some general characteristics become evident. On the one hand, holistic mission networks are truly global—there are network members on six continents—deeply embedded in civil society, and sufficiently organized to channel resources to places where they are needed. On the other hand, there is also an ad hoc nature to these networks. There is no central organization; many networks are overlapping and redundant. Lack of coordination within the movement creates inefficiencies. The great majority of networks do not venture outside of evangelical circles. Network characteristics thus appear on the positive and negative side of the ledger.

Analysis and Learnings

The networks we have just outlined help A-Brazo and other holistic mission organizations impact their religious and social environment. But how much? And do these networks also inhibit the movement's impact? We answer these questions by looking at the movement's interaction with two characteristics of El Salvador's religious context, followed by four key elements of El Salvador's social context.

TABLE 1: Impact of Holistic Mission Movement on Religion in El Salvador

Issue	High Impact	Low Impact
Catholic/Evangelical Divide		Few holistic mission networks cross Catholic/Evangelical divide.
Evangelicalism's Exclusive Focus on Evangelism	Many evangelical groups now have a broader social agenda.	

Catholic/Evangelical Divide. As noted above, the Catholic/evangelical divide is among the most prominent characteristics of El Salvador's religious terrain. Crossing the divide could be of great strategic importance for holistic mission actors because of the Catholic Church's significant commitment to address social ills. Yet, with few exceptions, holistic mission networks do not attempt to include Catholic actors. We also interviewed Catholic actors involved in social engagement—they also demonstrated little interest in collaboration. The one area where some networks existed across the divide was among faith-based organizations. A-Brazo had been subcontracted by Catholic Relief Services on a construction project, but no lasting relationships resulted. The Seeds of New Creation quietly attempts to draw members of the two groups into informal conversation, but the demand for this program has not been high. On the whole, the holistic mission movement has done little to create a bridge between Catholics and evangelicals.

Evangelicalism's Exclusive Focus on Verbal Proclamation. The holistic mission movement has, however, significantly altered evangelicalism's exclusive tendency to focus on verbal proclamation—perhaps the movement founders' greatest goal. Evidence of evangelicalism's shifting approach to mission is everywhere. A Central American Mission church planter, for example, now works with A-Brazo on a community sewing project. At Enlace, fifteen years ago they could only find three or four evangelical church partners who wanted to participate in their holistic mission programming. Now they work with over sixty churches around the country, and many more, including heads of denominations, are interested. Elim, which is El Salvador's largest megachurch, preaches the importance of holistic mission and has numerous forms of social outreach throughout the country. In short, significant numbers of evangelical congregations are expanding their social engagement repertoires far beyond the traditional interest in evangelism. They have come to understand their participation in God's mission in the world differently.

The holistic mission movement's local and transnational networks have helped to foment this shift. Many churches and organizations in A-Brazo's networks receive educational material and curriculum through networks like the Latin American Theological Fraternity. CETI, for example, provided training for almost all of Elim's pastors. Hundreds of churches in El Salvador have partnerships with Compassion International, World Vision, and similar organizations. Denominations like the Church of the Nazarene, the Assemblies of God and others send short-term mission teams. These teams are often involved in evangelism; they also construct houses for the poor, put on medical clinics, and help with literacy programs. It is usually the hosting congregations in El Salvador that identify the ministry needs and partner with the teams in these endeavors. Such networks, and the ideas, people, educational materials, and other information that flows through them, have helped to change evangelicalism's mission orientation.

Does it matter that evangelicals now have a broader social agenda? If so, how does it matter? Put differently, is the holistic mission movement in El Salvador actually creating a more shalom-like environment? One measure of this is to look at the holistic mission movement's impact (or lack thereof) on El Salvador's most significant social problems: migration, violence, poverty, and natural disasters.

TABLE 2: Impact of Holistic Mission Movement on Social Problems in El Salvador

Issue	High Impact	Low Impact
Migration		Does not influence evangelical or other actors in their response to migration.
Violence		Saves some individuals from violence but has no systemic efforts and does not greatly impact national indices of violence.
Poverty	Reduces poverty in many Salvadoran communities.	
Natural Disasters	Channels significant transnational resources for disaster response.	

Migration: There is a deep literature on the role of religion in the transnational migration process (see Levitt 2007; Offutt and Miller Forthcoming). Religious groups of all types help new migrants get settled into their new countries and keep them connected to their families back home. Congregations and NGOs within A-Brazo's networks are involved in both of these processes. World Relief, for example, helps to settle immigrants in the US.

Many of A-Brazo's local church partners have connections with congregations in the US and channel communication, religious goods and services, and sometimes people back and forth between them.

It is difficult to discern the impact that the holistic mission movement has on this issue in El Salvador, as nearly all evangelical congregations there seek to facilitate transnational lifestyles. The distinction is much greater in the US, where those who spearhead the call for evangelicals to "welcome the stranger" are part of the holistic mission movement, and those who are not part of this movement often resist such a call. But in El Salvador, the reverse is modestly true. Given that some holistic mission members' rhetoric discourages migration, it is difficult to claim any measurable impact by the movement on addressing migration's causes and consequences.

Violence: In theory, the holistic mission movement has the potential to reduce violence. There are a few specific cases, such as the Ten Point Coalition in Boston, where principles embraced by the holistic mission movement (but not necessarily the movement per se) have had an impact on violence. Other institutions, leaders, and community infrastructure must also be in place for this to occur. In El Salvador, evangelicals have rescued young men and women from being victims and perpetrators of violence. Evangelicals have brought youths out of gangs and former gang members now serve in various evangelical churches and ministries (Brenneman 2012). This work can be dangerous, miraculous, and is to be much commended. Women have also been rescued from domestic violence by concerned evangelicals in El Salvador. Sometimes this has meant removing women from abusive situations; other times it has meant the conversion and restoration of the abuser. In these ways, numerous individuals in El Salvador have avoided violent acts or have stopped committing violent acts because of holistic evangelical ministries and the networks that support them.

However, it is also true that holistic mission actors find many sources of violence to be impervious to their efforts and that they are themselves vulnerable to violent acts. A-Brazo has been forced out of one community by gangs; in another community, the children of a pastor who works with A-Brazo were forced to leave the school they were attending by gang members. High numbers of women who attend evangelical churches remain victims of domestic violence. Unfortunately, in some of these cases, the abuse is perpetrated by men who also attend evangelical churches and sometimes can be found in leadership positions in those churches. Our research thus indicates that while there are numerous individual cases in which the holistic mission movement has helped specific individuals escape violence and violent lifestyles, it has done relatively little to change the violent nature of contemporary Salvadoran culture. A correlation between the increase of the holistic mission movement in El Salvador and the decrease in indices of violence does not exist.

Poverty: The holistic mission movement is particularly interested in poverty reduction strategies. Its extensive networks penetrate Salvadoran communities across the country. A-Brazo has partnered with local churches and nonprofit organizations that have run microfinance projects, installed water and sanitation systems, and implemented successful latrine projects. Other members of A-Brazo's networks have started schools, orphanages, and literacy and (the afore-mentioned) computer literacy programs. Still others within the holistic mission network run successful drug and alcohol rehabilitation programs and are deeply engaged in El Salvador's almost inhumane prisons. Health is yet another area of activity for A-Brazo's partners; community health seminars and medical clinics are provided by numerous congregations and organizations. The extent and diversity of poverty reduction programs, as well as the quantity of local and transnational, human and financial resources that pour into these efforts, is considerable.

The collective efforts of holistic mission movement members have clearly impacted poverty levels in El Salvador. Although national level measurements of this impact are not available (and are probably unobtainable), larger organizations such as World Vision and Compassion International carefully measure the impact of their activities within communities. Data collected by smaller NGOs like A-Brazo show the number of houses built and the number of people benefitting from the different economic, health, or education programs. Often, congregations involved in holistic mission activities do not collect such data, but evidence of their impact can easily be found in their neighborhoods.

Not all poverty reduction efforts are successful. Indeed, many are ill-conceived, completely ineffective, and can sometimes exacerbate poverty. But after decades of implementing community development strategies, members of holistic mission networks are getting better at what they do. Evidence of their impact can be seen in hundreds of communities around the country.

Natural Disasters: Holistic mission actors and networks have also significantly reduced the human pain and suffering associated with natural disasters. Many organizations in the network, including A-Brazo, got their start by responding to disasters. The donor networks that are part of the holistic mission movement respond particularly well to disasters, channeling money from multiple continents to organizations throughout El Salvador. It is again difficult to measure the impact of faith-based organizations in this area, but the national government, USAID, local governments, and other civic organizations are eager to partner with evangelicals during natural disaster responses. A-Brazo and other groups in the La Roca network have also made many communities across the country safer from future disasters through their disaster mitigation projects and education seminars. These are evidences that the financial and educational resources that come through the holistic mission networks, and the local congregational and organizational programs they empower, do in fact make a difference.

Conclusions and the Future

By examining the local and transnational networks of A-Brazo, we have learned how they enable and inhibit the holistic mission movement's efforts to create religious and social change. The most enabling factor is that local and transnational networks knit together a global faith community. They periodically bring actors together for worship, Bible study, and mutual encouragement. They facilitate long distance communication that includes spiritual reflection, efforts to more deeply understand the character of God, and prayers of praise and petition. Those who are embedded in these networks share an identity in Christ.

The shared faith identity and the high levels of trust the networks facilitate allow the holistic mission movement to effectively operate in different contexts around the globe. In El Salvador, network actors have greater exposure to theological education and they are more equipped to address a variety of social issues because of their transnational interactions. As a result, they have been able to more deeply integrate faith and social action, diminish poverty in communities across the country, and respond to numerous natural disasters in recent years.

But networks have also created limitations for evangelical organizations and individuals in El Salvador. Global networks do not always know the challenges that confront local actors. In El Salvador, where migration and violence are among the most acute social problems, holistic mission actors remain largely unequipped to address such concerns. Second, holistic mission networks do not tend to develop sophisticated solutions to complex social problems. The current organizational structure provides freedom for local actors to solve problems, but it does not foster the more sophisticated (and probably resource intensive) innovation necessary to combat more intractable social problems. Even in areas where it has experienced success, the movement often implements strategies that were created by actors outside of these networks. Finally, the holistic mission movement has not shown an ability to mobilize its members for political advocacy. In countries where social structures create oppression, political solutions can be necessary to solve social problems. While global leaders of the movement are strongly in favor of advocacy, its networks have generated little activity in this area.

These weaknesses diminish the global networks' ability to enable local actors to be effective. They do not, however, negate the fact that the movement is a truly booming area of revitalization in countries around the globe. Its impact has been felt by millions.

Because the broader evangelical movement is increasingly adopting the holistic mission movement's agenda, its impact is likely to continue to grow.

References:

Brenneman, Robert E.
2012. Homies and Hermanos: God and Gangs in Central America. New York: Oxford University Press.

Coleman, K.M., E.E. Aguilar, J.M. Sandoval and T.J. Steigenga.
1993. "Protestantism in El Salvador: Conventional wisdom versus the survey evidence." In Rethinking Protestantism in Latin America, edited by Virginia Garrard-Burnett and David Stoll, 111-142. Philadelphia: Temple University Press.

Corbett, Steve and Brian Fikkert.
2009. When Helping Hurts: Alleviating Poverty Without Hurting the Poor and Yourself. Chicago: Moody Publishers.

Hagopian, Frances.
2009. "Social Justice, Moral Values, or Institutional Interests?" In Religious Pluralism, Democracy, and the Catholic Church in Latin America. Ed. Frances Hagopian, 257-331. Notre Dame: University of Notre Dame Press.

Instituto Universitario de Opinión Pública Encuesta de Evaluación
2010. IUDOP El Salvador. http://www.uca.edu.sv/publica/iudop/Web/2010/informeval126.pdf.

Lakhani, Nina.
2013. "Violence against Women Rises in El Salvador." Al Jazeera. Published June 7. http://www.aljazeera.com/indepth/features/2013/06/201364931359564 22.html

Levitt, Peggy.
2007. God Needs No Passport: Immigrants and the Changing American Religious Landscape. New York: New Press: Distributed by W.W. Norton & Company.

1998. "Local-Level Global Religion: The Case of U.S.-Dominican Migration." Journal of the Scientific Study of Religion 37, no. 3 (September):74-89.

Malkin, Elisabeth.
2015. "El Salvador Cracks Down on Crime, but Gangs Remain Unbowed." New York Times. August 11, on line edition. http://www.nytimes.com/2015/08/12/world/americas/el-salvador-cracks-down-on-crime-but-gangs-remain-unbowed.html?_r=0

Miller, Donald E. and Tetsunao Yamamori.
2007. Global Pentecostalism: The New Face of Christian Social Engagement. Berkeley: University of California Press.

Myers, Bryant.
1999. Walking with the Poor. Maryknoll, NY: Orbis Books.

Offutt, Stephen.
2015. New Centers of Global Evangelicalism in Latin America and Africa. New York: Cambridge University Press.

Offutt, Stephen and Grant Miller.
Forthcoming. "Transnationalism." Handbook of Religion and Social Institutions. Second Edition. Edited by David Yamane. New York: Springer Publishing Company.

Offutt, Stephen and Amy Reynolds.
2014. Religion and Poverty Database. Unpublished.

Reynolds, Amy and Stephen Offutt.
2014. "Evangelicals and International Economic Engagement." In The New Evangelical Social Engagement. Edited by Brian Steensland and Phillip Goff, 242-261. New York: Oxford University Press.

Samuel, Vinay and Chris Sugden, eds.
2009. Mission as Transformation: A Theology of the Whole Gospel. Eugene, OR: Wipf and Stock Publishers. Reprint.

Smilde, David.
1998. "'Letting God Govern': Supernatural Agency in the Venezuelan Pentecostal Approach to Social Change." Sociology of Religion 59, no. 3 (Autumn): 287-303.

Stearns, Richard.
2009. The Hole in Our Gospel: The Answer that Changed My Life and Might Just Change the World. Nashville, TN: Thomas Nelson.

Steensland, Brian and Philip Goff, eds.
2014. The New Evangelical Social Engagement. New York: Oxford University Press.

Swartz, David.
2012. "Embodying the Global Soul: Internationalism and the American Evangelical Left." Religions 3: 887-901. http://www.mdpi.com/2077-1444/3/4/887.

Tizon, Al.
2008. Transformation after Lausanne: Radical Evangelical Mission in Global-Local Perspective. Eugene, OR: Wipf and Stock Publishers.

Williams, Philip.
1997. "The Sound of Tambourines: The Politics of Pentecostal Growth in El Salvador." In Power, Politics & Pentecostals in El Salvador, edited by Edward L. Cleary and Hannah W. Stewart Gambino, 179-200. Boulder: Westview Press.

Wuthnow, Robert.
2009. Boundless Faith: The Global Reach of American Churches. Berkeley: University of California Press.

CHAPTER 7: WORLD CHRISTIAN REVITALIZATION AND THE CIRCLE METHOD[47]

Bryan T. Froehle with Karla Ann Koll

47 This is an adapted form of a chapter published by Bryan Froehle with Agbonkhianmeghe E. Orobator, SJ in Steven O'Malley and Philomena Mwaura, eds., Emerging Patterns of African Christian Identity in Urban Settings (Nairobi: Acton Publishers, 2015). It was adapted for the consultation in San José with the help of Karla Ann Koll together with input from Sara Baltodano Arróliga.

What is God doing today around the world? Where is God leading Christians and the world Christian movement today? How are Christians responding to God's call, and how are societies changing as a result? What is new in the world Christian movement, and what are important trajectories for the future? How can more adequate theology and theological reflection be developed to take account of these emerging realities?

Such questions are at the heart of the design and conduct of the consultations on the reality of world Christianity designed by Asbury Theological Seminary's Center for the Study of World Christian Revitalization Movements (CSWCRM) under its research director and consultation coordinator.[48] After an initial series of consultations on World Christianity that included gatherings during Edinburgh 2010 and in Toronto, Asbury Theological Seminary's Center for the Study of World Christian Revitalization Movements initiated a second round of case-based consultations in East Africa (Nairobi, July 2013), South Asia (Dehradun, July 2014), Southeast Asia (Quezon City, July 2015), and Central America and the Caribbean (San Jose, January 2016). What follows describes the methodology of the consultations and discusses the Circle Method, which is at the heart of the consultations themselves.

Methodological Reflections

Approaches to World Christian Studies

The growth and challenges faced by Christianity around the world today may be studied from many different disciplines, all of which have something important to say. Demographic studies that look at the levels of affiliation and participation across time and place offer new consciousness about the global reality of Christianity. General historical narratives within particular countries or regions as well as confessional or denominational contexts have offered new in-depth descriptions of the trajectory of Christian life. The discipline of religious studies has brought its narrative, descriptive focus along with its

48 Bryan Froehle has served in the role of research director and consultation coordinator throughout this round of world Christianity consultations.

sensitivity to phenomenologically oriented comparative study of meaning systems behind diverse traditions. Political and social studies of various kinds have explained political implications and social transformations tied to various contemporary Christian expressions around the world. Finally, theological approaches have provided insights critical to understand emerging Christian self-understanding in contemporary contexts around the world. These include critical hermeneutics necessary for both deconstructive and reconstructive interpretive approaches.

All these are helpful in their own right, yet limited. They often tend toward a focus that is more general than specific, more an outsider than an insider perspective, and offer a single disciplinary approach rather than an interdisciplinary one. The result is competing methodologies, conflicting methods, and warring conclusions.

The consultation approach

For these reasons, the CSWCRM developed its unique consultation approach. Designed to examine world Christian contexts—that is, specific broad cultural areas of renewal or revitalization, growth or innovation within world Christianity today—each consultation was aimed within a specific geography with a preferential nod toward urban contexts given global population realities. By itself, this already brought a stronger sense of context. Each consultation engaged very specific cases of "revitalization" movements. Thus, the "case" became the unit of analysis for advancing understanding of world Christianity. Such a case-based approach is resolutely inductive from beginning to end.[49] The goal has been to be discern what God is doing in specific contexts as sensitively as possible.

Each case is ideally a local level expression with features of renewal, revitalization, innovation, or growth. They were chosen to complement the others featured during the consultation as well as those considered in previous consultations. Placed in conversation with each other, the cases opened up to comparison and in-depth

49 At the same time, it engages deductive and abductive approaches. When held in proper relationship, these various traditions are able to contribute to each other's strengths.

consideration in their own right. Above all, the goal for each consultation has not been a predetermined set of comparisons or assumptions but a conversation that advances theological and social understanding in an integrated manner. A critical part of this conversation has been between the cases themselves, even while acknowledging that these cases themselves may be influencing the conversation. All levels, including this level, are therefore subject to a hermeneutic of suspicion (Gadamer 1984, Baltodano Arroliga 2013).

Outsider perspectives can offer the possibility of a claim of "neutrality" but typically sacrifice insider insight. This is all the more problematical in areas so richly imbued with meaning such as the life of faith. Oftentimes only insiders can fully appreciate what is happening. In any case, all research by and with human beings involves some particular personal perspective. True third-party objective observation is simply not something humans can do. All are shaped by experience and pre-existing understanding. On the other hand, a purely insider approach can easily miss critical issues as well precisely because insiders naturally take their own reality for granted. A combined insider-outsider approach offers an opportunity to engage multiple voices, including insiders, for deeper insight and new levels of collaborative learning.

The limitation to a single discipline needlessly impoverishes—even imprisons—understanding, all the more when theological or religious questions are at the heart of the inquiry. As already noted, without contextual understanding, theology is inevitably segregated into a space of speculation and abstraction, potentially far from the living God who acts in history. However, mere contextual understanding from experience can all too easily bring an impoverished understanding of theology, one too thin to substantially advance the theological conversation. In addition, an approach to theology as a single discipline in itself rather than in dialogue with other disciplines from the beginning can lead to an uncritical adoption of ideas from other fields, thereby ironically denying the theoretical and methodological capacity of theology in itself. Ultimately, as an interpretive science, theology does not stand on its own but walks with dialogic partners in other disciplines (Osmer 2008), contributing something of its own to other fields of knowledge even while learning from those same fields.

The Consultation Model

The consultations were designed to advance learning from patterns of revitalization and transformation across world Christianity by understanding the context of specific cases of revitalization movements, whether within congregations or wider networks of churches, or specific forms of parachurch organizations or other expressions. Preparatory research thus collected data, quantitative and qualitative, on emerging initiatives or developments, seeking to help resource the emerging needs of theological education by providing narratives and paradigms to understand broad contemporary directions in world Christianity.

Such an approach offers an opportunity to build symbiotic relationships between academic settings globally so as to develop reciprocal learning ventures. In these ways, the consultations have helped Asbury Theological Seminary's Center for the Study of World Christian Movements fulfill its mission to "contribute to the vitality of Christian mission and local congregations by synthesizing learnings from past and present revitalization movements worldwide."

Institutional background

Every method has a specific origin, one that must be understood if the method is to be understood. The method in this case flowed from a project to explore the revitalization of the church in urban cultural contexts in Africa, Asia, and Latin America. Specifically, the project consisted of four consultations—Nairobi, Kenya; Dehradun, India; Manila, the Philippines; and San Jose, Costa Rica. The consultation model was therefore oriented toward encountering the Christian message at the intersection of religious and social change in the particularities of these contexts. Based at a leading Wesleyan institution for theological education, the Center naturally had another, ancillary goal focused on the relationship between renewal movements and theological education, one sensitive to movements of the Spirit as well as the quadrilateral insights from scripture, tradition, experience, and reason. As a center of theological education, Asbury understands firsthand the challenge for leaders to engage and lead movements of revitalization and renewal in a wide variety of ways. The Wesleyan tradition on which Asbury builds is well situated between diverse ecclesial contexts and historical expressions of Christianity, rooted in praxis from its very origins, making it a particularly well-suited host for a broad conversation across diverse Christian expressions. In addition, this focus on movements of the Spirit positions the method within the world Christian development of a more adequate pneumatology.

Consultation design

Each consultation included approximately 40 participants representing a diversity of backgrounds and intersecting backgrounds as academics, theological educators, church leaders, researchers, and renewal movement leaders. These participants were grouped into five teams, or circles, each of which was assigned one of the five cases over the days of the consultation. Each such group consisted of some eight members in all, two of whom were the writers and leaders who prepared the initial report. The other six were scholars and church leaders from a wide diversity of Christian traditions. Each consultation opened with a provocative address and discussion on a critical dimension of Christian experience and insight within the overall national or regional context of the consultation.

The learnings of the consultation were developed within each circle group and further deepened through larger plenary conversations among all participants. The conclusions were ultimately shared broadly in a public event held immediately after the consultation as well as through videos and ensuing publications. Speakers at the public event brought voices as overall synthesizers within the consultation, tying together overall insights across the individual cases and circles. These speakers were typically scholars in world Christianity or leaders within Asbury, the Center, or the project as a whole. Consultation participants and designated spokespersons from each team offered their new clarity about each of the five cases and theologically-imbued interpretations and correlates of those cases, together with provisional conclusions and insights generated through the consultation process.

Approximately a year before the consultation, each case selected for study was given over to two key collaborators who eventually presented the case at the consultation and served within one of the circles as the voice of that particular circle's case. These two collaborators were both writers and leaders—that is, leaders may themselves have been writers and the writers may themselves have been engaged participants—thereby emphasizing an engaged scholarship. They drafted an initial paper that was shared with all participants about two months before the consultation. Participants also received and reviewed brief audiovisual presentations of all the cases. The goal was not only for them to have an advance, in-depth understanding of their particular case but to cultivate a comparative framework across all the cases from the start. Such a comparative framework involved not only the five cases under consideration but all those cases known to each of the participants from their own experience and understanding.

Throughout the consultation, the comparative dimension continued in a dynamic way. At various points between the team sessions, all participants gathered together as a single group to discuss and hear reflections from the other cases together with comments and critique from designated discussants on particular issues that likely cut across the cases. Members of each case also sat with each other in small groups to explore and share emerging insights. The conclusion of the process was heightened with a collective consideration of emerging themes, even while recognizing that those themes themselves were limited to the specific backgrounds, contexts, and approaches of those present and the specific cases selected for the consultation.

The main work of the consultations, and therefore the great bulk of the meeting time, was dedicated to each specific case. Each circle worked on moving toward greater insight in interpreting the case from both social and theological perspectives. This was facilitated by the initial paper, which was in turn revised and expanded after the consultation to reflect responses to important questions raised in the circle, above all the theological insights that emerged from the work of the group. This process depended on very involved meetings over five different sessions, the first four of which were designed to correspond to the four main movements of the circle method. The fifth session was devoted to evaluation and summary for purposes of the consultation itself.

The Circle Method

Movements within the method

The Circle Method can be traced to the hermeneutic circle (Segundo 1976) and pastoral circle (Holland and Henriot 1981; Wijsen, Henriot, and Holland 2005; Wijsen 2005), among many other sources. Such an approach has been widely used for many decades, but the general form itself goes back to basic ways of human understanding that can be traced down through the ages.[50] Many variations of this approach exist, particularly within practical theology (Osmer 2008; Browning 1991; Whitehead and Whitehead 1995).[51] A common metaphor for this approach is that of the "cycle" (Green 1994) or "spiral" (Wijsen 2005), referring to its dynamic, transformative quality.

Thus, the Circle Method helps develop case-based, collective, and interdisciplinary forms of insight. It offers a dynamic way of proceeding for theological reflection, beginning and ending in the experience of God's action in the world. In the consultation, this takes the form of a structured conversation that allows for mutual learning and shared insight from insiders and outsiders, scholars and practitioners.[52] The point is not the originality of the method but rather its consistency with approaches to knowledge-

50 This method is often used to seek out the relationship between faith and justice. In a Catholic context, roots go back to Catholic Action and the "see-judge-act" approach popularized by Joseph Cardijn, though it may be traced considerably earlier than that and has ancient sources.

51 Within Africa, the Circle of Concerned Women Theologians (http://www.thecirclecawt.org/) regularly uses this method, following the influence of Mercy Oduyoye, as do other contextual theologians and pastoral leaders throughout the continent.

52 In this way it builds on associative learning approaches, one of the most basic ways of human knowing.

building found in Scripture and throughout Christian history. The movements of the method reflect ordinary practices of Christian discernment critical for leadership and scholarship, prayer and contemplation. Each context and people group that has engaged in this method adds something unique to its understanding, however, and these consultations were no different.

Calling the method a "circle" is a reference not to an abstract model of a "cycle of knowing" as much as a traditional way of knowing that builds on the contributions of all. In a "palaver" or circle sharing within a traditional African village, for example, all would gather in a circle, more or less equally, and offer insight from their perspective. Insofar as theology is an ecclesial enterprise, it depends on an approach such as this for the production of insight (Lonergan 1992).

Each aspect of the method can also be seen as a movement, one that effectively has neither beginning nor end, and with each of the movements themselves embedded in every single movement. As such, these movements are not a set of steps for producing new knowledge but rather dynamic pathways toward ever greater insight and more sure action. Rather than seeing them as a structure or machine—which is then almost inevitably reified, becoming a mechanical understanding of conscious activity—these movements simply represent elements or aspects on which focus should be given for a time to ensure that collective discernment is as complete as possible.

The Circle Method is named, then, not so much for a "circle" of steps to be completed or cycle to be followed as the circle of people who engage it—as in, for example, the consultation. Instead of diagramming these movements—though they certainly can be—they are best seen as simple building blocks of insight that ought not be missed nor slighted. They are embedded throughout the process rather than merely in a single recipe-like step. Each "movement" is therefore best understood as more heuristic than distinctive. There can be no insistence that the movements necessarily must always proceed in the same stepwise order. Ordinary human ways of learning and proceeding simply vary too much by situation, human choice, and their own internal and external logics to insist on any one such flow. Though the order of movements given here implies a certain logic, others exist: they are not the only one. The reality is that each "move" inevitably contains within it in some way elements of the other movements—they cannot be separated one from another without hopelessly reducing the entire process to a lifeless abstraction. Ultimately, the Circle Method is about phronesis—practical wisdom—and as such makes its path by walking rather than by following a preset formula. Recognizing that no movement can be adequately summarized by a single word, pairs are used below to describe each movement, word pairs that themselves reveal a certain creative tension in each movement.

First movement: Identifying and inserting

The initial focus is on the "what" of the case. What is happening? It seeks to tell the story at first glance, while at the same time identifying the actors involved and showing how they, including any "outside" researchers, are inserted into the case and its context. This movement has a particularly strong incarnational component, recognizing that God is present already in the situation. One both "inserts" oneself in a reality, and one finds that one is already inserted in it! To separate oneself from reality, after all, is merely heuristic: one is always part of reality and not separate from it. Action occurs within other actions, tied to a cascading, interrelated host of actions. Part of the work in this movement is about identifying one's position and biases so as to be suspicious of them.

Spiritual discernment, for example, calls to the comfortable to see how God sees—from the perspective of all God's people, including most particularly the poor and marginalized on the underside of history (Gutierrez 2004). Questions characteristic of this movement ask where and how one pitches one's tent, which must always be a response to where God has already pitched the divine tent (Sobrino 2008).

Questions that may be helpful in this first movement include the following:

- What is the setting of this case, including geographic, social, cultural, and other factors?
- What stories do people tell about themselves and the case of which they are a part?
- What organization(s) and organizational stories are part of the case, including origins, developments, and structures?
- What people and personal profiles are part of the case, including leaders, members, insiders, and outsiders?
- What understanding of God, God's action, and Christian renewal is part of this case?

Second movement: Assessing and analyzing

The focus in this movement is toward understanding why and how the case has developed as it did. The movement involves a blend of discipleship and discernment, requiring explanatory lenses that bring together personal and social frames. Sometimes young children innocently ask "Why?", a question they often then follow up with another "Why?" and still another. One way of thinking of this movement is to think of it as a dynamic encounter with this "Why?" question asked many times over, as an inquisitive child might.[53] This requires bringing a particular questioning of one's own actions, or that of one's group. Such actions and understanding must be held in a certain suspicion if one is to respond to the "Why?" question as fulsomely as possible.

Sometimes one can show these relationships in diagrams and tables, in carefully constructed sentences and paragraphs. However, these cannot be the final word—such dissection can become a lifeless, bloodless exercise. Tables and diagrams neither suffer and weep nor laugh and smile. The focus of this movement, as with the Circle Method as a whole, has to be incarnational, never

53 This is similar to the approach used in Six Sigma. See http://www.isixsigma.com/tools-templates/cause-effect/determine-root-cause-5-whys/.

separated from the only place where God can be found—in God's creation, among God's people. Revelation is about relationship. This movement emphasized seeing the depth and complexity of relationships more clearly rather than breaking them into pieces without remainder.

Questions that might be helpful in this second movement include the following:

- What is really going on within this case overall, from a "bird's eye" view?
- What specific difficulties and opportunities does the organization and people face, and how have they acted, including when they have been caught up short?
- How might observes analyze or theorize about the situation and actions undertaken?
- Where can divine action most readily be seen in this situation?

Third movement: Correlating and confronting

This movement emphasizes meanings and interpretations, ones that both inform and form. Consistent with the method, it looks at the interplay of understanding so as to further advance understanding. It links the development of understanding within the particular case to theological concepts, Biblical stories, and broad Christian themes. Insofar as God's revelation of Godself is encountered in creation itself, this calls for a broad, sacramental view open to the surplus of meaning in the encounter with God in everyday life. There is always more to be understood. This movement is ultimately about the art of play in linking understandings.

Using analogy (Tracy 1998), one of the most basic human forms of knowing, a different order of theological reflection arises—one already emerging in the other movements but which is here distinctively configured (McBrien 1994, 732). In some ways, what might appear to be a move to abstraction is a move to greater specificity: the correlations or affinities seen here lead to confrontations as one is caught up short, both personally and in the context of a particular case. A clear confirmation of this movement is in feelings of awe and surprise, a sense of being animated by the Holy Spirit to see things differently and more completely (Elie 2004, 256-258). This is about a sense of dissonance as well as consonance. It involves a sharpening of understanding as well as wholly new understandings.

Some questions that might be asked in this third movement include the following:

- What theological or Biblical concepts, stories, or meanings can be related to this case in a way that helps advance a robust understanding of what God is doing in or through this case and context?
- What person, church, or other experiences can be related to this case?
- How does this situation challenge or expand specific understandings of Biblical/theological truth or experience?
- What deeper understandings of theological/Biblical truths seem to be emerging from exploring this case?

Fourth movement: Empowering and extending

The central question here is about next steps, the kind consistent with conversion or metanoia. There is a sense of being empowered and compelled toward action. In this movement, the critical question is quite simply "What to do?" In a pastoral context, the focus would be on pastoral planning and strategic action. In any case, the normative dimensions of this are explored in all the other movements, perhaps most intensively in the correlating-confronting movement. If the circle process is oriented toward theological understanding, then the action component must be more about transformative, creative work and relating that further advances understanding. It is about response to God's action in the world rightly understood. There is an element that must always be both personally and socially transformative.

Revitalization is communal, always more than mere structural adjustments—conversation that reshapes action as ongoing praxis. Thus, this movement is about much more than simply a pragmatic or strategic turn.

Questions that might be useful in this fourth movement could include the following:

- How does this new insight deepen energy for Christian renewal?
- What are the next steps for leaders and scholars, both in their own action and in the collection actions of which they are part?
- What could limit leaders and scholars in these next steps?
- What new kinds of cases or new questions is God prompting for future consideration?

Fifth movement: Evaluating and summarizing

This movement flows from the needs of the consultation itself, since the consultation depends on a collective and comparative consideration of multiple cases. The key question here is "What should we say?" Its goal is to put forth and refine the major, critical conclusions of the work of the team so that they might be briefly presented by the team members to all participants. After seasoning within the wider discussions at the conclusion of the consultation, these insights are ultimately presented at the ensuing public event and in emerging publications. This includes a book chapter that is a revised and expanded version of the paper initially presented to the team and consultation participants. What flows from this movement therefore needs to be as tightly worded and clearly presented as possible. Ideally, it will blend story with context and theological-biblical themes and understandings.

Questions that might be useful in this movement could include the following:

- What are the main takeaways from each of the four case sessions?
- How can this case be best summarized before the larger group?
- What directions for practical action and scholarship exploration does this case suggest for Christian renewal?
- How have these consultation case sessions been helpful, and how could they be improved?
- How has the circle method been helpful and how could its use be improved?

Conclusion

The framing underlying the consultations on World Christianity offer an opportunity to intentionally link case studies with theological work. In this way, the study of World Christianity is not merely descriptive and analytical but interpretive, ultimately directed toward understanding where the Christian tradition is being stretched and pulled by God's grace. Those in theological education may find this approach not only an expression of practical theological method but a source of insight for the next generation of pastoral leaders in a wide diversity of contexts.

Appendix I: Interview Protocol and Video Production

What follows are the key sorts of questions generally asked in the interviews of leaders and members, interviews that were typically video recorded. In addition, other videos and still images of worship and other activities and community events were taken, as well as related images reflecting the larger religious and social context. A link to a project video was provided with the case papers prior to the consultation. This initial video also included materials from previous consultations and the work as a whole, as well as other selected related footage not part of the project.

There are separate edited videos for each case, including the interviews. Another video of the cases with some of the interviews was also produced for the public event. After the consultation, a final video was produced to present the cases together with portions of the keynotes, plenaries, and synthesis presentations at the consultation itself as well as aspects of the public event.

I. Revitalization Story/Core Narrative

- What are the key events in the groups' development from the beginning to now, both positive and negative?
- What achievements most come to mind? What aspects are especially consoling in a spiritual sense?

II. Vision

- Why does this group, project, or movement exist? How does it fit within God's purposes?
- How might this group represent the church living out its life as a called community of God's people?

III. Organizational

- What are the predominant styles of leadership: tactical or strategic, hands-on or hands-off?
- How does the work or group grow? What have been some major difficulties? Why? What was the response?
- What lessons have been learned that could be passed on to similar efforts elsewhere?
- How does the group deepen a sense of discipleship, of living the Gospel? What are some points of conflict?

IV. Theological

- When you think of the group and its work, what scriptural references or stories most come to mind?
- What is the most important activity your organization undertakes? Why is this so?
- What is the most important achievement your organization accomplishes(d)? Why is this so?

- What does "salvation" mean to you? (What words would members tend to use?)
- What does it mean to live a "life of holiness"? Could you share a story or example?
- How would you say you experience God's grace? Could you share a story or example?
- Within God's purposes, what is the most important reason your organization exists?
- How is the church to be known or identified in the larger society?
- What are some of the theological distinctives, key ways of understanding yourselves theologically?

V. Social

- To what degree do you feel connected to other Christian groups outside of your own?
- What is the role of the Christian in transformation of the society or cultural changes?
- How does this work bring transformation to the larger society? Any stories or examples?
- To what degree can social or cultural change correlated with this group be said to be sustainable?
- How might your ministry connect with points of conflict: social, political, cultural?
- Thirty years from now, how might the local context be different because of this?

References:

Baltodano Arroliga, Sara.
2013. "La circularidad hermenéutica en teología práctica rompe el espejismo del paradigma positivista." In Pensar, Crear, Actuar, editado por José Enrique Ramírez Kidd y Sara Baltodano Arroliga, 397-432. San José: SEBILA.

Browning, Don.
1996. A Fundamental Practical Theology: Descriptive and Strategic Proposals. Minneapolis: Fortress.

Elie, Paul.
2004. The Life You Save May Be Your Own: An American Pilgrimage. New York: Farrar, Straus, Giroux.

Frykenberg, Robert.
2010. Christianity in India: From Beginnings to the Present. Oxford: Oxford University Press.

Gadamer, Hans-Georg.
1984. "The Hermeneutics of Suspicion," Man and World 17: 313-323.

Green, Laurie.
1990. Let's Do Theology: A Pastoral Cycle Resource Book. London and New York: Mowbray.

Gutierrez, Gustavo.
2004. The Power of the Poor in History. Eugene: Wipf and Stock.

Holland, Joe and Peter Henriot, SJ.
1983. Social Analysis: Linking Faith and Justice. Revised and enlarged edition. Maryknoll, NY: Orbis Books.

Lonergan, SJ, Bernard.
1992. Collected Works of Bernard Lonergan, Volume 3. Insight: A Study of Human Understanding. Toronto: University of Toronto Press.

McBrien, Richard.
1994. Catholicism. Revised edition. New York: Harper One.

Osmer, Richard.
2008. Practical Theology: An Introduction. Grand Rapids: Eerdmans.

Segundo, SJ, Juan Luis.
1976. The Liberation of Theology. Translated by John Drury. Maryknoll, NY: Orbis Books.

Sobrino, SJ, Jon.
2008. No Salvation outside the Poor: Prophetic-Utopian Essays. Maryknoll, NY: Orbis Books.

Tracy, David.
1998. The Analogical Imagination: Christian Theology and the Culture of Pluralism. New York: Crossroads.

Whitehead, James and Evelyn Eaton Whitehead.
1995. Method in Ministry: Theological Reflection and Christian Ministry. Revised Edition. Lanham: Rowman and Littlefield.

Wijsen, Frans, Peter Henriot, SJ, Rodrigo Mejia, SJ, editors.
2005. The Pastoral Circle Revisited: A Critical Quest for Truth and Transformation. Maryknoll, NY: Orbis Books.

Wijsen, Franz.

2005. "The Practical-Theological Spiral: Bridging Theology in the West and the Rest of the World." In The Pastoral Circle Revisited: A Critical Quest for Truth and Transformation, edited by Frans Wijsen, Peter Henriot, SJ, Rodrigo Mejia, SJ, 108-216. Maryknoll, NY: Orbis Books.

CHAPTER 8: EXPERIENCES OF REVITALIZATION IN LATIN AMERICA

Revitalization of the Micro-churches in Latin America and the Caribbean

Pablo Richard

The meaning of the word "revitalization" depends primarily on the context in which it is used and the social group where we find ourselves. It is not a magic word that says everything. More than anything else, it is a word that should provoke us to action, though the context is very important. The word revitalization can sound very different if we are talking about revitalization in Nicaragua or about revitalization in Cuba or in Guatemala or in El Salvador. It is very different to talk about revitalization here in Costa Rica or in the United States, or even to talk about revitalization in Africa or in Asia.

I want to speak about the micro-churches. Above all, I am referring to the base ecclesial communities. They are ecclesial and I want to underline this fact. They are ecclesial communities, that is to say they are the church. Many see these as marginal groups. However, they are church because they are base communities, churches of the grassroots. This is fundamental.

I have been reflecting on the last forty years of my life. The first period of my life happened in Chile. I am Chilean. In 1970, Salvador Allende was elected president, marking the beginning of the socialist project in Chile. Then came September 11, 1973, the first September 11th. It was a Tuesday, the day of the military coup d'tat by Pinochet. I had arrived in Chile after long years of study at the Pontifical Bible Institute in Rome, where I had done all of my studies in theology and philosophy. Then I spent a year at the Biblical School in Jerusalem, followed by a month in Turkey and Egypt. I spent time traveling. After all of this, I arrived back in Chile a week before the election of Salvador Allende. Very quickly, a movement sprang up and became very strong. It was an exodus of priests, of women religious, and of monks who moved out to the periphery. We left the center of the parishes and went to live in the periphery. These outlying areas were where the poorest of the poor were to be found, those who were living in the most miserable conditions. It was very important for us to go to the periphery. I became part of this movement as soon as I arrived from Rome. I went to live in an extremely poor community. I was there until I was thrown out. It was a huge change for me. In addition, for us as Catholics, the Second Vatican Council, from 1962 to 1965, was also very influential. The Council has been criticized by many for being too Lutheran. I said to them, "Yes, it was Lutheran," because it was the response of the Roman Catholic Church to the

Reformation. The first response had been the Council of Trent, which was horrible. The second response came 400 years after the Reformation, but it came.

Another event that was very important in our life was the meeting of the Latin American Episcopal Conference held in Medellin, Colombia in 1968. It was a space for rethinking the Second Vatican Council for Latin America. It was our council. There we had with us those whom Enrique Dussel calls the fathers of the church, some sixty bishops such as Helder Camara and Manuel Larrain, a whole generation of bishops who had been meeting in the catacombs and who at Medellin brought forth from the catacombs a project, a declaration of a reformation of the church in Latin America. In 1968, liberation theology was also born. The beginning of the 1970s was a very dense time that produced a new phenomenon, a convergence between the popular movements that had a leftist, socialist tendency and the church of the poor. This was very productive, because the grassroots socialist movements thought that Christianity was the opiate of the people. They discovered that Christianity wasn't opium, but rather dynamite and a tremendous force for liberation. As Christians, we discovered that the Marxists were not atheists and criminals. In the grassroots movements, there were very important values. This coming together of the grassroots movements with the church that was being born formed a movement called Christians for Socialism, which emerged in many places such as Argentina and Peru. In 1972, a congress of this movement was held in Colombia. We took the word socialism to mean post-capitalist. It had nothing to do with Lenin or Stalin, much less the Soviet Union. We understood socialism to be an effort construct a post-capitalist life in which the poor would be able to succeed.

This was a beginning, the Second Vatican Council, liberation theology and Medellin. My experience in Chile was the experience in all of Latin America. The emergence of liberation theology was a strong movement. Then came September 11, 1973 and the imposition of the ideology of national security and Plan Condor, a list of all the people in Latin America that the militaries sought to eliminate. Of course, I was on this list, because strangely, the militaries were more afraid—this appears in the Santa Fe Document and other documents related to national security doctrine—of liberation theology than of Marxism. They were much more afraid of this church of the poor than of Marxism or the Communist Party. It was awful, the death threats, the communities that were wipe out, the people who were disappeared. All of the community leaders in the poor neighborhood where I lived disappeared and we never learned anything about their fate. Five or seven priests of those of us who had moved to the periphery were murdered in a brutal way. One was put into a sack and dumped into the ocean from a helicopter. We never heard any more about him. I also had to go into exile. First, I went to Peru, but I was thrown out. I went to France and asked for political asylum. I also received death threats in France.

My true story and the history I am trying to tell has to do with these base communities, not as a theological abstraction, but as something that emerged in life. I think everything changed and my life changed as well, especially here in Central America. During the 1970s, things were hot in Argentina, Chile, Peru and Uruguay. Movements and military coups were happening in the south. Later, things heated up in Central America and Mexico, and in Colombia to some extent. The movement moved. For that reason, when I had to leave France I did not hesitate for an instant. I came to Costa Rica. My principal motivation was that there is no army here. Glory be to God!

It began in Central America and I believe a starting point was Monseñor Romero. I had the privilege of working with him for a year and a half. What was going to be the role of the church during the war? I went many times to El Salvador and we conversed at length about faith and politics. I was very afraid that those Christians who joined the revolutionary movement would lose their faith. I shared from the experience we had had in Chile, the convergence between the leftist movements and the church of liberation theology where the Christians did not lose their faith. Instead, their faith became radicalized. The grassroots movements as well did not lose their revolutionary impulses by working with the Christians. The opposite happened. The Christians were very important for the movements. I know many economists, including some Marxists, who have said that change will not be possible in Latin America without the participation of Christians. This was fundamental. With liberation theology, and above all, with the work of Monseñor Romero, this became more evident. In this context, there was a resurgence of the base ecclesial communities, which we also call micro-churches. It was an important transformation because it brought together a social base—grassroots, the people, the indigenous, men and women—with the Word of God, the Bible, which led to liberating action. The Word of God was at this intersection between the social insertion of Christians and liberating action. As a biblical scholar, I have always had great enthusiasm for the Word of God, for the work of the Bible, for teaching the Bible and for giving the Bible to the people. I find it very illuminating that the first thing Luther did was to translate the Bible into the language of the people and to put the Bible into the hands of the people. This was the great accomplishment of the base communities, that the Bible went out of the churches, went out of the hands of the priests and the pastors and went into the hands of the peasant farmers, of the indigenous, of the young people. This movement of popular reading of the Bible has been the most solid movement within Christian circles in Central America even up until today. The secret has been, as Carlos Mesters says, to put the Bible in the hands, the heart and the mind of the people. One needs to have one eye on the social situation and the other eye in the Bible. I saw this biblical movement as something very important and I have dedicated my entire life, all of my strength, to this movement.

An important aspect of the base communities is that they are not established from outside or imposed from above; they are born from below. They are groups of peasant farmers or indigenous, there in Guatemala or El Salvador, who come together to pray. They come together because they are feeling anguish, because they are being persecuted. Their interests bring them together, as they face repression or persecution. As they come together, the communities are born as a very natural grouping. Our function has been to put the Word of God in the heart of these communities, of these small churches. The communities were born with the old method of see, judge and act. To see is to analyze the social context. To judge is to discern what is happening in the light of God's Word. See, judge, act. Later, we added celebration. See, judge, act and celebrate.

The base communities also generated ministries. The first ministry to emerge was that of the catechists or of the delegates of the Word as they were called in Guatemala. Catechists, delegates of the Word of God, deacons. These different ministries emerged from the communities themselves. Our mission was to instruct these delegates of the Word, to give the Bible to them, to strengthen them in their use of the Bible and their reading of the Bible. I remember, for example in Nicaragua after the triumph of the revolution, how my friend Fernando Cardenal, the brother of Ernesto Cardenal, organized the literacy campaign. They used Paulo Freire's method, which not only teaches people to read and write, but also to change their mindset. The main reason for the literacy campaign was that ninety percent of people in the countryside could not read. Their principal motivation for wanting to learn to read was to be able to read the Bible. Poor me. After the triumph of the revolution, I spent two years going from one community to another, here and there, leading courses on the Bible. There was not room for the people in the places we tried to teach, so we had to set up under the trees because there was so much interest in the Word of God. The same happened in Guatemala, in the Peten, in Quiche, and in Honduras as well. The base communities and the popular reading of the Bible go together.

There was conflict, and I need to be sincere about this, between the base communities and the hierarchical church in the Catholic Church. There was tension, but it was a good tension. There were some bishops, certainly not all of them, who accompanied us and encouraged us. However, in general there was tension, but we managed it well. We never reached the point where relationships broke down. I had a slogan that we used often, "Avoid confrontation and grow where your strength is." So, if a bishop struck us on one cheek, we would say, "Here is the other cheek, strike us again." We did not enter into confrontation. However, if a bishop wanted to strike us a third time, we would say, "No, that's not in the Bible." We tried to avoid confrontation and manage the tension. Undoubtedly, an important concept appeared at that time. We no longer spoke of "the Church" as a theological concept. What exists are different ways of being church, new forms of being church. Therefore, we defended our way of being church in the base communities. We saw that there were two models of church. There was a pyramidal model in which the authority is at the apex; there is the pope, the bishop, the priests and finally the poor lay people who have to obey. We rejected outright this model of church. There emerged a new model of church as a communion of communities, in which the authority does not come from above, but is rather in the heart of the communities. Those bishops we obeyed and we said to them, "Look, sir, come down from your throne, come here and we will recognize you." However, the tension is always there. Since I work on the Bible, I study St. Paul a great deal. The tension between the Gospel and the law is eternal. Today even the pope is affected by this tension between the Gospel and the law. We need to break with the law. Faith comes from breaking with the law, not out of obedience to the law. To believe and to have faith means to break with the law. As St. Peter says, the law gives strength to sin that carries us to our death.

This biblical movement uses the prayerful reading of the Bible or lectio divina. The communities meet to pray and to commit to each other, but at the heart of the movement is the lectio divina which has the following steps. The first step is to put the Bible in the hands of the people. Everyone arrives with his or her Bible. Then we read Mateo 25 and the beatitudes. The first question is, "What does the text say?" We ask instead, "What do you read in the text?" The second question is, "What is the text saying to us?" The text, once it has been read, is transformed into the Word of God. Then comes the question, "What is our response to the Word of God?" If we listen to the Word of God, we cannot remain the same. We cannot remain indifferent to our context. This is the path. At the end, there is a communal prayer. The method began to spread and we were not the ones guiding it. Instead, the delegates of the Word or catechists were leading. We were not the owners of the communities, nor were we any kind of hierarchy in the communities. The communities existed in networks. We would say jokingly that previously it had been the time of the elephants, but we were living in the time of ants and spiders. What is it that spiders do? They build webs. The elephants were the theologians, the bishops and the politicians. Now we are in the time of the spiders. Webs or networks, that is the key word. We need to bind ourselves to others in networks.

An important point in our work was to define the subject. Who was the subject of this entire process? Liberation theology gives us an important clue by insisting that theory is the second step. The first step is action and the subject of this action are the people themselves, the ministers who are leading this biblical movement. They are the subjects of the biblical movement, not me and not a theologian. We visited and we helped, but we tried to work in such a way that the poor themselves were the ones interpreting the Bible. This was fundamental.

As we worked with the Bible we also used a phrase from St. Agustin, who said the Bible is the second book of God. The first book of God is life. In this book, we find all of those who are the subject of life in all areas, in all contexts: family life, social life, in the neighborhood. They are the subjects of the book of life, and we start from this book of life when we read the Bible. The Bible shows us where God is, where God is revealing Godself. The Bible reveals God's Word, but the Bible also reveals to us where God reveals Godself. We had another guiding phrase that comes from St. Irenaeus, who said, "The glory of God is the human being fully alive" and "the glory of the human being is the glory of the vision of God." Monseñor Romero believed deeply in this and he changed the Irenaeus' phrase to read, "The glory of God is the poor person fully alive" and "the glory of the poor person is the Word of God, the vision of God." This opened up the curtain and changed the image around. The church is no longer the hierarchical church where the bishop is above and the miserable lay people are below. The image has been flipped on its head.

Now we come to the most difficult problem, the topic of spirituality. A lot has been said about the spirituality of the small base communities centered on the Word of God, but the word spirituality has been very important in the actions carried out by the subjects. But what is spirituality? We developed an important definition. Faith in God has an opposite. It is not atheism, but rather idolatry. The atheists are not the problem. The atheists are our friends. The idolaters are the problem. We published a book with the title, La lucha de los dioses (1980). It was published in English as The Idols of Death and the God of Life: A Theology (1983). It also came out in French as well as other languages. Monseñor Romero had a copy among his books and I wrote a dedication to him. The struggle of the gods: The God of life and the idols of death. There are two types of idolatry. The first, perhaps the most dangerous, involves deforming the image of God, deforming the face of God. It is very dangerous to speak of God. Many times we say, "Lord willing," or "God bless," or "God is here." Be careful! We always need to contextualize and speak of the God of Jesus, the God of life, the God of the exodus. If we don't talk in specific ways about God, we can fall into idolatry. When someone says to me, "I believe in God," I always ask, "In which God do you believe? When an atheist says to me, "Father, I am an atheist," I ask, "From which god are you an atheist? It could be that we atheists from the same god!" Once, a twelve-year-old boy came to my office and he said to me, "Father, I am an atheist." I responded, "How wonderful!" His head was free of images of God, so he would be more open to finding God. Faith is not believing in God, but it is the search for God, this God that Moses found in the burning bush. "I have heard the cries of my people and I have decided to liberate them." (Exodus 3: 9-10) This is the God in whom I believe.

The other kind of idolatry, one that is opposed to the faith in the God of the poor, in the God of Jesus, in the God of life, does not deform the face of God. Instead, things or people are seen as divine. God's face in not deformed, but things, people, structures, teachers, priests or pastors are deified. This is the most dangerous form of idolatry, is it not? We live in a world that is very idolatrous. A short time ago, there was a North American theologian who talked a lot about the death of God. However, one day he said, "God is not dead; God has been transformed into gold." In other words, gold became God and money has been turned into an idol. Our world is tremendously idolatrous. Banks are the new cathedrals. The supermarkets are the new churches. Neoliberal ideology is deeply idolatrous because it turns products into idols. A product is good if it sells, not if it is useful. We live in a market that is deeply idolatrous. I have another friend who is a priest. He tells me that he likes to go into large supermarkets. I asked him why. 'Yes," he told me, "I go to see all the things I don't need and to confront idolatry." This is very important, because we should not allow ourselves to be carried away by the idolatry of the market. Neoliberal ideology is deeply idolatrous. It is economic idolatry and political idolatry, but worst of all it is also religious idolatry.

In liberation theology and the base communities, we have struggled a lot against idols. Our struggle has been against idols, not against atheists. The problem is idolatry. Therefore, to announce the Gospel is to act against idolatry. And the Gospel, the God of the Gospel, the God of Jesus, the God of the Exodus, is deeply opposed to idolatry. This is a fundamental characteristic of the Gospel. So, you need to be careful when you speak of God! You have to always qualify God: the God of the Exodus, the God of Jesus, the God of life. When I speak of God, I believe in God and I want to bring people to God. But what God are we talking about? Is it possible that we are talking about a God that we have invented? There is nothing easier than inventing a god, and suddenly we are carrying out the will of a god that we ourselves have made. Idolatry, not atheism, is very dangerous.

In liberation theology, we always speak of a preferential option for the poor. It is not just an option for the poor; it is a preferential option for the poor. With the rich, we follow what we might call the politics of Jesus, who said, "It is easier for a camel to pass through the eye of a needle than it is for a rich man to enter the kingdom of heaven." (Mathew 19: 24) And "Blessed are the poor, for the kingdom of heaven belongs to them." (Mathew 5: 3) Therefore, we don't exclude them, for they exclude themselves. What we have to do is open our hands, invite them and work with them. I don't reject this social class, but I do propose that they convert and follow Jesus. It is radical conversion that means putting their riches at the service of the life of the people and not at the service of the market. If they are in the market, there is no salvation for them.

Today, in addition to a preferential option for the poor, we talk about an option for gender, an option for the indigenous, and a preferential option for youth. It is not a question of trying to force people into the church, because many do not want to know anything about God or about the church. Therefore, you have to try to reach them another way. You have to listen to them. The option for young people is very important. Many young people are joining small communities. They are involved in youth movements of all kinds, but not in youth movements that are very connected to the churches.

Another problem right now is violence. I have worked on this topic a lot in El Salvador, where there are three large gangs. Our policy has been to listen. In seminary, we were taught to talk, but they never taught us to listen. I have sat down at two o'clock in the morning with gang members. They know I am a priest and they respect me. I talk about Monseñor Romero. For the celebration of the 35th anniversary of Romero's murder and for the beatification of Romero, they declared a truce of three days without violence in honor of Romero. It is important to listen, but it is difficult. These gang members are criminals. To join a gang, they have to kill three people and they say this outright, but I began to listen to them. I began to think, how is it possible for there to be such violence? Later in Mexico, I went to a meeting of the base communities followed by a seminar about violence and transnational organized crime. We worked off a text from St. Paul that is very important, the Letter to the Ephesians, which says, "For our struggle is not against flesh and blood, but against the powers of this dark world." (6:12) Therefore, the most important struggle is against the supernatural forces of evil. It is something very curious, that there are men who slit the throats of ten people and then go to their homes and drink coffee with their wives as if nothing has happened. The same happened with the man who dropped the bomb on Hiroshima. He arrived home and said that nothing had happened. This happens as well with those of ISIS and the Islamist terrorist movements. They kill people and it is as if nothing has happened. Therefore, there exists a supernatural evil force. This is the problem. It isn't found so much in people, but rather in the structures. I have come to see that the work with the gang members as an attempt to liberate them above all from this supernatural evil force. There is a supernatural force that leads them to kill with a clear conscience. It's incredible! When I sent to Guzman City, there were twelve bodies hanging from a pedestrian walkway. The local priest said to me, "Look, we know exactly who did this. Do you want to meet with them?" Of course, I did. I began to ask them questions. They told me that there was a demonic force that surged within them and made them kill, even though they didn't want to kill anyone. Thus, I discovered a little bit about these supernatural forces of evil. It's not a question of simple fighting against those who are armed, or of sending in the police to take them prisoners or to beat them. It is necessary to listen to them and to discover where these supernatural evil forces are lurking. I spend hours listening to them, listening to them to try to purify them from these evil forces.

As a final point, the election of Pope Francis has encouraged us greatly. I believe this more and more each day, because he is being attacked, a sure sign that he is doing good things. If Opus Dei is attacking, that is a sign that he is doing good things. This pope has opened up many new spaces. The critique that he has offered of the market economy is the strongest one the church has put forth. He has also focused firmly on the ecological problem. When he went to the Congress of the United States, he spoke very strongly. He also spoke harshly at the Assembly of the United Nations. He met with the social movements in Santa Cruz, Bolivia: he met with the social movements in Rome. Truly, he has moved the church out of the traditional hierarchical spaces. Therefore, he has opened up a lot of new spaces for us.

So, what would a revitalized faith community be like? In the first place, we have to do what the pope has said. "Leave, leave the church! I want priests that smell like sheep! Leave!" I think the principal first step in revitalization is to go out the church and go into the barrios, to go out to where the peasant farmers are instead of holding masses on Sundays in the center of the cities. Revitalization means emptying out the churches. We have to clean up the church. We have to rebuild the church in other contexts and in other spaces. These days I work with street people, with homosexuals and prostitutes. I go at seven o'clock in the morning and we hold a meeting of a base community with prostitutes who are finishing their work to listen to them and to listen to the gays, etc. When I am asked where my parish is located, I say my parish is in the street. I never go into a parish church. I believe that we are revitalizing the church, by getting people out of the parish churches. The greatest enemy that we have in the work that we are doing in the Plaza de la Dolorosa is the parish church. Our principal enemies are the members of the parish, because they say that we are making the area dirty, that the plaza fills up with prostitutes and transvestites with their miniskirts. For this reason, they don't allow us to enter the parish church. So, to revitalize the church we have to open up the door and go outside. I have never seen anyone from the parish church, which is right in front of where we meet, come out to help us. We gather together more than 120 men and women. To revitalize the church is to go outside of the church. That is what it takes.

References:

Gómez V., Jorge I.
1996. El crecimiento y la deserción en la iglesia evangélica costarricense. San José: IINDEF.

Richard, Pablo, et. al.
1980. La lucha de los dioses: los ídolos de la opresión y la búsqueda del Dios liberador. San José: DEI y Managua: Centro Antonio Valdivieso.

Richard, Pablo, et.al.
1983. The Idols of Death and the God of Life: A Theology. Translated from the Spanish by Barbara E. Campbell and Bonnie Shepard. Maryknoll: Orbis Books.

CHAPTER 9: REFLECTIONS ON REVITALIZATION

I. A Word about Revitalization

Herbert Mauricio Alvarez López

II. Revitalization of Mission?

Karla Ann Koll

III. From Local Impact to Cultural Change

H. Fernando Bullon

IV. Paths of Resistance and Transformation in the Search for Life

Priscila Barredo Pantí

I. A Word about Revitalization

Herbert Mauricio Alvarez López

When you walk through the jungle or the forest, you might come upon the skin of a snake. Snak)es shed their skins to be able to grow, as their skin cannot grow as fast as their bodies. The shedding of the outgrown skin keeps the snake healthy by getting rid of any parasites on the skin as well as eliminating any parts of the skin that have been damaged by lack of moisture or poor nutrition. A new skin is a new beginning, a revitalization. In this process, however, the snake is very vulnerable until the new skin has hardened. A snake that has just molted protects itself by remaining inactive for a time. In this case, revitalization prolongs a healthy life.

For the indigenous communities, who are farmers, the basic food crop is corn, which for us is sacred. Each year they repeat the process of sowing, using the same techniques to prepare the soil. They revitalize the land, that is to say they clean it, they stir it, they mix the weeds they have pulled or the stalks from the previous harvest into the soil to produce the humus that is needed. They make a new furrow. In our ancestral words, we feed the sacred mother earth so that she can give us once again our daily sustenance. Here, revitalization is the food needed to continue to live.

According to the Royal Spanish Academy, the word revitalize means to "give more strength and life to something." Humans have an innate desire to search for life, to promote life. Life itself is in a constant process of evolution. The experiences of revitalization in Christian churches imply, above all, the renewed ways the Spirit provides to live the message of Jesus of Nazareth, the Christ, within specific contexts. This means new impulses, new methods, old practices used in renewed keys, new ways of understanding, new concepts, new pastoral actions, new options, a new spirit in a Christian community open to ongoing transformation as history moves forward.

It is also necessary to emphasize that revitalization must be understood in relationship to resurrection. Revitalization means not only to give more strength and life, but it can also mean a radical change. It should eradicate the practices that impede the emergence of God's Reign and create something radically new. The children of light (1 Thess. 5:5) should not be afraid. The Spirit of God, the great Mother and the great Father, is always present in the community. When the snake changes its skin, it experiences a time of vulnerability. When new pastoral practices or new conceptual understandings emergence, often there is fear and condemnation, but if the new ways are faithful to the spirit of God's Reign, then there is nothing to fear. The logic of life itself will provide confirmation. Communities moved by the Spirit will perceive the lucidity and relevance of that which is radically new.

We must dare to allow ourselves to be carried away by the Spirit, to believe in the Spirit, to trust in the Spirit. How many years and how many times have we preferred to settle into norms over which we have power, to remain "safe" in what maintains a structure or a vision without seeking to transform society? The Holy Spirit moves us, or should move us, to dare what may be unthinkable yet faithful to the Good News. If this happens, when this happens, when radical proposals emerge that are faithful to the Spirit of the Good News, we are faced with a choice. I hope we can make a positive choice. In the spirit of our ancestral Maya words of the Popol Wuj, "May we all arise, may all be called, may no group nor two groups remain behind the rest."

The Revitalization Process in Christian Communities

Latin America has had 523 years of experience with the Christian church. This experience continues and influences our current historical moment. The reality that we are living through today, with the specific characteristics of postmodernity, brings its own challenges when we confront our past and current forms of faith experience and seek to elucidate if these practices continue to respond to the demands and the questions of today.

Time itself, as epochs change, obliges us to shed our skin to grow. The essence, the passion for God's Reign that was announced by Jesus of Nazareth, continues, but the ways we make this Reign present, the skin, are renewed and revitalized to make Jesus' proposal congruent with the signs of the times. We can find the signs of the times in cultural, political, economic, ecological, and religious realms, as well as in the increasing awareness of human diversity.

Boredom and exhaustion can accompany the lack of answers to the questions the believers in a Christian community are asking. Therefore, we need to search for, create and organize new responses. There might be both old and new changes in our context such as the continuing presence of poverty, the ecological disaster, the emergence of Christian and human subjects with diverse sexualities, migration, modern armed conflicts that have religious overtones, the existential vacuum felt by many in contexts of material abundance, corruption in government structures, the deep internal desire for spiritual experience in our postmodern context, the excessive violence in diverse contexts, scientific advances, etc.

As Christians, we are immersed in these different realities. The need for Christian revitalization is part of life's evolution. We may be motivated by the sense of unease brought about by Christian practices that no longer make sense in our lives. Perhaps we are pushed by specific social contexts that demand a spiritual answer that is human and Christian. The five case studies in this project represent five experiences of revitalization. All of them are valid, creative, based in human solidarity and reflective of the Gospel. These are five attempts to renew our experience of Jesus, of fellowship, of being sons and daughters of God.

The current situation is determined primarily by a model of globalization based on neoliberalism. The principal features of this system at different levels are the cult to the individual, the production and growth of capital as the measure of success for human action at the cost of marginalization and exploitation of large groups of people, the technification of human action on a large scale, and the global reach of the communications media which mold specific lifestyles at the same time they provide information. We see the practical results in the existence of a sector of the human population that has access to high standards of living while at the same time large masses of people, the majority of human beings, live in conditions of poverty and exclusion in environments that have been severely degraded.

There is no one model of Christian revitalization that addresses all of the challenges faced today by believers and nonbelievers. Each context demands its own response. Models for revitalization might be found in large ecclesial communities such as megachurches or in small-scale ecclesial communities such as the base ecclesial communities or other movements.

Though Christianity has been declared by some to be on its way to extinction, we are seeing the growth of religious practices, both Christian and of other religions, around the world. Yet, we need to ask whether or not this is beneficial for human development.

How do we measure a revitalization that is consistent with our faith?

Despite the variety of contexts in which Christian experience must respond, in spite of the different perspectives that exist about the process of revitalization itself, there is something, there must be something that serves as a guiding light, inspiring and defining the path.

I believe what is central to Christian communities is the proclamation of the Good News of the Reign of God. We find it expressed thus in the Gospel according to St. Luke 4:43-44. "But he said, 'I must proclaim the good news of the kingdom of God to the other towns also, because that is why I was sent.' And he kept on preaching in the synagogues of Judea." (NIV) Jesus was sent on a well-defined mission.

I understand God's Reign as the efforts of Jesus of Nazareth's to show us what the Father is like and how we should be as human beings, for Jesus is the one who reveals the Father and also serves as a model for being human. If we understand who the God of Jesus is and what this God is like, and if we can become like Jesus was, salvation will come to us and to all of creation. This salvation will extend the Spirit and the experience of living as daughters and sons of God to all human beings who are believers and who have open hearts.

In this salvation, my life will find meaning in my relationship to God by following Jesus as I am inspired by the Spirit. But what are we inspired to do as believers? We are inspired to enjoy living as we seek life's full realization within our own personal histories in diverse social contexts.

The promotion of life, both the aim and the task of the Reign of God, must have specific reference points related to the individual person and to social life. At the individual level, the promotion of life seeks to heal the wounds that have been inflicted by life such as abuse, low self-esteem, illness, discrimination, divorce, etc. To promote life at a social level means to fight for social justice.

For many years, we have pointed to the lack of incarnation of the Christian message in social realities as a divorce between faith and life. This is very clear in this Latin American and Caribbean continent where the vast majority of us are Christians and at the same time the vast majority of people live in situations of poverty and social exclusion. This is a contradiction and a scandal. The evidence around us screams at us that we are busy being church rather than working for the Reign of God. As the sincere and truthful prophetic voice of Jon Sobrino has said, the Reign of God has come close, the Reign of God is here, but nothing or almost nothing has changed. (Sobrino 2000, 179)

Given that Christianity is a religion of love and justice, we are not living what we preach. Christianity is incompatible with situations of injustice. We have become accustomed to a double moral standard and a lack of commitment that allow us to not be affected by the suffering of the majority.

I suspect that most Christian experiences today are focused on the individual and respond to the need for acceptance, healing, self-esteem, or integration into a family or a church community that becomes an oasis that isolates one from other people and their questions. We emphasize celebration and liturgy as a collective experience, which is good, but which cannot be the exclusive focus. We forget that we are beings-in-relation and that our relationships extend beyond our families and churches. We affected by what the social and political structures create with or without our conscious collaboration.

We should take advantage of the opportunities offered by today's experiences of revitalization. In addition to reinventing methods, we must become aware of a need that is often consciously or unconsciously ignored, namely that change at a personal level takes place within a context of social change and often in tension with that context. As Jesus comes close to me, I must respond on two levels, with an individual personal response and with a commitment to work for a better world by promoting social justice.

This is what Jesus wanted his disciples to grasp, that we are to love God and our neighbor as ourselves (Mk 12:28-31; Mt 22:34-40; Lk 10:25-28; Jn 13:34-35). It is such a central theme for Jesus' disciples that all four gospels remind us of it and ask it of us. It is incredible how we like to worship God with our liturgies, prayers, readings and studies, while at the same time we forget about our neighbors and do not love them as we love ourselves. Both should be part of Christian life; if one or the other is missing, we are not being faithful to the Reign of God and we have betrayed the Good News.

The new skin on the snake predicts a new beginning. The soil prepared for the sowing of the corn awaits the seed that will satisfy hunger. The experiences of Christian revitalization offer the hope of meaningful human life in both individual and social dimensions. We have the challenge of creating a new heaven and a new earth in the spirit of Revelation 21, a place where we will be the people of God and God will be with us, as Uk´u´x K´a, Uk´u´x Uleu (Heart of Heaven, Heart of Earth) so that we might all produce life.

II. Revitalization of Mission?

Karla Ann Koll

I am a missiologist. As such, I reflect on the experiences of churches and faith-based organizations in Latin America, including the cases presented in this book, with the eyes of a missiologist. I often think that missiology, an interdisciplinary field by definition, is the last refuge of those of us who refuse to specialize. Being a missiologist allows me to be a bit of a historian, a bit of an anthropologist, a bit of a sociologist, a bit of an ecologist, a bit of a Bible scholar and a bit of a theologian. Missiology is this way precisely because the mission of God embraces the entire world, not only human life but all of creation as well.

Following David Bosch, I affirm that it is impossible to offer a definitive definition of mission because mission expresses the dynamic relationship that exists between God and the world. All areas of human life and the entire creation are the object of God's salvific love. In our time, which Bosch identifies as the ecumenical era, the concept of mission includes many facets. There are many ways proposed for the collaboration of churches and believers in God's salvific project (2012, 24-25, 451). The invitation to participate in God's mission comes from Jesus. In John 17:18, as part of his prayer for his followers, Jesus says to God, "As you have sent me into the world, so I send them into the world." When Jesus appears to his disciples after his resurrection, he repeats these words of sending (John 20:21). There are no limits imposed in these texts. All persons who wish to follow Jesus are sent into the world. For this reason, we affirm that the mission is God's mission, because God sends us into the world through Jesus Christ.

This process of consultations started with the premise that God is at work in the world. The question that brought us together is about what God is doing in different contexts. We have sought to discover the answer to this question by looking for signs of revitalization as indicators of God's action. However, revitalization does not offer clear theological criteria for discerning divine action in the world today. We must continue to ask, "Revitialization of what?" Without a doubt, lives have been transformed in each of the cases presented in this book. Is mission being revitalized? It could be that we are seeing a revitalization of subjects in each of the case studies. Still, we must ask if the persons who are being transformed understand themselves as subjects of God's mission.

In Latin America, several movements focused on the revitalization of mission have made important theoretical and practical contributions. I worked in Guatemala for thirteen years with the Evangelical Center for Pastoral Studies in Central America (Centro Evangélico de Estudios Pastorales en Centroamérica—CEDEPCA). This institution emerged out of an evaluation of a previous experience in evangelization. Evangelism in Depth, a project begun by the Latin American Mission in 1959, sought to mobilize the members of evangelical churches to evangelize their neighbors. To this end, Evangelism in Depth used communications media in a way that was innovative at the time and organized national campaigns in various countries with the active participation of several denominations. After ten years of accumulated experience, some leaders within Evangelism in Depth—Plutarco Bonilla, Guillermo Cook and Orlando Costas—began to raise questions about what they were doing. It was evident that the project had mobilized people from the churches to evangelize their neighbors. The evangelical churches had grown. However, there were no noticeable changes in the communities around the churches. Living conditions for the majority of Latin Americans were deteriorating. These leaders concluded that there was a problem with the model of church among the evangelicals. The churches were pastor-centric, in other words, the ministry was thought of as belonging to the pastor and not to the members. Evangelism in Depth had managed to fill up the pews, but the movement had not mobilized people to get actively involved in missionary efforts outside of the churches. Bonilla, Cook and Costas borrowed ideas and language from the pastoral renewal taking place in the Roman Catholic Church in Latin America at the time. They defined pastoral work as the organized work of the church in carrying out God's mission, what we would call missional action today. This led to the founding of a new continental organization based in Costa Rica, the Latin American Evangelical

Center for Pastoral Studies (Centro Evangélico Latinoamericano de Estudios Pastorales—CELEP), and a regional organization, CEDEPCA, to promote missional action and train members of the churches, not just the pastors, to participate in God's mission (Costas 1984).

Some models of mission and evangelization are centrifugal, sending people out from a center, the church in this case, to the surrounding areas. Other models are centripetal, attracting people to the churches. As a first attempt at analyzing the revitalization of mission, we can examine the relationship between the centrifugal and centripetal movements in each of the case studies. This is important, for being sent into the world does not necessarily involve a change of location, but rather has to do with one's relationship to the world. The Catholic Church in Cuba, which for many years did not have any possibility of developing a public presence outside of the church buildings, was still being sent into the world by God. To what extend can we perceive a revitalization of mission in each of the case studies? Do the persons who feel themselves attracted to the churches also feel themselves to be moved to work in their communities?

For A-Brazo, the evangelical churches serve as an entrance point into the communities. They mobilize people in the churches to serve their neighbors. In a very deliberate way, A-Brazo trains people in holistic mission and as subjects of mission. It would be interesting to have information on at least two more points. Does the mobilization of church members in service to their community continue once a particular project has come to an end? Is there a centripetal component as well? Does the involvement of the churches in meeting the needs of the community also attract people to the churches?

In the Belice Bridge Labor and Educational Project, an effort is made to avoid explicit religious language. However, this leaves many questions unanswered about the relationship that exists between the life of the parish and the project. Surely some of the young people who have received an education and gotten access to employment are active participants in the parish.

Are they being trained as agents of God's mission? How do they understand the responsibility to work for the transformation of their community and their country?

The centripetal and centrifugal movements can be clearly seen in the history of the New Jerusalem Church in La Chureca. Pastor Magdalena began by preaching to people, attracting them with a proclamation of God's love. Together they worked for a transformation of their living conditions and they were able to achieve very visible improvements in the community. Do they continue to be mobilized for such missional action? Does their vision extend beyond their own community?

The Catholic Church in Cuba has experienced various stages that allow us to visualize a changing relationship between centripetal and centrifugal movements. The church lived through a period of being silenced in which it had no public presence. It was a time of deepening and purifying the faith in Jesus Christ of the people who had stayed in the churches. The efforts of this remnant, many of whom were lay women, not only kept the church alive, but also transmitted the faith within families. Once religious faith was permitted, it was possible for the church to reach out and occupy small public spaces, such as the feeding programs for older adults. Today the outward movement is seen in various mission activities, including the mission houses, the outreach efforts to visit house to house and listen to the people, and the work of Catholic Relief Services in responding to disasters caused by natural phenomena. In addition, there has been movement toward the church. Many people who have little or no religious formation continue to enter into the parishes.

The remaining case study is of Abundant Life, a megachurch I have visited twice. I confess that I have many reservations about this style of church that seeks to attract people and, in fact, attracts many people. The centripetal movement is very evident. People arrive for services from many places, but what is happening in those neighborhoods where the people live? A friend of mine was pastoring a Mennonite church in Guatemala City for a time. She told me how a megachurch sent a bus to the neighborhood every Sunday morning to pick people up for the worship service. The folks would put on their best clothes and escape from the barrio for a few hours. The worst thing, my friend told me, was that these folks would not make any commitment to work to improve the conditions in the barrio. That was not a part of their faith commitment. The people who responded to the survey carried out in Abundant Life indicated that they were satisfied with their spiritual lives. On the basis of this survey, the authors of the case study conclude that the Abundant Life church represents an experience of spiritual renewal. But is it a revitalization of mission? The slogan of Abundant Life is "Making every member a disciple of Christ". However, this does not answer the question of what it means for this church to be a disciple. The report mentions some efforts by the church to care for women who have been abused and for children who have been abandoned. However, the survey did not ask questions that would have made the level of commitment by the church members to mission efforts outside the church visible. Could it be that the majority of those who attend Abundant Life are merely spectators?

Dr. Ondina Cortes has insisted that we should not seek a spiritual revitalization. Instead, she argues, we should seek an evangelical revitalization which combines internal spiritual renewal with a communal dimension. Pablo Richard affirms that revitalization happens when we leave the church buildings. I firmly believe this. However, in the case of the base ecclesial communities, there is also a movement toward the center. Reading the Bible in community and prayer constitute the heart of base community movement.

In order to analyze more deeply the question of the revitalization of mission, I want to return to two interrelated aspects of the Central American context: violence and economic inequity. We cannot forget that Latin America is the region of the world where the highest percentage of the population identifies as Christian, yet at the same time it is the region of the world that displays the greatest inequity in the distribution of wealth and income. The northern triangle of Central America—Guatemala, El Salvador and Honduras—are experiencing the highest levels of violence in the world for a region without an active armed conflict. Could it be that God is calling to us through these statistics to rethink how we are participating in God's mission in this region?

In terms of violence, Offnut and Romero point out the A-Brazo's work has not had much success in lowering the levels of violence in Salvadoran communities. A much deeper analysis of the causes of violence is needed. Who is benefiting from the high levels of violence in the region? The youth who enter the gangs are not organizing to change the structures of their societies. Instead, they are constructing their own structures. For the elite who are seeking to generate profits through megaprojects that require very little in terms of labor, the fact the gang members are killing each other while thousands of young people flee the region to escape the violence perpetrated by the gangs reduces the political and economic pressure to change the development model and incorporate more sectors of the population into the active labor force. It is also important to remember that the gangs are only the visible face of the violence. While the young gang members carry out extortions and murders, the leaders of organized criminal organizations become wealthy. The high levels of violence also justify the expansion of police and military forces. Terrorized populations easily give their votes to the conservative political forces that promise a hard line on crime. What are the churches doing in such a context? In Guatemala, people speak in whispers of the "narco-offerings" some churches receive. If the blood of Christ can wash the stains of sin away from a human soul, can it not do the same for money? Pastors I know in Honduras have to decide each day if they are going to pay the "tax" to the local gang so people will be permitted to come to the church service. How is it possible to speak of the revitalization of mission in such contexts? How can we develop an adequate analysis and missional action that is not only capable of saving lives but also of challenging the systems based on violence?

The image of the bridge has caught my attention. I wonder if we still have an idea of mission as a rescue effort, even though today the goal of mission is not to rescue souls from hell, but rather to allow individuals and occasionally communities to escape from the hells that are created by our societies. Bridges are very important because they allow people and resources to move from one side of a chasm to the other. But at the end of the day, the chasm still exists. Thus, some young people in Guatemala are receiving an education that allows them to compete for jobs in the formal economy. In El Salvador, some communities have been able to improve their crop yields and raise their income levels. Even though the case study on the Abundant Life church did not explain the specific actions involved in that church's ministries with women who have been abused and with abandoned children, it is likely that such services are directed toward individuals rather than addressing systemic causes. Without a doubt, responding to the concrete necessities of individuals is an important part of the revitalization of mission. The concept of holistic mission has made a vital contribution on this point by insisting that the gospel is directed to the whole human person. Holistic mission also speaks about the importance of working for justice (Padilla 2006). However, holistic mission has serious limitations as a theological framework because it does not incorporate a social analysis capable of making visible the structural sin that generates societies marked by high levels of exclusion, violence and inequality.

I believe that Pastor Magdalena of the New Jerusalem Church in La Chureca gives us an important element for the revitalization of mission. I am going to call this element "indignation". This was the strong feeling Magdalena experienced when she realized that people in her country were living in the garbage. Indignation rises up from the gap that exists between what we experience and the way we believe the world should be.[54] Human beings should not be looking for food in what has been thrown away by the inhabitants of the city! It is a protest against a society and a globalized world that, as Zygmunt Bauman has noted, produces disposable people (2004). I believe that this indignation connects us with the God of the Bible. This is where we encounter the God of Exodus who hears the cries of the enslaved community and acts to free them (Ex. 3:7). We hear Jesus, God among us, protest against the social exclusion of his time by announcing the arrival of a reign in which those who are last shall be first (Luke 13:30). The Holy Spirit enables us to hear the groans of

54 It is interesting to note that the last book of educator Paulo Freire, who dedicated his life to social transformation and whose work greatly influenced the development of liberation theology in Latin America, is titled Pedagogy of Indignation (2004).

the entire creation (Rom. 8:22-23).

Our capacity to feel indignation is directly related to the eschatological horizon that we have. Bosch noted the importance role that an eschatological vision plays in defining the model of mission (1991, 498-510). Revitalized mission as "action in hope" (Bosch 1991, 498) does not seek to return to an idealized past. Instead, it is oriented toward the future that God desires for all of creation. One of the major contributions of Latin American liberation theology has been the recovery of the historical Jesus and the centrality of the Reign of God in all of Jesus' actions.[55] Today we speak of the Reign of God to place the emphasis on God's action and to move beyond a territorial idea of kingdom. In truth, none of us live today in a kingdom; it is a political structure that we have never experienced. Brian McLaren has an interesting article in which he looks for new metaphors to speak of the Reign of God (2006). Of the suggestions offered by McLaren, my favorite is "the dream of God", that is to say the sum of the intentions and desires God has for all of creation. To the extent that we grow closer to God to share in God's dreams, we should feel more and more dissatisfied with a world situation in which economic inequality is growing, in which more than 800 million people do not have enough to eat, in which violence takes the life of thousands of young people each year, in which women and children suffer abuse and in which elderly people are abandoned.

In closing, I offer a translation of the words of a hymn written by Edmundo Reinhardt of Brazil:

Longing for an earth without evil, an Eden of feathers and flowers,
Of peace and justice embracing, a world without hate or pain.
Longing for a world without owners, without weak or powerful,
The overthrow of every system that creates palaces and shacks.
You gave us, Lord, the seed, a sign that the Reign is now,

55 The work of the Jesuit theologian Jon Sobrino (1978, 2001) has been key.

The future that illuminates the present, you are on your way, without delay.
May your Reign come, Lord, to recreate the festival of the world,
And transform our waiting and our pain into full joy.[56]

III. From Local Impact to Cultural Change

H. Fernando Bullon

Prior Considerations

I offer this reflection from my perspective as a specialist in social ethics, mission, social responsibility and development. As such, I am most interested in some of the points raised in the set of questions that were asked in relationship to the case studies:

- What is the role of a Christian in the transformation of the society or in cultural changes?
- How does the work of this group contribute to the transformation of the society?
- To what extent can the social or cultural change related to this group be considered sustainable?
- How could this ministry be connected with points of social, political or cultural conflict?
- In thirty years, what differences will exist in the local context as a consequence of this group's action or presence?

The analysis of the case studies, with the exception of the study of the church in Cuba, shows a major emphasis in the social arena as a fundamental aspect of revitalization. I observe a certain focus on "projectism". Three of the cases presented are special service projects or NGOs, as if the nature of the answer to the question about revitalization would be special "projects" with a social focus ("projectism"). The case of the megachurch shows the needed growth of the church (the incorporation of new

56 "Jesucristo, esperanza del mundo" in the hymnal Celebremos juntos #95 (San José: SEBILA, 1989).

believers) for spiritual renewal and for reaching the middle class, but the education, the ministries and the various services offered also emphasize "projectism".

Reflections and Suggestions

Holistic mission involving action by the whole people of God (versus the risk of putting a professional team in charge of revitalizing action/"projectism")

The so-called "cultural mandate" (Gen. 1:28) implies that God has charged human beings with care for creation and development of society and culture. Therefore, there is a tacit affirmation of the legitimacy and importance of all of the vocations and all of the disciplines of knowledge—humanities, natural sciences, social sciences, the arts—and their multiple derivations, developments and applications, all of which are produced through the exercise of the special faculties given to human beings to fulfill this cultural mandate. The Fall did not annul this mandate, but from that point on, it must be considered within the redeeming perspective of the salvific project of God, the life-giving message of the Gospel and the eschatological horizon of the values of the Kingdom of God.

The people (laos) of God, as a "royal priesthood", is fundamentally the laity with a diversity of gifts, preparation and life experiences who are inserted and dispersed in the daily activity of the world. This charismatic and diaconal body manifests the diversity of gifts and resources in service to the body and for mission. Therefore, to speak of the church is basically to speak of the whole laity, with the exception of the clerical position of the "ordained" pastor, or the associate pastors in the case of a large church.

It is the whole people (laos) of God who are to be missionary and who are called to "ministry". Each member is linked to a vocation and a body of particular disciplinary knowledge which he or she should exercise within society in fulfillment of the cultural mandate and in service to society: in industry, in commerce, in the service sector, in the public sector with its multiple branches, in the private sector with its diverse types of organizations, etc.

To summarize, the people of God are to be found throughout the institutional web of society, which in the modern and urbanized world tends to be complex and very diversified. Inspired by the vision and values of the Kingdom of God, the people of God will seek to validate fully the fruits of the transformative impact of the Gospel in all dimensions of their existence, manifesting the multiform grace of God through the gifts they have received and taking on their identity as God's people in their mission "to be a blessing for the world" in the fullest sense.

Implications for leadership formation for multidisciplinary action and social impact

In general, the people of God in Latin America appear not to be missionally oriented toward social impact because they have not understood the dimensions that are implied in the exercise of their diverse vocations and the application of associated disciplines in connection with the values of the Kingdom of God and for the improvement and transformation of society: justice, integrity, solidarity, excellence in service, all of which should be articulated through daily action within society. People are not equipped to think about and reflect on human responsibility in light of the challenges of this age because they do not have criteria available to them with which to test the attitudes, the behaviors or successes of contemporary daily life. This would require drawing upon diverse areas of knowledge. The research showing the lack of significant contributions by Christians, in spite of their numerical growth, in addressing or solving a variety of social problems is due in large part to their lack of understanding in these areas.

Therefore, it is indispensable that church leadership at different levels receive a formation that is interdisciplinary in order to mark the mission of the church in Latin America with a more holistic perspective. By discovering and learning to work with the interdisciplinary potential present in the congregations, the people of God should be transformed into a missional force dispersed throughout society.

Based on this consideration, it seems unbelievable that in today's world the "seminary" model is still considered the principle institution for the training of church leadership or that there is any justification for keeping ministerial formation isolated from contact with other institutional spaces for higher education. What is worse, some circles still believe that to transform a seminary into an educational center offering an interdisciplinary formation would be a deviation from the mission of the church.

I affirm that the university model is the best setting for training the leadership of God's people, dismantling the clerical focus of the current vision and adopting a more holistic vision that corresponds to the situation of the world and the development of the society and the culture that the Creator placed in our hands from the beginning. In this way, more open and ecumenical educational settings will prepare church leadership for dialogue and constructive action in a globalized and plural world such as the world today.

Dangers of the Protestant "mega" phenomenon: Ahistoricity due to the lack of incarnation and the absence of parish-based organization in the congregations

One of the recent phenomena is the emergence of the large local church, the so-called "mega" or "kilo" churches. In and of themselves, these churches seem to respond to the mass society that is typical of large urban areas, where the population is accustomed to events for large audiences in stadiums, movie theaters or parks, etc., for entertainment or other purposes. Those who participate in these churches generally do not live in the neighborhood where the church building is located, but rather come from different points in the metropolis or large city. Some of these churches have organized to facilitate transportation by providing a fleet of buses that pick up people in different areas of the city.

Those who have analyzed the missionary dynamics of churches with congregations that are not strictly parish-based have be able to discover a double fragmentation that affects the development process for the membership of these churches. On one hand, the members ignore their own neighborhood or community—both evangelization and social development—because their church is located in another neighborhood. Yet, on the other hand, the believers also don't evangelize in the neighborhood where the church is located because they actually live in a different community. Thus, the members live in the "limbo" of a church-centered life focused primarily on worship. If for some reason, some of their neighbors become interested in the gospel, it turns out to be difficult to convince them to travel voluntarily to travel across the city to participate in congregational life. There is a disarticulated and ahistoric vision which is connected to a lack of understanding or a reductionistic picture in terms of the holistic nature of Christian mission.

Given the importance of a parish base for the church, the building in which the church meets should serve as a physical base from which people move out to serve the community in which the meeting place is located. This makes other alternatives imperative. If the model of "large church" is to be pursued, it should be supported by a disperse structure of cell groups in which the members can develop closer relationships (koinonia) and fulfill their historic role in the communities where they live. These cell groups should foment the development of independent, formal churches in their own localities.

From local impact to cultural change: Broadening of renewed moral, ethical and social densities

It appears that we hope to transcend the mere local case studies to discern a more systematic influence in the society and in the culture. One problem is the nominalism found in elements of popular religiosity in both Catholicism and Protestantism. This problem is reflected in the culture and its deficiencies in a broad ethical and social dimension.

For this reason, it is useful to take into account the studies that analyze the impact of religion in the culture and the development of peoples and look at how religion transforms the visions and behaviors of believers who begin to permeate the society with their ethics and morality and provoke economic, political and cultural consequences (for example, the case of the Protestant Reformation in certain European countries, or the Wesleyan revival in England).

There are specific studies done by Mariátegui (1980) and Zea (1970) on the contrast between the two Americas—North America (Protestant) and Latin America (Catholic)—concerning economic, social and cultural development. Gramsci investigated the contrast between northern and southern Europe and recognized the impact of the Protestant Reformation, which generated differences in terms of development (F. Piñón G. 1987, 63-79 and R. Díaz-Salazar 1993). These studies pointed to a type of Christianity incarnated in Protestantism that had a greater consistency reflected in the systemic effects it caused. This was so much so that Gramsci affirmed the need for a cultural and moral reform in order to bring about lasting transformations and an advance in civilization (though he stated this from a secular, socialist perspective rather than a religious one).

It is possible that Protestantism, rightly understood according to its best historical precedents, could be an alternative that would contribute to increasing development in the Latin American region. For this to happen, various aspects need to be overcome to permit Protestantism access to the spheres of public influence (politics, communications media, etc.), conditions that do not currently exist because of the hegemonic weight of Catholic corporatism that is still present (Bastian 1990).

However, the Latin American Protestantism of today reflects contradictions between its manifestations in historic Protestantism (enlightened) verses massive millennialist Pentecostalism that is removed from the political sphere. On the other hand, a vast sector of Protestantism defines itself still primarily within the modernist liberal project, yet it has not been able to open itself in a significant and rational way to the contributions and channels for reconstruction offered by the socialist option (neither of the Marxists nor of any other group), which promote structures that are more caring and more in keeping with the testimony of Scripture (Trinitarian theology, understanding the church as a charismatic and diaconal body).

Adding to this is the lack of unity. Taken together, atomization and the lack of unity have weakened the Protestant movement so it is incapable of more effective action that would permit more balanced thinking and more coordinated intervention at the strategic and methodological levels. These weaknesses have stopped and continue to be an obstacle to the contributions Protestantism could make to the transformations the continent requires.

In the ecumenical subsector, the unbalanced focus on mission, which sidelined the importance of evangelization, has led over time to a numerical reduction, which means they have little social weight or influence, in the first place among Protestantism itself and much less in the general population. So, it happens that in the crucial moments of electing representatives for political office, in spite of being perhaps the sector that is most conscious of and best prepared in social matters, in reality they don't have enough support in among the citizens to provide a vision for the country based on Protestant perspectives. On the contrary, those of the subsector who have less consciousness and are the least prepared in terms of social matters (especially from popular Pentecostalism), given their broad social base, are able to elect representatives who for many other sectors of Protestantism (ecumenical and evangelical churches) do not represent the best of the tradition or the historical social contribution of regional and worldwide Protestantism.

In the evangelical subsector, apart from atomization and association with dogmatisms of various stripes (some of which are still not very clear in terms of their position of social issues), and perhaps due to a lack of precision about the place of specialized and technical knowledge in social transformation, the broader frameworks invoked of "holistic mission" or the "Kingdom of God" (as utopia, historical project, or values) do not lead to concrete viable alternatives, beginning with the lack of vocations in specific fields and the corresponding lack of theoretical and praxiological contributions in relationship to this vision.

Currently, the northern countries where Protestantism prevails are the hegemonic center of the neoliberal economy. This merits serious reflection and committed transformative action by northern Protestants themselves. At the same time, it merits a dialogic and transformative tension between Protestants from the south and from the north as we seek a systemic change on a global level.

IV. Paths of Resistance and Transformation in the Search for Life

Priscila Barredo Pantí

God calls us today to a new moment,
To walk together with God's people.
It is time to transform what no longer works,
Alone and isolated it is not possible.
God still invites us to work,
To share God's love and join forces.[57]

Our liberating biblical and theological reflection begins from the contexts and concrete situations in our Latin American and Caribbean countries with their history of oppression, subjugation and colonization. The effects of this history are evidenced today by the economic, political and cultural inequalities, imposed as a form intranational colonization, that keep thousands of people pushed to the margins of society. We find the cause of this inequality in the powers of domination representing deeply-rooted structures that exercise control in politics and the economy. In Paul´s thought, these structures are called "principalities and powers."

Even though these powers oppress, sometimes with discourses and actions that appear to bring progress and benefits, we are certain the forceful and tangible proclamation of the Gospel that brings hope and resistance will promote liberation from these forces by denouncing and unmasking them. In other words, the good news of salvation produces transformation in concordance with the example and message of Jesus, who proposes a new way of life and a countervailing logic by confronting the established dominant system that promotes inequality and exclusion.

57 Translation by Pablo Sosa of a fragment of the song "Momento nuevo", a collective creation from Brazil based on Ecclesiastes 4:12. Found in the hymnal Celebremos juntos #129 (San José: SEBILA, 1989).

How to resist evil in the world?

How to resist evil in the world is a constant challenge that calls for specific forms of action. It is true that many projects and initiatives taken up by different Christian groups reveal the character of the liberating message of Jesus in his preferential option for impoverished people. At the same time, it is also true that we should strive to be consistent with the gospel and work to remove the power structures. It is not at all an easy task. We are so permeated by the system that is colonial, capitalist, patriarchal, adult-centered, anthropocentric and individualistic that we become unwitting accomplices to the neoliberal model. Sometimes we enter into contradictions in our spiritualities, thoughts, practices and discourses that are imperceptible to our own eyes. Therein lies the complicity. These powers can utilize the good will of our faith communities and our calls for transformation by masking their real intentions behind policies and programs to help those in need. Thus, they seek "to change so that nothing changes", a concept made famous by Giuseppe Tomasi di Lampedusa in his novel, Il Gattopardo.

Of course, I do not think we are facing a simplistic situation of "good guys" versus "bad guys". Those of us who are committed to justice are not completely exempt from incoherent practices. I also don't believe that this ideological manipulation penetrates easily as if the population, lacking their own criteria, were an inert prisoner in the hands of the powerful. Definitely, I believe we need to put more faith in people. We should challenge their conscience, humanity and sensitivity with critical reflections promoting a cooperative style that does not allow ideas, feelings and actions to remain abstract.

The message expressed in Ephesians 6: 13-17 gives us important clues using the image of the armor of God as a means of resisting the evil of the world: the belt of truth, the breastplate of righteousness, the shoes of the gospel of peace, the shield of faith, the helmet of salvation and the sword of the Spirit, which is the word of God (the message of Jesus, the Christ).

> If we perceive in this text an incitement to the Christian communities to take up a struggle of active, non-violent resistance to all the ways in which the institutions and systems govern society and impose dehumanizing conditions that destroy the lives of certain sectors of the population, we can use this basis to build a Christian practice of discernment for political and social action today. The descriptors applied to the different pieces of armor recommended for this task point to the qualities and values that should characterize the people and the communities that confront these powerful adversaries (Foulkes 2011, 142).

Irene Foulkes proposes we read this text backwards. In other words, we should ask ourselves how to reject lies, injustice, evil, intimidation, and oppression within the dominant religious, political and economic structures. This is a subversive proposal that gives power to those of us who follow the movement of Jesus, the Christ, with a logic of resistance, not of domination. We have seen movements that denounce and confront from academic, artistic and farmworker platforms. There is undeniable evidence that these organizations destabilize the scaffolding of the powerful. The Uruguayan journalist Raúl Zibechi explains:

> In the last two decades, movements have taken a series of directions. . .It is not about a single path or a single movement, but rather about tendencies that seem to move in related directions. . . .In some cases, they move along pathways that don't seem to lead anywhere, or they move directly where no permanent (exterior, visible) pathway exists, although there is always a flow (or silences instead of words and actions, as the Zapatistas teach us) (Zibechi 2007, 93).

We run the permanent risk of ignoring the passages and divisions that we experience as groups in struggle. Instead, we concentrate on "the results" and we feel ourselves to be discredited because we believe we have not achieved anything important.

As collectives and committed faith groups we should affirm, in the first place, that our hope comes from the companion God who does not pull all the strings of the world. Secondly, we should focus our work on transforming our interpersonal relationships and our relationship with nature. Thirdly, we should give priority to intimacy and solidarity to strengthen our ties of friendship and joint efforts. If we do not do so, even our urgent and legitimate projects will start from a base that will be too fragile to withstand the perverse beatings that will come from that machinery of coercion and discrediting orchestrated by those who only seek their own interests no matter what the cost to millions of people and to the environment.

Silvia Rivera Cusicanqui insists that even in the midst of our failures we should keep the flame of change burning and not let it be extinguished. We need to keep it covered like the ember that is blown on to start the fire the next day.

> This is the great metaphor for the bad times. We have to care for this glowing ember; we have to embrace it and cover it so it will keep breathing and not go cold. In the future, that ember will give off a spark that will start a fire. The problem is that in defeat people let the flame go out; the people emigrate or leave, or they dedicate themselves only to their personal lives (Rivera Cusicanqui 2016).

Independent Communications Media: The Opening Horizon

Independent communications media offer faith communities concrete ways to revitalize through a proclamation of life. To clarify, I am not referring to the so-called "fourth power" tied to the media oligopolies with their ideologically controlled content that plays a fundamental role in strengthening the oppressive structures.

Given this situation, one of the most effective ways to resist evil is through the use of alternative communications media (webpages, blogs, social networks, online radio and television, among others) to produce and support content that is critical, thoughtful, non-conformist and agile. Throughout our continent

Christian communication groups are emerging that have a political commitment, gender consciousness, and biblical and theological preparation. They are collaborating with other collectives and like-minded groups, including secular movements.

Youth Movements That Are Tearing Down the Walls: The Chaos of Revolution

It is key to focus on the youth movements that are emerging with critical thought and social commitment fitting for our times as we work for the revitalization of the churches and their action in the world. Sometimes I hear phrases that express a marked disdain and latent distrust toward young people: "Youth today are very apathetic." "They are always on the internet." "They have a crisis of faith and don't want any commitment to the church." In contrast to what some adults affirm, the new generations are not homogeneous. Instead, they represent a kaleidoscope of youth movements.

Young people exist who, far from leaving behind belief and abandoning spiritual practices, are constantly searching for faith experiences that evoke and represent freedom, creativity, solidarity, purpose and community. We can count on young people who remain within the traditional structures of churches and Christian organizations, yet are committed to the transformation of those structures through proposing new forms of being church and taking collective action. In addition, they are seeking training that will allow them to contribute from social commitment, biblical studies and theological reflection with an interdisciplinary approach that transcends ecclesiastical spaces. Other young people place themselves in public spaces where they engage in positive public advocacy as activists and initiators of processes of transformation. They are citizens with a social and political consciousness that comes from their belief in the God of justice, freedom, love and diversity.

No, these young people are not experiencing a "crisis of faith". The crisis is with religious institutions, with what is established, with the inequity and the lack of purpose in the macro structures. As the anthropologist Jose Martin Barbero has said, "The youth continue to want to be citizens, but of another planet, another society, another family, another school." I follow his lead and say that young people continue to want to be believers, but of another church. They are questioning the traditional models of family, work, relationships, education and church. Based on the analysis offered by Barbero, I insist that this distance from what exists does not require the earphones of an iPod or smartphone. Young people are not removed from reality because the digital world has captured them. No. Young people are in their own world creating codes within and beyond social networks that seem chaotic to many adults who don't understand them. "We must stop being afraid of chaos, because from chaos a social order can emerge that will be less unjust, less dishonest, and less oppressive. We need such chaos to reinvent this old society that is experiencing the most cruel and licentious phase of capitalism."[58]

Undoubtedly therefore, it is the institutional forms, constructed from above in a patriarchal and colonial logic, that are being disrupted by the movements of youth, feminists and farmers. These groups are exploring new forms of organization outside of the labor unions or insurgent groups that have, despite the contributions they have made, become part of the same centralized and vertical structure.

Paths toward Revitalization: Routes to Decolonization and Depatriarchalization

It is not easy to talk about decolonization and depatriarchalization of our societies, churches, mission and theology as paths toward revitalization. However, I need to mention them in reference to the changes we wish to experience as believers. I remind you that there is no decolonialization without depatriarchalization. To overturn these paradigms, we must begin by recognizing that our Christian faith, even though today we are rereading it and reinterpreting it in terms of liberating justice, has its origins in the genocide of our indigenous ancestors carried out in the name of "evangelization". It is a history of the subjugation and plunder of populations who boldly resisted such disgrace and knew how to reorganize their practices, beliefs and identities.

This rereading of our history brings us to a reflection that leads to concrete acts of decolonization in our discourses, ideas,

58 See the interview by CLACSO TV available at https://www.youtube.com/watch?v=VdvwSHvEob0.

proposals and lifestyles. The gospel proclaimed by Jesus Christ is against any condemnation and mistreatment of life in all of its forms. The feminist writer Silvia Federici describes the violent agenda of powerful groups operating at an international level that exude this patriarchal and colonial vision (the principalities and powers mentioned above).

> There is a very direct relationship between the attempts of the State today. . . to deepen its control of and vigilance over the bodies of women and the extractivist policies. . . I believe the common element is found in the attempts by governments today, in the new wave of primitive accumulation, to extend their control over all the natural wealth, all of the rural and urban territories and over the bodies of women. Capitalism and the governments that represent the objectives of capitalist investors have tried to control the bodies of women because they are seen as a natural resource, as a machine to reproduce the labor force and therefore something that should be controlled (2016).

Of course, the pressing task we have before us to defend the lives of people and of nature requires simultaneous collective efforts. Within the Christian faith, the starting point should be the decolonization and depatriarchalization of the theology from which we derive our concepts of God, of God's Word and of our mission as Christ's body. The Brazilian theologian Silvia Regina De Lima Silva forcefully underlines the delegitimate nature of this racist theology and points to the recovery of a Black theology that recognizes the black face as "image and likeness of God".

> The struggle against discrimination and racism means this theology is rooted in the movements and organizations of impoverished men and women who join with other groups that share the same experience of exclusion. Aware of the growing exclusion promoted by neoliberal globalization, we affirm blackness and the feminist commitment arising for the world of the poor to search together

> for another possible world, a society that respects life, protects the weak, and allows each to live with dignity in our differences (2010, 92).

Conclusion

We are moving toward the construction of a world in which many worlds are possible: worlds without discrimination based on ethnicity, class, gender, age, or sexual orientation; worlds that move toward utopias of equality and recognize diversity, justice, solidarity and love toward humanity and the creation of which we are a part; worlds that unmask the systems that promote the depredation of life in the name of "development" and "economic growth", that promise "quality of life" for the people yet only serve the interests of the elite and the oligarchies. These are the oppressive forces that artisan from an insignificant town in Galilee confronted with his subversive message and practice when he proposed a new order in which there is no room for "those who are considered rulers of the nations and oppress their subjects, and high officials that abuse their authority." Instead, Jesus took the side of those who, like him, lived out a logic of solidarity and who incarnated the gospel to serve and give their lives "as a ransom for many" (Mk 10: 41-45). As the Chilean theologian Pablo Richard points out, "The subject-individual says, 'If there is not enough for everyone, there should be enough for me.' The subject-community says, 'If there is enough for everyone, there will be enough for me.'" (2004, 24) This subject-community is the people, the persons who change history, who actively build the bases for dethroning the dominant and oppressive systems. The transformation of history is not a facile, partisan, irrational or vengeful struggle of some against others. Instead, it is rebellion characterized by the search for justice and equality, our hope in a reachable utopia in which no one will live at the expense of those who are weak. The Argentine philosopher Enrique Dussel puts it this way.

> Articulated within the question of "the people" we find the question of the exercise of "popular power",

> with a political system that creates new forms of participation in all levels of the political structures, in civil society and in the policies of the State, as well as constitutionally. Real democracy is linked with the effective organization of grassroots political participation (2013).

To close, I want to call to mind that afternoon in the first century, when the teacher of the people showed his hands and his side as a sign that life had overcome death and exclaimed, "Peace be with you." Then he said, "As the Father has sent me, so I send you." (Jn 20: 21) In his resurrection, the liberating mission of Christians comes alive because his resurrection shows life as fullness that triumphs over injustice, evil and oppression.

What is this proposal for fullness of life offered in a context of violence, abandonment, discrimination and exploitation of all of creation? Is it good news to be practiced on the road or is it to be shouted from the balcony? It is good news that the God of the Bible has always proclaimed as the New Jerusalem, the city prophesied in Isaiah 65. It is a land in which people who build the houses will live in them and those who plant the vineyards will live from the fruits of the harvest. In God's dreams and within our reach there exists a different society in which justice, love, joy and celebration prevail.

References:

Bastian, Jean Pierre.
1990. Historia del Protestantismo en América Latina. México, D.F.: CUPSA.

Bauman, Zygmunt.
2004. Wasted Lives: Modernity and its Outcasts. Cambridge: Polity.

Bosch, David J.
1991. Transforming Mission: Paradigm Shifts in Theology of Mission. Maryknoll, NY: Orbis Books.

Costas, Orlando E.
1984. "El CELEP y la pastoral." Pastoralia 6, nos. 12 & 13 (julio-dic.): 81-90.

De Lima Silva, Silvia Regina.
2010. "Abriendo Caminos, Teología Feminista y Teología Negra Feminista Latinoamericana". Revista Magistro 1/1: 82-95. http://publicacoes.unigranrio.edu.br/index.php/magistro/article/view/1055/618. Accesado 10 junio 2016.

Díaz-Salazar, R.
1993. Gramsci y la construcción del socialismo. San Salvador: UCA Editores.

Dussel, Enrique.
2013. "Cinco tesis sobre el populismo". http://www.medelu.org/Cinco-tesis-sobre-el-populismo. Accesado 20 junio 2016.

Federici, Silvia.
2016. "Acumulación originaria y violencia contra las mujeres". Entrevistada por Manuel Bayón, 4 de junio. https://resumen.cl/articulos/silvia-federici-acumulacion-originaria-violencia-las-mujeres. Accesado 20 junio 2016.

Foulkes, Irene.
2011. "Autoridades, potestades, dominios... ¿Qué hacer con los 'poderes' en Efesios?" en Revista de Interpretación Bíblica Latinoamericana (RIBLA) 68: 130-142.

Freire, Paulo.
2004. Pedagogy of Indignation. Boulder: Paradigm Publishers.

Marátegui, J.C.
1980. Siete ensayos de interpretación de la realidad peruana. Lima: Ed. Amauta.

McLaren, Brian.
2006. "Found in Translation." Sojourners (March). https://sojo.net/magazine/march-2006/found-translation. Accessed January 15, 2016.

Padilla, C. René.
2006. ¿Qué es la misión integral? Serie del Camino No. 1. Buenos Aires: Kairós.

Piñón G, F.
1987. "Antonio Gramsci y el análisis del fenómeno religioso". Cristianismo y Sociedad XXV/91: 63-79.

Richard, Pablo.
2004. "¿Cuál es el sujeto capaz de construir 'otro mundo'?" En ¿Es posible otro mundo? Reflexiones desde la fe cristiana, ed. Dom Demetrio Valentini. Bogotá: Indo-American Press Service.

Rivera Cusicanqui, Silvia.
2016. "Una candidatura índigena puede alborotar el sueño de los poderosos: Silvia Rivera". https://desinformemonos.org/una-candidatura-indigena-puede-alborotar-sueno-los-poderosos-silvia-rivera/ . Accesado 29 de diciembre de 2016.

Sam Colop, Luis Enrique, trans.
2008. Popol Wuj. Guatemala: Cholsamaj.

Sobrino, Jon.
1978. Christology at the Crossroads: A Latin American Approach. Translated from the Spanish by John Drury. Maryknoll, N.Y.: Orbis.

1993. Jesus the Liberator: A Historical Reading of Jesus of Nazareth. Translated from the Spanish by Paul Burns and Francis McDonagh. Maryknoll, N.Y.: Orbis.

2001. Christ the Liberator: A View from the Victims. Translated from the Spanish by Paul Burns. Maryknoll, N.Y.: Orbis.

Zea, L.
1970. América en la Historia. Madrid: Ed. Revista de Occidente.

Zibechi, Raúl.
2007. Autonomías y emancipaciones: América Latina en movimiento. Lima: Universidad Nacional Mayor de San Marcos y Fondo Editorial de la Facultad de Ciencias Sociales, Perú.

CHAPTER 10: REVITALIZATION, RENEWAL AND REVIVAL

Achievements, Challenges and Promise

Nestor Medina

The five cases presented in this book have been analyzed within the framework of revitalization. In the following paragraphs, I want to reflect on some aspects of these cases as well as on themes that have emerged during the consultation. In some ways, the questions and the discussions are familiar territory. When I left El Salvador in the 1980s on my way to the United States, the churches were already facing tremendous challenges similar to those examined in this process. Guatemala, El Salvador and Nicaragua were in the midst of "civil wars"; Honduras had been converted into a U.S. military base. Countries from Panama to Chile were recovering from the trauma of a long list of military dictatorships. Guerrilla armies were still going strong in their fights against rightwing governments. The countries of the Caribbean were also experiencing social and political turmoil. From those days, I remember the conversion of Nicky Cruz and how the conversions of those who had been drug addicts or guerrilla fighters were used as examples of the advance of the Gospel.

Certain factors contribute to or prevent revitalization in the church. Some aspects that point to radical changes in the church's self-understanding. Various questions have arisen. For example, how do we respond to the challenges the church is facing? What is our vocation as the people of God in the Latin American context? What is our role at this historical crossroads? How shall we work in a way that allows people to be confronted by the Reign of God? This last question helps us remember the passage from Matthew 11:5 when John the Baptist asks the question, "Are you the one who is to come?" The answer Jesus gives could not be clearer. "The blind see, the lame walk, the lepers are healed, the deaf hear and the dead are raised to life." We also remember the passage from Isaiah 55:1 as a promise of the awaited Reign of God, "Come, buy and eat, come and buy without money and without price." This promise subverts the current system that codifies everything, including life itself.

A certain degree of suspicion is needed, given that methods used previously no longer respond to contemporary challenges. Likewise, the revitalization of the church should go beyond a simple spiritualization in which people see religion as a form of social escapism. In each of the cases, there are things to be criticized as well as contradictions to be found. Some cases appear to demonstrate a certain degree of "success". Other cases don't follow these patterns of success yet none-the-less represent examples of revitalization. However, we should not interpret these cases only as topics for study and analysis, but as expressions of a complex process in which Christians are becoming historical subjects. These examples provide us with a series of lessons from which we can learn and through which we can discern God's actions and God's will for the peoples of Latin America.

Reading the signs of the times

Of course, the church has often found itself at such a historical crossroads in which it has had to reinvent itself and rethink what it means to be church and what it means to follow Jesus Christ. Over and over again in different contexts, the church has had to remake itself to be able to respond to the social, political, economic and religious challenges of the day.

The changes that are interpreted as signs of revitalization of the church are often connected globally with forces related to major changes occurring at the geopolitical level, even if these changes manifest themselves in a way that is local and concrete. For example, with all its limitations, the Catholic Church in Cuba helps us see how the tide of political and social changes impact the participation of the church or the church's abstention from participation in national processes.[59]

Enormous changes have occurred in the church since the middle of the twentieth century. Though it appears that the Second Vatican Council (1962-1965) has lost some of its

59 In this case, there has been a direct impact from the exodus of church leaders, particularly clergy and ministers, who left the island fleeing the conditions that were created after the triumph of the revolution. In the same way, the Catholic Church in Cuba, more than any other denomination, has achieved a degree of recognition by the government. The approach of the revolutionary government to the Catholic Church has been very different than that towards the Protestant or Pentecostal churches. The Catholic experience in the Military Units to Aid Production should be complemented with the experience of Protestants, and especially the experiences of Jehovah Witnesses, Mormons, or any other groups that opposed the dictatorial format of the revolutionary government.

renewing force, in Latin America the general conferences of the Latin American bishops—especially the last general conference held in Aparecida, Brazil in 2007—preserve the original force of Medellin in 1968. Aparecida sought to focus directly on the lives of the peoples. Echoes of this focus can be heard in the recent pronouncements by Pope Francis in Laudato Si.[60] Coincidentally, this same pope played a very important role in Aparecida when he was still Cardinal Jorge Mario Bergoglio. At the local level, movements such as the Cuban National Ecclesial Encounter (Encuentro Nacional Eclesial Cubano - ENEC) have proven to be a revitalizing force for the church.

Among Protestants, the World Council of Churches, the congresses of the Lausanne Movement and other ecumenical efforts have offered diverse expressions of these changes. The most recent event, held in Edinburgh in 2010 to mark the hundredth anniversary of the World Missionary Conference (1910), sought to rethink what it means to evangelize in the twenty-first century.

In Latin America, the Latin American Council of Churches (Consejo Latinoamericano de Iglesias – CLAI), formed in the 1980s as an effort to renew in the church in a climate of a rejection of ecumenism, has become a force for renewal. The Hispanic-American Evangelical Congress held in Havana (2009) brought together representatives from many countries to celebrate the diversity of expressions of Christianity in Latin America. The Latin American Congress on Evangelization (Congreso Latinoamericano de Evangelización - CLADE) and the National Evangelical Christian Council (Consejo Nacional Cristiano Evangélico - CNCE) in Argentina have been re-energized.

Nor can we forget that Pentecostalism is now one-hundred-years-old. It is entering a new stage of theological construction, looking in particular to articulate the connection between being filled with the Spirit and pouring out one's life for those who are the disinherited of the earth, as Frantz Fanon would say (1963). We see this expressed, for example, in the Latin American Network for Pentecostal Studies (Red Latinoamericana de Estudios Pentecostales - RELEP). Pentecostals form a large

60 Http://w2.vatican.va/content/francesco/en/encyclicals/documents/papa-francesco_20150524_enciclica-laudato-si.pdf.

segment of the Latin American population. At the same time, many megachurches hold enormous economic resources, many Pentecostals, according to Yamamori and Miller (2007), are reconfiguring their understanding of the Gospel to include a greater social commitment. It seems to me that a Pentecostal theology of liberation is about to emerge (Medina 2016). We cannot ignore this, because Pentecostalism, together with the charismatic renewal movement and the Neopentecostal churches, is growing by leaps and bounds. Jenkins (2011) would say that the face and the character of the church and of Christianity are being reconfigured by new actors.

These are just a few small examples of a major turning point in Christianity at a global level. This represents a historic change of direction. The majority of Christians now live in the misnamed Third World. The local and global religious marketplaces are diversifying, and we can even say that with this change it has become even more true that the poor are becoming the privileged recipients of God's mystery in Africa, Asia, Oceania and the Americas, as Professor Wanjiru Gitau would say (chapter 1). Theology itself is changing; new theological subjects are opening up spaces for their voices to be heard.

Part of the complexity of this analysis arises from the category of revitalization, inherited from Anthony Wallace, that covers three aspects to revitalization. First is the larger social aspect, which studies different sectors of the society to determine how to introduce or contribute to change. Secondly, there is the personal aspect, which emphasizes the changing processes people experience and how these processes are lived in different individual contexts. Finally, revitalization can be explored from a theological perspective, as an act of discerning what God is doing today in our midst. We are looking for those seeds or signs of divine activity that can help other groups in other places learn from our experiences. It is clear that revitalization encompasses much more. Sometimes it seems to function as shibboleth, enclosing complex phenomena that refuse to be reduced to fixed categories. In fact, revival and renewal share the same semantic space with revitalization, yet they suggest other aspects that magnify the complexity of the phenomena we are trying to describe. For these reasons, I want to propose that we understand revitalization not as something negative, not as a reality in which something is missing, but rather as an action, a way of living the faith that arises from a social consciousness. It is a process of rethinking, of restructuring and reorienting how we see the world. Therefore, revitalization implies a conscious recognition of changing social processes, to which the response is not a reaction, but a pro-action, that is to say actions that seek to prevent the church from becoming irrelevant.

Three Theological Criteria

I wish to elaborate on three positive elements to see how they enrich our understanding of revitalization. Then I will offer some comments related to challenges we still need to consider. I want to suggest that these three elements can serve as criteria for determining what we can consider to be real revitalization.

New theologies and other forms of knowledge

The different cases demonstrate the inconclusive nature of our theological reflection. This is so, in spite of the advances or levels we have reached in our discussions. It is a sign that the church is confronting a mix of intertwined challenges that demand theological rethinking to respond in a way that is relevant.

The worldwide expansion of Christianity has been accompanied by not only profound geopolitical changes, but as well by theological changes that fall to us to address today. It is no accident we often hear that each generation must rethink theology for itself. I am speaking of theology not as a form of hidden knowledge or as something to which only experts have access, but as a part of the dynamic exchanges of reflection that happen in the faith communities of which we are a part.

We have realized that there are no universal formulas that we can import from elsewhere. What concerns me, however, is not so much what class of theories or theologies we might use, but rather what is implicit in each proposal. In other words, what are these positions able to say to us without resorting to foreign theories or theologies? It is imperative that we think about our own problems with tools that belong to us rather than using borrowed frameworks.

To do this, we need to immerse ourselves again in the in the Biblical text. The Bible, our sacred text, is subversive and transforming. This is the only way we will be able to confront idolatry inside and outside of the church, as Pablo Richard would say (chapter 8). Our social, political and material context invites us to rethink the Gospel in new ways that can respond the challenges we face today. In the same way, we need to reconsider the role of culture, not as something apart from people's faith activities, but as a constitutive part of how people weave their lives, incorporating religious aspects as they construct meaning and confront their situation. From the grassroots level, we could see that we do not need an uncritical repetition of the elements of our faith. Instead, we need the creation of a lively theology that will be prophetic and relevant within its own social context.

The need to construct theologies from below is obvious. I am not referring to positions that negate our inherited theologies. Instead, we need new reflections that can enrich these theologies and, in some cases, correct the degree to which they are Eurocentric or irrelevant. In fact, the Methodist quadrilateral is a useful tool for constructing our theology. Reason, tradition, Scripture and our experiences truly are key sources that can help us think theologically in more holistic ways.

Our experiences and our challenges are our own, for which imported or borrowed theologies are not sufficient. Our theologies need to speak from our own cultural spaces and from our experiences of faith in a living God who renews our lives. This consultation process challenged us to imitate Christ in a concrete way, a praxis of holiness, in other words, an action that results from deliberate reflection that seek transformation, as María Pilar Aquino would say (2002, 37).

The meaning of church is being redefined

As I have already mentioned, the question of what it means to be the church is not new. However, the basic definition of the church as the people of God or the Body of Christ can serve as a criterion to help us reclaim the role we have within a complex network of factors, elements and actors. Many written resources exist to help us understand what we mean by church. It is much easier, however, to develop of theology of the church in the abstract than it is to take into account the various contexts and the at times contradictory aspects in the voices of the people who are busy being the church. Two points stand out for me. One is the church as a space for community and family. The other is the church as a collective engaged in social transformation.

The examples of the Abundant Life Church (chapter 5) and the church located in La Chureca (chapter 2), each within their own particular horizon, show us the importance of the church in responding to the needs of family groups. In this case, the church does not focus on individuals apart from their family and social connections. Thus, the church focuses on all types of relationships people can have and attempts to reproduce them as part of a larger community and in ways that protect the family nucleus. From this perspective, the church becomes a space for enriching personal relationships that are made possible through a shared faith, but also as well by shared interests (Abundant Life Church) or by shared struggles [the church in La Chureca, the Belice Bridge project (chapter 3), the A-Brazo organization (chapter 6), and the Catholic Church in Cuba (chapter 4)]. As a confirmation of this, Roberto Goizueta (1999) would say that the church is a space of accompaniment in which people identify with the sufferings of Christ and seek to accompany him, while at the same time Jesus accompanies them because he knows their suffering and struggles.

The programs of A-Brazo, the Belice Bridge project, and the church in La Chureca show how churches can take an active part in processes of social transformation as they respond to immediate challenges. As we have seen, the churches cannot turn their backs on the situations produced by natural disasters or the social disruption caused by crime and entrenched poverty because these phenomena of social fragmentation also touch the lives of the churches and of Christians. Misery and pain occur both inside and outside of the church. Therefore, the response of the church to its members or participants is, by extension, also a response to the context and the social problems that surround the church. Thus, the church takes on a double role. On one hand, the church as a space for social transformation presents believers as ambassadors of the Reign of God. On the other hand, the members of the church act as social and cultural agents. This is a way for us to recover the notion of the priesthood of all believers (1 Peter 2:5-9).

One of the most innovative aspects that has emerged in some of the cases is interchurch collaboration, this intense work through networks and bridges that cross denominational boundaries. Though many leaders often won't consider working together with others, at times because they want to protect their own territories, the projects at the Belice Bridge, La Chureca and A-Brazo prove that sometimes the church will have to reinvent itself and break through religious and denominational boundaries. As Jesus says Luke 9:50, "The one who is not against us is for us." These projects show us that people make up the church. Limited by its context, the Catholic Church in Cuba is has had to recover the notion of the people of God as the church (ekklesia) rather than the institution as it responds to the phenomena of the mission houses. Given their wide geographical distribution, these mission houses offer another model of church with lay leadership as a contrast to vertical structures led only by clergy.

Every case study shows that the attitude of the church toward people has changed. Earlier, the church waited for the people to come and be attended to within the church building. Now, the church in different contexts is going outside of itself to find people where they are. In the process, the understanding of holiness has broadened as the distinction between sacred and secular spaces has disappeared. The world is our parish, as the folks with A-Brazo would say. The church, by going into the world, is converting "secular" spaces into spaces where God manifests Godself. In my way of thinking, this is a new way of doing mission.

A new theological understanding of our humanity

One of the very particular characteristics evident in the different cases is the broader focus on people. In the Abundant Life Church, there is a clear commitment to accompany people in their lives through a wide network of services. In this church context, we found it important to be critical of some of the positions and the ideas of supply and demand centered in an individualistic spiritualization of Christian experience. Though Bible study, prayer and fasting play an important role, in some of the cases it appears that spirituality or people's spiritual health cannot be reduced to these practices. A person's spirituality embraces their multiple relationships with their family and in their community, as well as one's sense of ministry and attitude of service toward others. A-Brazo, for example, invests its energy in creating networks of cooperation at an interchurch level to reach people in various ways. The church in La Chureca and the project at the Belice Bridge reach out to people at the basic levels of education, food and personal security. Meanwhile, the Catholic Church in Cuba rediscovered what is essential in its faith once its social position was relegated to the margins of the society.

One way or another, we are seeing a redefinition of the Gospel or of evangelization as a holistic social response and a life-giving proposal that rests on the evangelical values of compassion, grace and love. In addition to providing spiritual instruction, efforts are made to meet basic needs such as food, security, counseling or support groups, as well as needs for personal development like education or training in computer skills. Somehow the available resources multiply, just as Jesus did in John 6 when he fed thousands with resources provided by the people themselves. We need to remember that it was a poor boy, one from whom no one could have expected a contribution, who offers out of his poverty and his limited resources. This disinterested action culminates in a miracle; the small amount he had was multiplied for the good of the multitude. That is how I see the renewal that is happening in our time. Through their actions, the people provide us with glimmers of divine intention and allow us to glimpse the Reign of God.

In these diverse projects, we see people recovering their dignity and, in some cases, their human rights and the right to work. This is not just a question of demanding human rights, but rather a profound affirmation that all people are created in the image and likeness of God. We can see that the revitalization of the church will continue and gain more force to the extent the churches stop seeking souls to convert and look instead for people beside whom they can walk as part of Christian life itself. The projects under study are already doing this to a greater or lesser degree. We should affirm that these examples reflect God's will for persons. In other words, it is not God's will that people be poor, suffer from oppression, experience violence, live a life of scarcity without access to a basic education, or live without employment. This does not mean a rejection of direct assistance, even though we recognize such efforts are not sufficient to lead to social transformation. We must go further until we impact the fabric of society. Churches that reflect this commitment to the whole person become signs of the Reign of God. People need to be valued for the simple fact they are created by God. We saw this attitude, for example, in Pastor Magdalena. The unhealthy conditions of poverty and misery of the people working in La Chureca did not impede her from seeing them as God's creations. As she would say, "Before they are good citizens or people who can vote, I want them to be children of God."

When the church turns toward persons, especially the poor and marginalized, and seeks to improve the conditions in which they live, the church itself becomes a prophetic voice. The church's preaching of the Gospel includes addressing the social structures that render a large portion of the population disposable. By doing this, the church incarnates the eschatological promise Jesus voiced in the synagogue. "The Spirit of the Lord is upon me, because he has anointed me to bring good news to the poor. He has sent me to proclaim release to the captives and recovery of sight to the blind, to let the oppressed go free." And Jesus goes on, "to proclaim the year of the Lord's favor." (Luke 4:18-19).

In other words, our humanity that has been taken up by Jesus in the incarnation becomes a prophetic space for the proclamation of God's jubilee, of the restoration of human beings, of renewal based in God's desire for love, hope and dignity for people over against the forces that destroy life. This logic that restores human beings and life opposes the global culture of consumption, the hording of material goods, the concentration of wealth in few hands, technological monopolies and the exploitation of nonrenewable natural resources. It rejects this system that is built on the backs of those who have been cast aside, as Pope Francis says in Laudato Sí.

This takes us to a new encounter with the biblical text. I remember Maria Alarcon, one of the people who worked in the dump at La Chureca. In her interview, she expressed herself with great dignity as she interpreted her experience of leaving the dump as being comparable to God's liberation of Israel in the book of Exodus. At the same time, Pastor Magdalena Herrera invites us to trust in God's power. The use of Exodus as an interpretive key had been developed years before by Latin American Liberation theologians.[61] However, in the interview with Maria the idea comes to life. God has come to the least of these! The church in La Chureca and the project at the Belice Bridge demonstrate the power of God; God continues to save those who are alcoholics, drug addicts, and criminals, but at the same time God restores them as human beings and as citizens, converting them into a positive force for social transformation. One of the key aspects of the project at the Belice Bridge is the work with the young people to break the cycle of violence and poverty. This, together with the church at La Chureca, highlights how young people, and believers in general, can become agents of change within their own communities, despite enormous obstacles.

I want to propose, therefore, that the construction of our own theology, a new understanding of the church, and a new vision of our humanity based on the example of Jesus Christ can serve as three key theological criteria for examining the revitalization of Christianity. The objectification of the church, the commercialization of the Gospel and the cooptation of the mission remain clear and present dangers, but revitalization understood as pro-action will keep the church from becoming paralyzed.

61 For example, see José Severino Croatto (1978, 1983).

Threats Posed by Social Imbalances

In these case studies, it is obvious that the church in Latin America, and particularly here in Central America, is facing enormous challenges. In the following lines, I mention a few of these as aspects that should be rethought as a way of promoting a revivification or renewal that will be permanent.

The humanization of misery

We need to understand that poverty, crime, corruption, unemployment and so forth are symptoms of a major social imbalance. Hunger, unemployment and poverty do not exist. What do exist are men, women and children who are hungry, who do not have work, or who live in conditions of scarcity and poverty. The church can help the larger society understand that these are not just social, economic or political problems; they are fundamentally spiritual problems.

The church has its own voice that it should use to challenge and push the entire population in the direction of a more just society and a better quality of life. "For I was hungry and you gave me food, I was thirsty and you gave me something to drink, I was a stranger and you welcomed me, I was naked and you clothed me." (Matthew 25:35-36) These words serve as a calling for the church. "For I desire steadfast love and not sacrifice, the knowledge of God rather than burnt offerings." (Hosea 6:6). This passage serves as a guide to what it means to follow Christ. At the same time, these texts transmit social values. The church can provide a broader theological framework in which salvation in Christ includes material liberation, space for physical health, economic improvement for the poor and, of course, spiritual restoration. For this reason, our theology should be a "biotheology" that expresses our concern for the lives of persons. This goal would be in keeping with the original intentions of our creator.

As the Pueblo document affirms, the church becomes a force for evangelizing the culture. The continuation and advancement of the revitalization of the church requires that we adopt a self-critical attitude. In other words, the revitalization of the church also includes the evangelization of our culture inside and outside of the church, as

Pope Paul VI said in Evangelii Nuntiandi[62] and Pope Francis has now repeated in Laudato Si. We have seen how the Catholic Church in Santa Clara, Cuba is focused in this way. We can also affirm that when the church seeks to transform the larger context the church itself is evangelized. The church comes to realize that responding to social problems is not a marginal or peripheral aspect of the Gospel, but rather a constituent element of Christian life and of the model that Jesus Christ gave us.

Facing the pain of migration

Much is said today about the masses of human beings who are crossing political borders, leaving behind worlds, friendships and ways of life in the search of a place where they and their children can have a better future. In some cases, it is the only way to get out of poverty. The obstacles are enormous and people end up risking their lives, the stability of their families and the possibility of ever seeing again the loved ones they leave behind in their native countries. The church is being called to respond to the reality of migration, to extend its hospitality and help to those who emigrate or leave their countries and to those to stay behind when a member of the family migrates, as well as to those who enter the country from other nations. In each case, the challenges are different, but the church should be a space of consolation, accompaniment and help for those who seek to establish themselves in a new country. In both immigration and emigration, the church should take Jesus seriously when it comes to hospitality and be a good Samaritan (Luke 10:25-37).

The reconfiguration of the church is occurring at various levels. The church has become a transnational phenomenon. If at one time we talked about internationalism, today we can't avoid referring to the way churches are connected across national political borders. In fact, when people migrate, they take their faith traditions and culture with them, which they use to confront the challenges of their new context. The church is also being reconstructed because now it inhabits multiple national contexts

62 Http://w2.vatican.va/content/paul-vi/en/apost_exhortations/documents/hf_p-vi_exh_19751208_evangelii-nuntiandi.html.

with fluidity. For this same reason, we can longer speak of fixed religious borders or identities. Identities have become fluid and borders are now porous.

Along with immigration, the changes that are occurring deeply impact the culture. Young people are being affected by the importing of different cultural elements and values that cause intergenerational tensions in terms of music, the understanding of worship and respect for sacred spaces. It is important to develop open spaces where our youth can express themselves without feeling restricted or judged while they are encouraged not to abandon values related to devotion, social commitment and service.

A prophetic social voice

Social evils, the violence of the gangs, poverty, the lack of medical care and migration cannot be separated from the larger context of free trade agreements and the expansion of a voracious capitalism that devours everything in its path. We all participate in this system, but at the same time we are its victims as our peoples, our work, our natural resources and our life itself are being reduced to consumer products.

In some cases, the churches accommodate themselves to reflect the logic of the market by emphasizing numbers as a measure of the spirituality of their people. In these cases, the assumption is made that the size of the church is a sign of divine activity and that the "prosperity" offered by God can only be marked by the accumulation of material goods and ostentatious displays. In other cases, people participate in the church based on the social capital with which they entered. If for Dietrich Bonhoeffer the question had to do with cheap grace, for us it is life itself which is being cheapened. As Sister Ondina Cortes and Laura Maria Fernandez Gomez would say, "The revitalization of the church is not measured by institutional growth. Instead, it is marked by the quality of Christian life and communion resulting from reconciliation that is human, spiritual, personal and social."

The example of Cuba, though very particular in comparison to the rest of Latin America, helps us to understand how the church can see itself as a social force that contributes to the building of social character for a whole country. In the video from La Chureca, Pastor Magdalena says that when people would come to the church they learned how to be citizens. Kevin Lewis O'Neil, in the study he carried out in Guatemala, also speaks of how the churches serve to incorporate people as better citizens.

However, it is not a question of becoming involved in an acritical fashion. The church should recover its prophetic voice by condemning the root causes of poverty, illiteracy, the lack of access to medical care, etc. It is appropriate for the church to take up the task of questioning the social mechanisms that make it so difficult for people to get out of poverty, to be secure in their own neighborhoods, or to prevent easy access to drugs. Isaiah 58:6 helps us to remember the question that God asks. "Is this not the fast that I choose: to loose the bonds in injustice, to undo the thongs of the yoke, to let the oppressed go free and to break every yoke?"This is also what it means to be a citizen.

Self-critique of our internal structures

Part of the revitalization and recovery of the church's prophetic voice will be to work against the social and cultural structures that cause discrimination against our indigenous peoples and those of African descent. Social classes are still dominant within the church, and in some cases the racialized differences are very notorious. The revitalization of the church will depend on how we appropriate Galatians 3:28, where in Christ there is a humanizing and democratizing effect that recognizes all persons as equals who can contribute richly to the reign of God. No one is pushed aside because of their culture, their social or educational background, or their gender. The church should do as Paul did when he celebrated the life of Phoebe (Romans 16:1-2). Our theology has to make space to value the contributions and enormous work of our sisters, mothers, wives and daughters in the church. Christianity has the potential to transform men and break down the cultural patterns of machismo (Santos 2012, Brusco 1995). It also has the potential to re-educate our society.

Care for nature

The evangelization of our culture will have to include the rediscovery of our responsibility toward nature. We need to abandon approaches that are centered only in human interests and realize that the human race is part of creation. In other words, we need to recover the balanced relationship where we are sustained by the earth instead of destroying it. Franz Hinkelammert would say that the forces of predatory capitalism are in the position of cutting off the branch of the tree in which we are sitting (1995, 215). In the same vein, James Cone (2000) reminds us that the struggle against other forms of injustice has to take into account the destruction of nature as another form of injustice in which all of us are implicated and for which all of us are responsible. The church should be able to renew itself by being an example of the divine mandate to care for the earth (Gen 1:28). Now more than ever before we cannot ignore what Paul said almost two thousand years ago. "The whole creation is groaning in labor pains." (Romans 8:22). As Christians we should cry out, together with the Spirit, for our earth because it is God's creation.

Conclusion

The future of revitalization for the church in Latin America looks promising. At the same time, we must remember that a growing number of non-believers are abandoning the institutionalized expressions of Christianity. The study of the Abundant Life church demonstrated that the majority of the "new converts" or new church members came from other churches. Going forward, a question will be how to reach those sectors that have separated themselves from the church.

However, we cannot overestimate the importance of providence, divine grace, and the work of the Holy Spirit in the revitalization of the church. Love, peace and hope. At this point we can adopt a profoundly Wesleyan sense of the presence and activity of the Holy Spirit. In fact, what is happening should more appropriately be called a revitalization, renewal and revival of the church. We must not forget that our frameworks are imperfect. We need to think about the activity of the Spirit outside of ecclesial spaces that is also a sign of the times. We must do so in a holistic way, taking into account physical, emotional, social, political and other aspects that can contrition to and affect the ability of people to hear the invitation from God in the Gospel. The Spirit is guiding us to live our humanity. The Spirit helps us to imagine ourselves within the divine plan and purpose, the example of which we have in Jesus Christ. It is the Spirit who moves the masses and who causes movements to irrupt. The Spirit calls us to a deeper communion among religious traditions. It is the Spirit who promotes community among the children of God.

References:

Aquino, María Pilar.

2002. "Latina Feminist Theology: Central Features." In A Reader in Latina Feminist Theology: Religion and Justice, ed. María Pilar Aquino, Daisy L. Machado, and Jeanette Rodríguez, 133-160. Austin, Texas: University of Texas Press.

Brusco, Elizabeth E.

1995. The Reformation of Machismo: Evangelical Conversion and Gender in Colombia. Austin, TX: University of Texas Press.

Cone, James.

2000. "Whose Earth is It Anyway?" Cross Current 50/ 1–2: 36–46.

Croatto, José Severino,

1978. Exodus: A Hermeneutics of Freedom. Trans. Salvator Attanasio. Maryknoll, NY: Orbis Books.

1983. "Biblical Hermeneutics in the Theologies of Liberation." Trans. Robert Barr. In Irruption of the Third World: Challenge to Theology, ed. Virginia Fabella and Sergio Torres, 140-168. Maryknoll, NY: Orbis Books.

Fanon, Frantz.

1963. The Wretched of the Earth, preface by Jean-Paul Sartre, trans. Constance Farrington. New York, NY: Grove Press.

Goizueta, Roberto S.

1999. Caminemos con Jesús: Toward a Hispanic/Latino Theology of Accompaniment. Maryknoll, NY: Orbis Books.

Hinkelammert, Franz J.
1995. Cultura de la esperanza y sociedad sin exclusión. San José, Costa Rica: Departamento Ecuménico de Investigaciones.

Jenkins, Philip.
2011. Next Christendom: The Coming of Global Christianity. Oxford, UK: Oxford University Press.

Medina, Néstor.
2016. "Entre (Otros) Conocimientos and the Struggle for Liberation: Remembering the Legacy of Otto Maduro (1945–2013)," Perspectivas 13: 82-89. http://perspectivasonline.com/downloads/entre-otros-conocimientos-and-the-struggle-for-liberation-remembering-the-legacy-of-otto-maduro-1945-2013/.

Miller, Donald E. and Tetsunao Yamamori.
2007. Global Pentecostalism: The New Face of Christian Social Engagement. Los Angeles, CA: University of California Press.

O'Neill, Kevin Lewis.
2010. City of God: Christian Citizenship in Postwar Guatemala. Berkeley, CA: University of California Press.

Santos, José Leonardo.
2012. Evangelicalism and Masculinity: Faith and Gender in El Salvador. Plymouth, UK: Lexington Books.

www.ingramcontent.com/pod-product-compliance
Lightning Source LLC
Chambersburg PA
CBHW071953040426
42447CB00009B/1318

* 9 7 8 1 6 2 1 7 1 8 7 8 9 *